ANOTHER **MIND-
BODY** PROBLEM

SUNY series, Philosophy and Race

Robert Bernasconi and T. Denean Sharpley-Whiting, editors

ANOTHER
MIND-BODY
PROBLEM

A HISTORY OF
RACIAL NON-BEING

JOHN HARFOUCH

SUNY
PRESS

Published by State University of New York Press, Albany

For information, contact State University of New York Press, Albany, NY
www.sunypress.edu

Library of Congress Cataloging-in-Publication Data

Names: Harfouch, John, author.
Title: Another mind-body problem : the history of racial non-being / John
    Harfouch.
Description: Albany, NY : State University of New York, 2018. | Series: SUNY
    series, philosophy and race | Includes bibliographical references and index.
        Identifiers: LCCN 2017032626| ISBN 9781438469959 (hardcover) |
        ISBN 9781438469973 (e-book) | ISBN 9781438469966 (paperback)
    Subjects: LCSH: Philosophical anthropology. | Mind and body. | Human
    beings. | Race. | Physical anthropology.
Classification: LCC BD450 .H28725 2018 | DDC 305.8001—dc23 LC record
    available at https://lccn.loc.gov/2017032626

10 9 8 7 6 5 4 3 2 1

CONTENTS

ACKNOWLEDGMENTS

This book is dedicated to my Sittoo. I would also like to thank my mother and father, who supported me throughout the process of writing this book. I also thank my wife, Shanhai, who supports and encourages me always. I appreciate everyone I met at Catholic Charities, including Dieudonne Nahigombeye, Evelyne Rusagabandi, and Constance Kabaziga. Thanks to Robert Bernasconi for supporting this project throughout. Thanks to Emily Grosholz for helping me with portions of chapter 1. Thanks also to the anonymous reviewers for their charitable reading of my draft and giving me the constructive criticism necessary to improve my ideas. I am also grateful to Andrew Kenyon, Tracy Sharpley-Whiting, and State University of New York Press. I appreciate the philosophy department and the University of Alabama in Huntsville for giving me the platform necessary to complete this research. An earlier version of chapter 1 was published as "Descartes on the Disposition of the Blood and the Substantial Union of Mind and Body," *Studia UBB Philosophia: Descartes' Scientific and Philosophical Disputes with His Contemporaries* 58, no. 3 (December 2013): 109–124. An earlier version of chapter 1 was published as "Arthur de Gobineau on Blood and Race," *Critical Philosophy of Race* 2, no. 1 (2014): 106–124. An earlier version of chapter 3 was published as "Kant's Racial Mind-Body Unions," *Continental Philosophy Review* 48, no. 1 (2015): 41–58.

INTRODUCTION

Imperialism was and still is a political philosophy whose aim and purpose for being is territorial expansion and its legitimation. A serious underestimation of imperialism, however, would be to consider territory in too literal a way. Gaining and holding an *imperium* means gaining and holding a domain, which includes a variety of operations, among them constituting an area, accumulating its inhabitants, having power over its ideas, people and, of course, its land, converting people and ideas to the purposes and for the use of a hegemonic imperial design; all this as a result of being able to treat reality appropriatively.

—Edward Said, *The Question of Palestine*

When you have no knowledge of your history, you're just another animal; in fact, you're a Negro; something that's nothing.

—Malcolm X, *By Any Means Necessary*

How can we marry our thought so that we can now pose the questions whose answers can resolve the plight of the Jobless archipelagoes, the N.H.I. categories, and the environment?

—Sylvia Wynter, " 'No Humans Involved':
An Open Letter to My Colleagues"

A RACIAL NON-BEING

Malcolm X makes the preceding statement on June 28, 1964, at the founding rally of the Organization of Afro-American Unity (OAAU). His reference to the Negro as a kind of nothingness is not a stray remark.

He is making a historical, political, and philosophical point about non-White people, and it is a theme that runs through many of his speeches and interviews from the early 1960s. The sort of non-being X invokes is not a logical negation where one might begin with p and then derive not-p. Nor is it the nothingness one encounters in daily affairs, as when checking the mailbox and finding nothing. It does not find precursors in the history of philosophy in Nietzsche's nihilism or the nothingness Heidegger claims one faces in anxiety. As he makes clear, the non-being X is concerned with is distinctively racial. This singular experience of the nothing, unique to those denied history, land, culture, and identity, is captured by the word Negro insofar as that name "attaches you to nothing."[1] In this case, 'Negro' is a racial non-being.

A commonplace holds that racism is a doctrine representing certain peoples as inferior, as less than human, or even as animals. X is not testifying here to that experience of racism. He will not say that once a person is identified as a Negro they are stripped of their humanity and treated as an animal. Notice that X corrects himself in the preceding quote and draws a sharp distinction between the animal and the Negro. Rather, 'Negro' strips a person of any existence whatsoever, as he makes clear in a speech from January 24, 1965:

> Negro doesn't tell you anything, I mean nothing, absolutely nothing. What do you identify with it? Tell me. Nothing. What do you attach to it? Nothing. It's completely in the middle of nowhere. It doesn't give you a language because there is no such thing as a Negro language. It doesn't give you a country because there is no such thing as a Negro country. It doesn't give you a culture—there's no such thing as a Negro culture, it doesn't exist. The land doesn't exist, the culture doesn't exist, the language doesn't exist, and the man doesn't exist. They take you out of existence by calling you a Negro.[2]

It is not that the Negro is somehow 'less-than,' as if one could measure intelligence, skull size, or IQ and then plot it on a scale below the White race. 'Negro' is beyond measurement. The Negro X is talking about does not exist to be measured. Denied history, culture, and existence—this is how one is chained to the nothing. Whence this nothingness?

Malcolm X is among the first to comment on this question of a racial non-being, but he is not the first, and he is certainly not the last. One finds references to an experience of a racial non-being dating back at least to Sojourner Truth's testimony from 1850.[3] It would not be surprising were X himself expounding on a theme found in Marcus Garvey's writings. Garvey agrees that the narrative of racial inferiority does not do justice to the meaning of 'Negro,' and he too wants to dissociate the word from that interpretation. On April 16, 1923, Garvey publishes an article called "Who and What Is a Negro?" in which he criticizes the anthropologist Franz Boas for refusing to identify as Negroes the Moroccans and Algerians employed by France to invade Germany in World War I. Garvey points out that, according to the logic of Boas and other European anthropologists, as soon as one is "recognized in any useful occupation or activity,"[4] he or she ceases to be a Negro. In other words, the Negro is, by definition, without purpose. One ceases to be a Negro once one is given a purpose, even if that purpose is to merely serve as a thing or tool. Garvey makes this clear in his definition of 'Negro': "A person of dark complexion or race, who has not accomplished anything and to whom others are not obligated for any useful service."[5] He goes on to state,

> If the Moroccans and Algerians were not needed [...] to save the French nation from extinction, they would have been called Negroes as usual, but now that they have rendered themselves useful to the higher appreciation of France they are no longer members of the Negro race.[6]

By this logic, the non-White, non-Negro is identified as a tool; they render a reason to Europe. With a use, a purpose, a reason, the Algerian and Moroccan become a kind of thing, however minimal that might be in the eyes of the anthropologists. But the Negro is without reason. The Negro is not even a thing. *Nihil est sine ratio*—Nothing is without reason.

It is no accident that when Malcolm X concludes his presentation on the problem of non-being at the Hotel Theresa in Harlem, he goes on to announce the schedule for a number of regular classes offered by the OAAU in Arabic, Swahili, and Huasa.[7] For if that with neither culture nor history is nothing, it is logical to develop those characteristics in order to escape non-being. Of course, X's resistance to this nothingness is diverse and nuanced. It includes not only the 'ballot and the bullet' but above all a program aimed at becoming human through historical self-determination. It could even be said that the overriding motivation behind all X's political work is to reclaim a kind of destiny for non-White peoples around the world. This idea, which is not unique to X and can be found throughout the works of Marcus Garvey and others, concerns the future insofar as it addresses the political and economic prospects of a people. However, this future is not possible without a rigorous reckoning with the past, a point X make clear when he states, for example,

> Armed with the knowledge of our past, we can with confidence charter a course for the future. Culture is an indispensable weapon in the freedom struggle. We must take hold of it and forge the future with the past.[8]

The future being forged is humanity. That is, X seeks a metamorphosis from the nothing to the human. Of course, Islam, politics, and even violence remain essential to X's program. Yet, if a people are to become human, then one must recognize the "inalienable right of all our people to control our own destiny."[9] And that future requires a methodical consideration of the past, since it is precisely the lack of history and the racist construction of a people that have supposedly neither accomplished anything in history nor even served any purpose, that binds one to non-being in the first place. I am talking about Malcolm X here, but one can just as well find nearly identical decolonial strategies in Latin America and the Middle East. Gustavo Gutiérrez writes that liberation in Latin America must include not only economic and political reform but also the creation of a society that "will be the artisan of its own destiny."[10] In Lebanon, Sayyed Hassan Nasrallah, Secretary General of Hezbollah, declares the primary aim of America's 'war on terror' has been to deny Arabs the right to "assuming the historical roles that people select for themselves."[11] One might begin to wonder if Malcolm X's 'Negro' is a not global phenomenon, the product of an imperial ideology aimed at colonizing time and history just as much as territorial space.

The problem of racial non-being is certainly broad. However, the ambition of this book is to cultivate a new understanding of philosophy's mind-body problem. I concede it is not entirely obvious the extent to which Malcolm X is articulating and thinking through a particular mind-body problem. However, X comprehends philosophy's mind-body problem exceedingly well if readers are open to the possibility that professional academic philosophy has not entirely grasped the history and contours of that problem. As a result of that oversight, the field is not well positioned to recognize a range of solutions and experts, of which Malcolm X is but one. The intersection of X's 'Negro' and the mind-body problem can be clarified if one considers the possibility of a mind-body problem that is, at its roots, a problem of racism. In this book, I trace Modern Europe's invention of a hereditary and racialized mind-body union. This racial union, deemed in some cases to be born 'without reason,' becomes the site of a racial non-being. The institution of a racial non-being, conceived as a mind-body union without reason, does not begin with Descartes, as is often claimed for philosophy's orthodox mind-body problem. The overlap of a certain brand of racism with the question of the mind-body union is only fully realized in Immanuel Kant's work. In Kant's essays on race from the 1770s and 1780s one discovers the orthodox mind-body problem is solved when he manages to formulate a theory of race that simultaneously accounts for the sexual regeneration of the human being and the union of mind and body. Accordingly, a key premise in the extrapolation of another mind-body problem is that 'race,' as Kant conceives it, effectively solves the problem of how mind and body relate. However, Kant's solution is not fully appreciated if one does not also see it opening onto another mind-body problem. Specifically, once Kant offers a theory of sex that accounts for the mind-body union, this science instantly strips certain racial mind-body unions of any relationship to being. Hence the problem of a racialized union without being, a problem that both grows within and yet is heterogeneous to the problem of how a being, composed of mind and body, can be united.

This other mind-body problem is grounded in its own history, with its alternate protagonists and innovators, but perhaps more importantly this problem is grounded in a distinct testimony. When one speaks of the orthodox problem of *a being* that is *not one*, this discourse refers to certain basic experiences such as the death of another or even sleep, wherein the body is present but the functions of the intellect, be it a soul, mind, or consciousness, are no longer animated. These experiences suggest human existence is a composite, leading to philosophical speculations on the nature of the conjunction between these parts. In more contemporary terms, one might highlight the experience of consciousness insofar as it reduces to neither neural processes nor the elements of the physical world as they are currently understood. The longstanding question for philosophers has been just how the experience of consciousness can arise from the purely physical systems of the brain, a problem David Chalmers famously calls 'the hard problem of consciousness.'

To some extent this is a legitimate question, grasped by nearly every lay person. Although phenomenologists might point out how this problem was long ago dissolved in the early works of Heidegger or Merleau-Ponty, my aim is neither to defend nor outright reject the orthodox problem, but rather to use it as a pivot to move in a new direction. As I will continue to emphasize throughout the book, the experience of a single being that is nevertheless composed of supposedly irreconcilable parts is not the only way for the human being to experience him- or herself as 'broken up,' nor is the meaning of the phrase 'mind-body problem' necessarily determined or governed by this experience. When one speculates on the problem of *a* (one) human being, certainly the oneness of the being is not the only point in question. What experience is there of the (non-)being of the one? Is there not conceivably a unity of mind and body without being, a notion just as baffling and contradictory as that of a being that is not one? Is this other experience not possible? Can anyone testify to it? When was it instituted? When Frantz Fanon says, "Let us endeavor to create a man in full [*l'homme total*], something which Europe has been incapable of achieving,"[12] the kind of brokenness of those not *total* is not the same kind of fracture or damage referred to by advocates of dualism, panpsychism, or materialism. The problem Fanon is pointing to is imposed by a colonial violence upon one "broken in the very depth of his substance."[13] As I argue, this is a brokenness peculiar to those races deemed 'without purpose' and thus disposable. The intersection of unity, non-being, and violence is essential to what I understand as a mind-body problem in the Kantian tradition. Moreover, because the problem addresses itself only to a racial union of mind and body that is non-White—and thus stands without reason, without purpose, and is thereby a non-being, a nothingness, or a waste—it can be solved neither by doctrines of materialism, dualism, nor monism, nor by those currently recognized as 'mind-body experts.'

THE THESIS AND GOAL OF THIS STUDY

In tracing the historical development of the experience of another mind-body problem, I return to a discounted, mostly abandoned outpost in the history of the race discourse. In 1933 a political theorist named Eric Voegelin published two books, *Rasse und Staat* (*Race and State*) and its later companion, *Die Rassenidee in der Geistesgeschicte von Ray bis Carus* (*The History of the Race Idea from Ray to Carus*). *Race and State* is a survey of the theoretical foundations of White supremacy from the late nineteenth to the early twentieth centuries, while *The History of the Race Idea* covers the development of race thinking from the late seventeenth to the mid-eighteenth century. Although his works are largely snubbed by contemporary anthologies and surveys of racism, Hannah Arendt,

for instance, once cited *Race and State* as "the best historical account of
race-thinking in the pattern of a 'history of ideas.' "[14] Over six decades
later, Arendt's estimation still holds some truth. At a time when many of
my contemporaries in philosophy are motivated to dissociate canonical
thinkers from their writings on race, Voegelin's works remain relevant
insofar as they accomplish a most thorough integration of philosophy's
Modern historical canon with the emergence of race and racism. He
examines the contributions made by figures such as Descartes, Leibniz,
Herder, Kant, Goethe, and Schiller, orchestrating a broad range of texts
and concepts while demonstrating their roles in the construction of racial
concepts and political practices. In this way, Voegelin incorporates not
only familiar philosophical figures into the history of the development
of racism but their concepts and precepts as well, many of which were
not explicitly theorized as ideas about race or racism.

Voegelin's study of racism is motivated by his desire to subvert
National Socialism by scrutinizing the ways in which it is founded upon
certain understandings of racial difference. In brief, Voegelin's interest in the race idea and racism is grounded in his belief that the State
is organized around certain racial myths of the body. Although these
myths are based on common experiences, throughout their long history
they have transformed into a political ideology that goes beyond empirical biological or anthropological analyses.[15] This approach, known as
Staatslehre, assumes "that the roots of the state must be sought by the
nature of man,"[16] and thus the historical conditions for the rise and fall of
a racial state will be found in the emergence of a racialized human being.

This is not a book in *Staatslehre*, nor do I measure up to Voegelin's
ambition to grasp the racist foundations of society. Nevertheless, the
conceptual framework of Voegelin's research is of such relevance to the
present work that it must be recognized as the thread guiding my entire
investigation. This is particularly true of one assertion from *The History
of the Race Idea*, where Voegelin states, "The race concept is a part of
the body-soul problem; the former requires for its adequate understanding complete clarity about the latter and therefore about the nature of

man."[17] The second half of that text is then dedicated to a demonstration of "how the modern race idea gradually grew out of the problem of body and mind in the eighteenth century."[18] My study of the mind-body problem will return to this hypothesis repeatedly. In Voegelin's work, the claim refers to a race idea that can only emerge in the eighteenth century once Cartesian mind-body dualism has been imagined anew and the supernatural, transcendent soul has been reconceived as immanent in the development of organic matter.[19] My own study, while significantly indebted to Voegelin's research, seeks to advance his thesis in new directions and with the help of over eight decades of new scholarship. Accordingly, this work is much less a study of Eric Voegelin as it is a reengagement with his thesis in order to reassert the place of the study of racism in philosophy's mind-body discourse.

Although Voegelin's hypothesis is helpful, it cannot survive without some basic modifications. While to a certain extent Voegelin is justified in claiming that 'the race concept is a part of the body-soul problem,' his analysis does not go far enough. Upon uncovering another mind-body problem, that is, a mind-body union without being, I amend his hypothesis to more accurately reflect the status of the mind-body problem in the wake of Kant's contributions. What is at stake in the following pages is something much less benign than 'race.' What one will find in not only Kant's writings but also throughout the work of thinkers like Charles Bonnet, Edward Long, and Arthur de Gobineau is simply racism, and, more accurately, White supremacy. This important distinction would then lead to the following reformulation of Voegelin's thesis: 'White supremacy is a part of the body-soul problem; the former requires for its adequate understanding complete clarity about the latter and therefore about the nature of man.' Yet, that statement does not capture the thesis of my argument much more precisely than Voegelin's original assertion. As is well known, racism is hardly monolithic and it cannot be distilled to a simple formula and then wholly attributed to any one thinker. Many manifestations of White supremacy do not concern the representation of non-White people as a kind of non-being without reason that thereby invites a genocidal violence. There are varieties of racist violence that go well beyond the scope of this book, including racisms that are medico-biological as is the case of biopower, philological as with orientalist racism,[20] or 'auto-genocidal' narratives that depict indigenous peoples as self-exterminating.[21] Kant's racial non-being and the logic of its violence cannot be so casually conflated with these other forms of racist violence even though they all fall under the heading of 'racism' and (perhaps with the exception of biopower) 'White supremacy.'

That said, it is not satisfactory to claim, 'White supremacy is a part of the body-soul problem,' since many manifestations of racism do not depend on any theory of the mind-body union whatsoever. To accurately reformulate Voegelin's hypothesis in a way that does not give readers the impression that this is an exhaustive and final declaration on the proper definition and history of an abstract monolith called 'racism,' I submit the following statement as the thesis of the book: The body-soul problem is a part of White supremacy; the former requires for its understanding further clarity about the latter and therefore about the nature of the human being.

This is to say that a study of racism is prerequisite to any thorough and comprehensive engagement with the mind-body problem today, and specifically the racism that declares being the singular domain of Whiteness and relegates all others to nonexistence. If readers are convinced of my argument, then one should further recognize that given the relationship between the mind-body problem and racism, such that the former is a division of the latter, students and others studying the mind-body problem will require a training that diverges sharply with the one they receive today. In fact, beyond my main conclusion, I encourage philosophers to reckon with the possibility of a basic shift not only in the discursive elements of the mind-body problem but, more importantly, with the nondiscursive economic aspects of the industry. This includes questions of just who testifies to the experience of a racial non-being, what training students must receive to be employed in this field, who should receive funding to solve the problem, and above all, who best represents those most qualified to serve as paid experts in this research area. To better understand this essential point, I must address the nexus of history, problems, solutions, and those recognized as 'in the know.'

For philosophers today, the term 'mind-body problem' is hardly spoken univocally, and although the core problem is commonly grounded in the experience of consciousness, there are various subsidiary problems. Nevertheless, one can delineate some of the broad contours uniting the debate. Philosophers trying to solve the mind-body problem today commonly work within the landscape of solutions taking the form of materialism, property dualism, monism, and the like. Broadly speaking, these concepts are generated in response to a problem of *unity*: How do minds and bodies *interact*? What is their *relation*?[22] Or, if, like nearly all my contemporaries, one rejects the notion of distinct substances, the question becomes, 'What kind of thing is consciousness and how does it *fit* into the natural world?' These questions begin with minds or consciousness on the one hand, and bodies or nature on the other. The two then must be connected or put into some rapport that accounts for the unity of the human being. For instance, while mind-body dualism may struggle to provide a causal interpretation of the union, a materialist might identify 'mind' with the physical world and thereby account for the unity of the being. Then again, this attempt at a solution may be eroded by the introduction of certain ontological and epistemological gaps between the physical world and consciousness.[23] In general terms, much of philosophy's mind-body debate is aimed at closing these gaps through various renditions of monism, materialism, and the like. As Todd Moody frames it in a recent article on the exact terms of the debate, the 'mind-body problem' refers to "a problem of *accommodating* the facts about the mental into a physical world."[24] Similarly, in David Chalmers's formulation of the 'hard problem' one still detects the problem of how *two* can be scientifically known as *one*:

> The hard problem of consciousness is that of explaining how and why physical processes *give rise to* phenomenal consciousness.

> A solution to the hard problem would involve an account of
> the *relation* between physical processes and consciousness,
> explaining on the basis of natural principles how and why it is
> that physical processes are *associated with* states of experience.[25]

This is to say, on the one hand one finds physical processes and natural principles, and on the other, there is consciousness and states of experience. This problem of a single being that is nevertheless two will find its solution in the form of a 'relation,' a 'giving rise,' an 'association,' or as Moody phrases it, an 'accommodation.'[26] In much of Anglophone philosophy, Descartes's name is nearly synonymous with this problem. Of course, it should be noted the phrase 'mind-body problem' never appears in any of his writings or correspondence, making the problem as such entirely foreign to his corpus. In any case, thanks to Pierre Gassendi and Princess Elisabeth of Bohemia, at least the question of how the mind and body interact is present in his work, and he is routinely cited as an early precedent.[27] This is all a fairly stock assessment of the mind-body problem, but it is important to pay attention to all the elements at work and how they fit together: the mind-body problem is a problem of relations between minds and bodies (or consciousness and brain states), it maintains a long precedent in the history of philosophy (at least since Descartes), and experts on the problem and its solutions include names like Chalmers, McGinn, and Nagel.

I too am concerned with the mind-body problem, its history, and those best qualified to solve it. However, I am not concerned with investing myself in any of the current solutions on offer in the literature on the mind-body problem. Rather, what interests me is the way in which all of these solutions are organized along the same plane of discourse that allows each to stand in opposition to another. For instance, a Cartesian dualist might argue that mind and body are united through some kind of causal interaction between the mind and brain. In this case, the unity of mind and body is called 'causation.' At the same time, a functionalist might call this union a 'realizing,' insofar as the mental event of pain, for instance, is realized in the nervous system although it is not reducible to it. Yet another camp, the property dualists, will call the unity a 'dependence,' since mental and material properties are distinct, but the former depends on the latter. Whether one wants to call the union 'causal,' an 'identity,' a 'realization,' or anything else is not the concern of this book. Instead, I am attracted to the landscape upon which each of these camps operate, affording each a common ground upon which they can oppose each other and converse. This terrain, which is the problem itself, allows each hypothesis to be defined not only in relation to other camps but also relative to a very specific understanding of the history of philosophy from which the discourse draws. History grants philosophy this problem today, and even though philosophers may continue to invent new and plausible solutions, it is the problem as it is understood historically that provides a valid backdrop against which his or her statements can be heard as solutions. That is to say, a certain understanding of history and the problem philosophy has inherited calls these thinkers and their solutions to presence.

To date philosophers have been largely satisfied with a history of the mind-body problem that calls forth solutions to this question of unity. Without doubt, the contemporary philosophy of mind has not summoned this problem from thin air. If I were interested in writing a history of the orthodox mind-body problem, I might dwell on the problem of the mind-body union and trace its roots.[28] While this sort of project is not entirely foreign to what follows in this book, it does not accurately capture my aims. There are a number of books already detailing the history of mind and body in ways that go well beyond Descartes.[29] Instead, what follows is a study of the history of the orthodox problem and its overriding concern with unity and relations, but only to the degree that this history contains within itself another problem of mind and body. This opens the way to a kind of counterhistory. In other words, I will not be describing the historical emergence of the orthodox problem. Rather, I use that history, starting with Descartes, to discover within the orthodox history another mind-body problem that has long been enveloped and harbored by the orthodox problem. The goal is to discover the old roots of another problem, a problem that stands as the historical unconscious informing the statements of a thinker like Malcolm X. This is not to say that I am inventing another mind-body problem. It was the *Annales* historian François Furet who once wrote, "[The historian] constructs his own object of study by defining not only the period—the complex of events—but also the problems that are raised by that period and by the events that need to be solved."[30] On my understanding, however, Furet has the relationship between problems and history turned upside down. It is not I who institutes the mind-body problem of a racial non-being under evaluation in this book. Malcolm X, Sojourner Truth, Albert Memmi, Edward Said, and Frantz Fanon had all noted the experience of a racialized non-being long before this book was dreamt of. Still, they did not make the problem either. Rather, it is more accurate to say the problem made them, a problem that receives its first, most coherent formulation with Kant's writings.

If this work is worried about the historical roots of the mind-body problem, I am only excavating those roots in order to comprehend the contours of a problem this history continuously supports. If I am so concerned with the nature of the problem, it is not only because the problem delineates its appropriate and concomitant field of solutions. And yet, I did not set out to write this book with the sole ambition of altering a problem and its discursive field. While I can agree with Henri Bergson when he writes, "I consider a philosopher the one who creates the necessarily unique solution to a problem posed anew by the very effort to solve it,"[31] the overriding importance of the problem and its history is not limited to the discursive realm. At times in the pages to follow the reader will encounter various references to a 'job initiative,' or 'the economics of an industry.' If I am so concerned with the historical roots of the problem and the various solutions that branch off from it, then this interest ultimately derives from an overriding concern for the fruits of labor. By that I am referring to the money. A problem does not only call forth its own field of discourse in the form of concepts and solutions; it highlights those individuals most familiar with the problem and most qualified to alter it and formulate responses. In this way every problem has its economics insofar as it bears the fruits of labor, which is to say the jobs, for those most competent to address it. If philosophy departments did not employ, say, Malcolm X, to take just one example, to work toward a solution to the mind-body problem, that is in part a consequence of philosophers' limited view of the history of the problem, a myopia that cut X not only out of the discourse, but also academic employment. Accordingly, I cannot be entirely certain of where this project leaves those currently specializing in the orthodox mind-body problem. Nevertheless, I can say that insofar as philosophy has a long-established commitment to solving the problems defining its core areas, it would be productive to make room for those familiar with this other, most basic, mind-body problem enveloped in the history of European thought.

Beyond Malcolm X and those mentioned earlier, the fundamental experience of a racial non-being has already been described and elaborated by a broad range of qualified intellectuals from fields including liberation theology to critical race theory to postcolonialism. Scarcely any of these authors are or were employed as professional philosophers. However, beyond a range of published comments on a racial non-being (which I will visit in chapter 3), there exists a much broader field of qualified individuals currently at the margins of the profession and society as a whole. It would be a stretch to call these individuals 'unemployed,' since that would seem to imply a temporary condition. 'Unemployed' means, presumably, the individual will at some point return to work and again participate in society. The segment of humanity highlighted by another mind-body problem is more accurately captured by what the sociologist Zygmunt Bauman has referred to as 'human waste,' a group for which society's current projects and problems have no use. These individuals are thereby not just 'unemployed' but rather 'redundant':

> To be 'redundant' means to be supernumerary, unneeded, of no use—whatever the needs and uses are that set the standard of

usefulness and indispensability. The others do not need you; they
can do as well, and better, without you. There is no self-evident
reason for your being around and no obvious justification for
your claim to stay around. To be declared redundant means to
have been disposed of *because of being disposable*—just like the
empty and non-refundable plastic bottle or once-used syringe,
an unattractive commodity with no buyers, or a substandard
or stained product without use thrown off the assembly line
by the quality inspectors. 'Redundancy' shares its semantic
space with 'rejects,' 'wastrels,' 'garbage,' 'refuse'—with *waste*.[32]

These individuals are unneeded not just by philosophy and the problem
sets philosophy works to resolve, but they are disposable to modernity as
a whole. Moreover, this sector is not just unneeded, they are unwanted.
As such, 'human waste,' those 'without reason,' are often the objects of
worldwide security initiatives that designate redundancy not only as
'criminals,' 'felons,' and 'vagabonds' but also the closely related categories
of asylee and, above all, refugee. Other times, redundancy is made synonymous with a place—'Lampedusa.' Of course, one should add 'Negro'
as Garvey and X define it to this list of synonyms for the redundant. As
I will explain in more detail, this label is far from benign. It carries along
its own rationale for violence insofar as that which is 'waste' or 'without
reason' is thereby eliminable. In this counterhistory of the mind-body
problem, readers will witness the initial characterization of 'refuse' as a
peculiarly racial phenomenon, entitling this demographic to the role of
experts on the mind-body problem.

    With Bergson surely in mind, Gilles Deleuze once wrote of philos-
ophy as a problem-making discipline, one that runs the risk of leaving
thinkers in a subordinate position to masters or those in power, "so
long as we do not possess a right to the problems, to a participation and
management of problems."[33] In my recounting of the history of the mind-
body problem, I am open to the criticism from postcolonialists and race
scholars that in my reformulation of the problem I am only taking up

the role of the master myself and then nominating this 'refuse' to function as problem-solvers or 'servants,' to borrow Deleuze's language.
However, my intent is not to homogenize a 'redundant' class and invoke
a pure and authentic expertise on the problem of a racial non-being.
Without doubt this purity is immediately spoiled once I merely articulate the terms of the problem. In other words, I readily acknowledge
that the problem of a racial non-being operates as a kind of boundary
that gathers together certain discourses and individuals while at the
same time excluding others. As I wrote earlier, not every experience of
racism should be understood this way. However, part of the reason this
book is concerned with history and the mechanics of the problem over
and against its solutions is because I endeavor to bring to light various
forms of domination manifested in particular understandings of the
problem of mind and body. I intend to demonstrate the contingency of
a discourse on mind and body that has long rendered certain peoples
not only mute but entirely irrelevant. Philosophers will certainly argue
that what follows is not the only or the best account of the mind-body
problem. They might also argue that this is not even a good account.
Nonetheless, what I want to lay emphasis on above all is the question, For
whom is this or any formulation of the mind-body problem the 'best'?
Might there be some reflection among philosophers on how self-inter-
ested the orthodox mind-body problem is for those around whom the
academy, philosophy, and the mind-body discourse were built? Precisely
the point of this project is to reopen the space of the mind-body problem
in a way that permits the reformulation of how that knowledge is produced. That may very well include a reconsideration of the terms I have
laid out here so as to bring about a wholesale rejection of the problem
of a racial non-being. Yet, that is just to say that knowledge production
involves not only providing answers but, more importantly, a partak-
ing in the construction of the problems themselves. Furthermore, one
reason why I keep returning to the question of employment is because
the university platform affords a privileged opportunity for intellectuals
to reshape problems and the historical narratives from which they are

born. The question of who is qualified to occupy that platform is essential in all of this, much more so than whether anyone uses it to edify the problem I unearth. Thus, my reformulation does have its limits insofar as certain forms of resistance to racism cannot be seen as responding to the problem of a racial non-being. Nevertheless, I would consider this book a success if within those limits a space is opened up for those deemed a 'waste' and targeted by a particularly genocidal racist tradition to speak and be paid for their insights.

THE METHODOLOGY OF A CRITICAL HISTORY
OF THE MIND-BODY PROBLEM

To summarize a central claim of this book, I argue that the question of how mind and body relate is solved by Kant's invention of an unprecedented concept of race. Kant's particular formulation of the race concept should be seen as a solution to the orthodox mind-body problem insofar as he racially determines the mind and body in terms of those elements of the person that regenerate unfailingly and in unison across generations. This results in four mind-body unions corresponding to Kant's four races, such that, for instance, a Hindu mind incapable of abstract thought will forever repeat in unison with an olive-yellow skin. Furthermore, each of these races must obey Kant's 'principle of purposes,' which declares nature does nothing without reason. Regeneration, which is both essential to Kant's concept of race as an object of science and the very fabric of the mind-body union, must have a reason or purpose. Kant locates this purpose in the progressive development of reason through culture, which depends on the 'transmission of enlightenment' over the course of generations. Yet, by defining the races precisely in terms of their capacity for culture, Kant renders all non-White peoples without any relation to the purpose of the species. Without reason, Kant's non-White races stand without ground as a kind of non-being. That is to say that while other racisms are operative in Kant's corpus, one form that is unique to his thinking is based on a racial mind-body union with neither reason nor being. This is the historical backdrop to what Malcolm X will two centuries later call the 'Negro,' although Kant thinks this condition envelopes all non-White people. Of course, Kant does not develop this concept *ex nihilo*, and I will devote much of the book to a demonstration of how a Modern European discourse on mind and body developed around questions of sex, regeneration, historical progress, and early doctrines of human difference.

Given this argument, two questions arise. On the one hand, philosophers may wonder what will be done with Kant and Kantianism if he is in fact racist to the point of having developed a racism hitherto unknown by his contemporaries. At the same time, critical race theorists and postcolonial scholars may find it paradoxical that I propose a decolonization of the mind-body problem only to then go on and yet again interpret Descartes, Kant, and the like. These two questions are but two sides of the same coin.

Regarding the question of whether Kant (or any canonical Modern figure) is racist and what will become of him if he in fact is, I first point out that my ultimate aim in this book is not to convict Kant or any other thinker on charges of racism. Rather, in this book I have begun with the institution of a racism that systematically designates non-White people as useless and nonexistent. As an institution, I would like to understand when and how this racism was instituted. In pursuing that end, I begin with certain testimonies to a racial non-being and conduct a kind of genealogy, turning to history to clarify this racism and its inherent violence. Furthermore, I am attracted to antiracist opportunities that may lay within that narrative. I am hardly alone in this approach, but it is not the norm when it comes to philosophy's discussion around racism in the canon.

Currently, one can generally detect two approaches to the problem of racism in philosophy's canon. On the one hand, what seems to me a majority of philosophers seem to agree on two precepts guiding their methodology. First, any rigorous philosophical thinking must start with a set of clearly defined terms. Second, racism, however it is defined, manifests itself in the form of individuals' racist statements and personal beliefs. Together, these two principles lead some philosophers to examine whether this or that statement from some author or another is 'truly racist.' With a definition of racism already in hand, the focus shifts to the perpetrator, and questions are posed regarding the maturity or sincerity of the philosopher in question when he or she wrote the statement under review. In other words, researchers want to know if the philosopher's statement meets a standard of racism selected in advance, and if it does, can the philosopher legitimately plead insanity, or immaturity, or ignorance, or senility, or some other alibi.

Clearly for this methodology everything depends upon which definition of racism one chooses to then measure the philosopher against. An example is helpful to illustrate how this can play out. In Justin E. H. Smith's recent work, he attempts to exonerate Leibniz of charges of racism by pointing to the fact that Leibniz only makes distinctions within the human species on the basis of language, leaving physical characteristics to the side. According to Smith, Leibniz's linguistic taxonomy is not racial—and hence has no place in a history of racism—because 'race,' as Smith defines it, concerns corporeal differences.[34] Meanwhile, just a few years earlier, Pauline Kleingeld mounts a defense of Kant by underscoring how, supposedly, after 1794 Kant only racialized the body, leaving minds out of the taxonomy. Thus, according to Kleingeld, 'race,' the foundation of 'racism,' is predicated on a racialization of the mind. Because Kant only racialized bodies, he is not 'racist.'[35] Just taking these two examples, there is on the one hand a definition of racism grounded in a taxonomy of phenotypes and physical attributes from which Leibniz is exempted, and on the other hand, one finds a racism predicated on mental types that Kant does not support. Given the definitions of racism brought along in advance and the statements chosen for analysis, everyone is innocent. It scarcely merits mention that if one only switched around Smith's and Kleingeld's definitions of race and racism, both Leibniz and Kant could stand as exemplary racists. One begins to detect a kind of shell game.

Naturally, both Kleingeld and Smith are correct in how they define racism, which is only to say that racism is multifaceted and complex, always shifting along with the society it organizes. However, one of the many shortcomings of their approach is that it overlooks a number of firsthand testimonies to the experience of racism. Namely, it ignores the evidence from authors including, but not limited to, Frantz Fanon,[36] Kwame Ture,[37] Charles Mills,[38] and Kimberlé Crenshaw,[39] along with the rest of the tradition of critical race theory, all of whom agree that the machinations of racism operate primarily through a society's laws, institutions, histories, and discourse. This affords a second approach to the question of racism in the canon. As I mentioned earlier, insofar as racism is manifested institutionally, it behooves scholars to ask just when and how specific experiences of racism were instituted. The result is a fundamental reframing of the question of racism in the philosophical canon. Rather than asking, for instance, 'Was Kant or Leibniz racist?' and then measuring his statements against an anachronistic definition, one asks, 'What contemporary experiences of racism or manifestations of oppression are indebted to Kant, Leibniz, or other philosophical heroes?' The second question does not exonerate the individual or release a philosopher from responsibility. Rather, it contextualizes the philosopher's work so as to illuminate a network of oppression still operative long after his or her time.[40] This approach not only avoids the ahistoricity and arbitrariness the former approach struggles to avoid in choosing a definition of racism in advance; it also brings to light the logic, scope, and nuances of more or less obscure racist institutions.

If the reader understands what follows in this book, I am not entirely agnostic about whether Kant is racist, but I do not think that is the most significant question. Nor do I think the guilty/innocent dichotomy overshadowing the discussion of racism in the history of philosophy amounts to much more than a polemic. Kant, for example, can and should be preserved in philosophy's canon. After all, as I see it, he inaugurates the mind-body problem. And yet, he must be preserved along with all his racist statements without attempting to relegate those works to personal biases or minor side-projects. This is the preferable route for those whose main concern lies in combatting racism. As I will demonstrate, by detailing and highlighting Kant's unique brand of racism and understanding where it fits in today's philosophical landscape, one finds a pivot around which jobs and resources can be reappropriated. Readers can then better understand why I am nearly indifferent to questions of whether Kant or any other philosopher is 'truly racist.' Whether that question is answered up or down, the more pressing issue is how these authors can serve antiracism and the reappropriation of material resources that in large part defines the antiracist project. This is the decisive advantage of a genealogical method: one must begin with and come back to the lived experience of racism as it is experienced by the victim. Moreover, within that history one can discover the contingencies or possibilities for antiracist alternatives. Insofar as Kant's writings on race cannot be unwritten and yet provide a foothold for that endeavor, they must be conserved.

Accordingly, this is not an attack on Kant, Leibniz, Descartes, or the philosophy of mind. In fact, insofar as I am addressing the history of the mind-body problem I would insist that I am working in the philosophy of mind. For readers having difficulty coming to terms with a mind-body problem focused so intently on sex, racism, and violence, allow me to pose the following question: What will the mind-body problem look like in the coming century? I believe the answer to that question depends in part on what role the critical philosophy of race decides to take up in the field of professional philosophy. Will the field run alongside the core areas of philosophy, which includes the philosophy of mind, metaphysics, and epistemology, insisting on its purity? Or will it perform the work of a critique and engage the philosophy of mind, metaphysics, and epistemology so as to reorient the field according to the directives of antiracism?[41]

I wrote earlier that the problem of racism in the canon is the converse side of the question of why race theory or decolonial philosophy might spend time interpreting Descartes, Kant, and the like. Some may find it regressive or contradictory that a book intending to address racism ends up focusing so much on Descartes, Kant, the history of the philosophy of mind, and its mind-body problem. Yet, this is not by accident. This is a study in the critical philosophy of race. That remains the case even though I maintain that this is a work on the history of the philosophy of mind. This is not in spite of the fact, but rather this project is a work in the critical philosophy of race because it is a work in the philosophy of mind. If this seems paradoxical, the paradox derives from the meaning of the word 'critical' in the title of the disciplines known as 'critical race theory' or the 'critical philosophy of race.'

Clevis Headley is correct in stating that the legal tradition known as critical race theory is distinct from the Critical Theory of the Frankfurt School, and I would add that the critical philosophy of race is not entirely synonymous with either. Nevertheless, I can also agree with Headley that one cannot deny certain connections between these traditions.[42] Most pertinent to my study is the practice of 'critique.'[43] For instance, when Max Horkheimer defines critical theory, distinguishing it from the methodology of the sciences, he takes care to emphasize the essentially transformative effects of the critical attitude. In his estimation, scientific theories are descriptive insofar as they are primarily concerned with deducing consequences from a certain set of facts, such as when a biologist determines the processes that lead to a plant's wilting or a doctor deduces the events causing an illness. In these cases a theory is responsible for connecting a series of events, but whether the events can be altered is not essential to the theory. Horkheimer claims this kind of thinking is predicated on a distinction between subject and object such that the logical necessity of the chain of events under examination is not effected by the theory or the theorizing subject. In other words, the subject transcends the object under investigation. By contrast, Horkheimer argues the critical theorist studies society while consciously residing within that society, and thus the critique is immanent. It is immanent in the sense that the theorist works through the contradictions of society to not merely describe it, but rather, through description the theorist decisively changes society. As such, the critical attitude finds itself within the object under investigation, discovering the possibility of transformation within the very conditions it brings to light. This is clear when Horkheimer writes,

> A consciously critical attitude, however is part of the development of society: the construing of the course of history as the necessary product of an economic mechanism simultaneously contains both a protest against this order of things, a protest generated by the order itself, and the idea of self-determination for the human race.[44]

Thus, in opposition to both the quietist, descriptive theories of the sciences and a revolutionary fantasy positing a transcendent position from which one might remake society, the hallmark of the critical attitude is the remaking of society out of material found within society. This transformative movement working out of/within is the essence of immanent critique as I understand it. A similar theme is found in other critical fields. Critical Legal Studies, for example, as described by Roberto Mangabeira Unger, operates according to what he calls a method of 'internal development.' Explicitly opposed to a transcendent reordering of society, internal development "begins by exploring conflicts between ruling ideals and established arrangements, or among those ideals themselves"[45] to then use those materials as the tools of social transformation. Again, it is 'critical' insofar as it works within an established tradition in order to overturn it.

In this book I excavate the historical roots of a mind-body problem that calls forth comments such as those from Sojourner Truth or Malcolm X cited earlier. Insofar as this analysis intends to engage and overturn the philosophy of mind, and insofar as that field understands its rudimentary problem to have been inaugurated by Descartes, I follow along with these initial boundaries of the discourse. This is a key point, since I maintain that this work is *within* the history of the mind-body problem and yet this alternate problem develops *out of* the orthodox history. In other words, Kant's racial union without being is not 'another problem' in the sense that it runs parallel to the orthodox mind-body problem. Being in relation *to* the problem would imply that the discourse I trace in this book transcends the orthodox history. Rather, the race discourse I follow here is in relation *with* the orthodox history of mind and body. As such, a critical history of the orthodox mind-body problem demonstrates a more fundamental problem located within the discourse. This then calls for a displacement not only of the orthodox problem but also its solutions, experts, and resources. Therefore, it is fair to say that my study is a counterhistory in the sense that I will retain the language of mind, body, union, and the like in order to track how the development of those terms results in a problem very different from what is now understood as *the* mind-body problem. Yet, it is 'counter' or against the orthodox problem both in the sense that I oppose it, but also insofar as I am against it in the sense of being close to it, or 'right up against' the orthodox problem. My study is thus in the proximity of the orthodox history of the problem while working against it in order to turn it into something else. In that sense, a counterhistory is 'critical.'[46]

I do not intend to make the impression that critique is the only methodology available to race scholars. Nor would I deny that feminist and other minority discourses have had an uneasy and at times unfriendly relationship with the critical tradition.[47] I would also agree that one need not appeal to German philosophy for precedents to the methodology of this book.[48] Nevertheless, the aspect of the critical tradition that I have highlighted maintains a long-established precedent in race theory as well. For example, when Kimberlé Crenshaw and her cohort introduce the strategy of critical race theory, she first and foremost cites Said's production of 'anti-thetical knowledge,' which she defines as "the development of counter-accounts of social reality by subversive and subaltern elements of the reigning order."[49] But of course, Said's critique of knowledge production in books like *Orientalism* or the first half of *Culture and Imperialism* do not proceed by ignoring racist European traditions in order to construct an independent opposition discourse. In fact, *Orientalism* has little to do with Arabs and the Middle East as such and everything to do with how Arabs have been imagined in Europe.[50] Said's counter-account makes use of that European imaginary in order to appropriate its imperial ideology to his own ends.[51] This is similar to how critical race theorists find claims for reparations or affirmative action within an otherwise racist legal framework, or how, in this book, I locate similar claims within a racist European discourse on minds and bodies. Again, being within and yet against is what makes these discourses 'critical' insofar as they deploy an immanent critique.

Precedent is certainly not the only reason to adopt a methodology. I am only explaining why, although readers may find it paradoxical that I locate a race discourse and antiracist program within a history of the philosophy of mind that begins with Descartes, one should not find this approach unusual or surprising. I should think it more surprising to readers if I were to leave the core areas of professional philosophy alone and contribute to a race discourse that insists on talking only to itself.[52] Insofar as I am interested in the ways in which philosophical problems are inherited and who is paid to address them, a critical history of the mind-body problem is necessary if one is to discover *another* mind-body problem *within* the orthodox discourse and thereby locate another expertise within a paid academic industry. Finally, to return to the other side of this question—What to do with racism in the history of philosophy?—this is why Kant must be conserved in the canon no matter how offensive his ideas on race might be: the specific economic opportunities I seek are found within his writings and in opposition to his racism.

Since I started this introduction with a quote from Malcolm X, allow me to end with one. In an interview with A. B. Spellman on March 19, 1964, he states, "Revolution is like a forest fire. It burns everything in its path. [. . .] The German word for a revolution is 'Umwälzung,' which means a complete overturning and a complete change."[53] If the critical philosophy of race is an overturning, then those aligned with that movement cannot be characterized by a disengagement from the core areas of the field. A forest fire does not take up its position running alongside the trees, leaving them intact. It remakes the forest in its image and in accord with a desire all its own. It alters the trees, but also their historical roots. What follows is an overturning of the mind-body problem and the question of being and unity such that the discourse and industry surrounding it can be actively appropriated by those born 'without reason.' In the end, I seek at least a partial answer to the question posed by Sylvia Wynter, quoted at the opening of this introduction, as to where the governing problems of philosophy stand in relation to 'redundant' peoples. To accomplish that, I will engage the philosophy of mind by taking up its roots and scrutinizing its own historical foundations. Since the orthodox history of the mind-body problem begins with Descartes, I too will begin there in search of another mind-body problem.

Chapter One

Descartes's Fundamental Mind-Body Problem

The Question of Sex

The orthodox mind-body problem ignores the fact of a racial non-being. Of course, part of what it means to be 'nothing,' 'redundant,' or 'without reason' is that one is forgotten and obscure. All the same, the mind-body problem does overlook a racial non-being. It is true that all of modernity has forgotten a racial non-being, but the idea that others make the same oversight is not an alibi. Everyone looks past a racialized non-being in their own way, each contributing to a near-total invisibility. The orthodox mind-body problem plays its role in large part by forgetting its history. A history of the mind-body problem incorporating a racial non-being remains absent to this day, even though its primary sources are published, some translated, and lay in plain sight. That history is forgotten because the mind-body problem ignores a racial non-being. It forgets a racial non-being because it loses sight of its history. A vicious cycle. To realize the expertise a racial non-being holds over the mind-body problem, one must begin to see that if the mind-body problem begins with Descartes, then his problem is not what philosophy has hitherto believed it to be. In this chapter, I address the root of a problem that is not only more funda-mental than what philosophy has hitherto understood as the mind-body problem; this foundation will develop into a problem that highlights the invisibility of a racialized non-being.

Despite all the attention it has attracted, Descartes's mind-body problem is not entirely well understood. Among philosophers of mind, selected passages on mind and body in Descartes's oeuvre are often

lifted from their historical context and deemed similar if not identical to the twentieth-century study of consciousness and brain states.
What brief histories of the problem that are offered usually feature
statements that begin with 'Ever since Descartes...' or 'Descartes's
dualism has provoked a tremendous controversy...' Invoking Descartes
in this way, authors agree he institutes the mind-body problem such
that it turns on the question of relations or interactions between mind
and body in an adult human being. There are too many instances to
count, but consider, for example, John Searle's introduction to his Reith
Lectures in 1984:

> Since Descartes, the mind-body problem has taken the follow-
> ing form: how can we account for the relationships between
> two apparently completely different kinds of things? On the
> one hand, there are mental things, such as our thoughts and
> feelings; we think of them as subjective, conscious, and imma-
> terial. On the other hand, there are physical things; we think
> of them as having mass, as extended in space, and as causally
> interacting with other physical things.[1]

For reasons that will be made clear throughout this book, I strongly
disagree with the notion that Descartes's mind-body problem is similar
to philosophy's mind-body problem in the twenty-first century, but
nevertheless there is at least some reason to think that Descartes was
confronted with a question of mind-body interaction. Quite famously,
evidence of such a problem can be found in Pierre Gassendi's reply to the
Meditations and Descartes's correspondence with Princess Elisabeth of
Bohemia in 1643.[2] Further evidence supporting the idea that mind-body
interaction is a particularly Cartesian problem is found throughout the
seventeenth century. For instance, both Leibniz and Spinoza comment
on the issue, along with many others.[3] To note just one example, in 1696
Bernard le Bovier de Fontenelle found "an extreme disproportion between
that which is extended and that which thinks." This disproportion led

him to ask "how bodily motions cause thoughts in the soul" and, "how thoughts in the soul cause motions in the body."[4]

Based on these passages certain authors might see themselves justified in framing the debate in terms of mind-body interactions that occur most conspicuously in sensations. For that reason, it seems appropriate to consider Descartes's mind-body problem identical to or a precursor of philosophy's current mind-body problem, which also is framed in terms of relations and interactions. However, a number of scholars agree there is no problem of interaction in Descartes's philosophy. A growing school of thought generally doubts that Descartes's correspondence with Princess Elisabeth even addressed the causal interactions of heterogeneous substances. Instead Descartes coherently explains the union of mind and body, a union that is not to be understood on the model of causal interaction.[5] Under this interpretation of Descartes's work, authors commonly refer to scholastic vocabulary found throughout his writings on the mind-body union, an indication that he believes the mind-body relation is a substantial union on the model of Aristotelian hylomorphism.[6] These scholars cite passages where Descartes writes, for example, "the mind is substantially united with the body,"[7] or, the

> human being is made up of body and soul, not by the mere presence or proximity of one to the other, but by a true substantial union. For this there is, indeed, required a natural disposition of the body and the appropriate configuration of its parts.[8]

Similar comments from the correspondence with Arnauld, Mesland, and others have been marshaled to support the notion that the Aristotelean metaphysics of substantial forms strongly influences Descartes's understanding of the mind-body union.[9]

By characterizing the relationship between mind and body as a 'substantial union,' Descartes is supposed to have overcome the problem of interaction and resolved the mind-body problem. As the argument goes, God institutes certain correlations between mind and body such

that, for instance, the thought of pain in my foot will arise along with
some harm done to my physical foot. This interpretation dissolves the
problem of how heterogeneous substances interact because Descartes
never intends mind and body to interact mechanically as two physical
substances. To assert such a causal connection, or even to seek such an
interaction, fundamentally misunderstands the natures of mind and body.
The mind, which is not in space, simply is not available for the same kind
of investigation one might carry out in the study of two causally inter-
acting physical bodies. Descartes is well aware of this, and that is why
he appeals to God as he who instituted the system of correlations constituting a substantial union, a system that cannot be made intelligible but
is nevertheless experienced. Gordon Baker and Katherine Morris do an
exemplary job of developing this position and explaining just why interaction is not a problem for Descartes's substantial union when they write,

> 'Our Nature,' or the pattern of correlations [between mind
> and body] ordained by Nature, is described as 'what God has
> bestowed on us.' There can be no intelligible relation between
> a mode of thinking and a mode of extension, and he expressed
> this point by claiming that they 'bear no resemblance' to each
> other. [. . .] Any discernable patterns of correlation between a
> person's thoughts and movements must be God's handiwork
> precisely because both logical and causal connections are out
> of the question. [. . .] Descartes' use of occasionalist idioms
> manifests his intention to stress this feature of mind-body inter-
> action: without God, the substantial union would be dissolved.[10]

Without question, this interpretation of Descartes's mind-body union is
both charitable and firmly grounded in a bevy of textual evidence. Were
it valid, it would be the case that not only is Descartes not a forerunner
of the twentieth-century mind-body problem, but there would be no
'Cartesian mind-body problem.' However, if Descartes truly understands
the mind-body union in terms of a 'substantial union,' on the model of

Scholastic physics, then one must reckon with all this concept involves. Closer inspection reveals that Descartes does not—and cannot—invoke the notion of a substantial union without attempting to account for the sexual generation of the mind-body union.

Although Descartes is rather important to Modern Europe's mathematization of nature, that is not the picture of nature he has in mind when he claims that the nature of the human being is a substantial union. In this Aristotelian framework, the study of nature does not begin with a set of abstract mathematical laws that are then applied to specific cases; rather, it starts with the fundamental experience of movement and change.[11] From this perspective, a substance's changing its predicates or moving in space are common occurrences in nature, but there is no change more notable than when an entirely new being appears. This sort of change is of course none other than the birth of a new substance. As the most abrupt and extraordinary experience of change, birth holds a preeminent place in the Scholastic study of nature, a privilege that is expressed in the very language of the natural world. In Latin, this kind of change is *natio*, a term that must be heard in the same key as *naturalis*, and that is simply because when the Scholastics study nature, they study 'births.' Étienne Gilson emphasizes this point when he writes,

> If [Scholastics] recognize changes in quality or space on the model of that which designates birth, it is because they spontaneously perceive them as generations or quasi-generations of an effect by a cause. Physics as a whole, insofar as it is above all an explanation of change, is going to entail a biological aspect because the fundamental notion on which it rests is going to be modelled on a biological fact: an ordinary physical phenomenon will always be explained by a cause analogous to animal reproduction.[12]

'Nature' is that which gives birth, even if those 'births' are just changes experienced as growth and locomotion. In the Aristotelian tradition, a substantial form is responsible for these behaviors, and for that reason it is the primary object of physics.[13] Even though the term 'substantial form' never actually appears in any of Aristotle's writing, nearly every one of Descartes's contemporaries owes a debt to him when they state that the movements and generations of any being must be studied on the basis of a corresponding substantial form. Although the demolition of this science is one of Descartes's main objectives, when he describes human nature in the Scholastic language of a substantial union, one must recognize that this is an approach to human nature and the physiology of the union rooted in a science of generation.

This context is of crucial importance to Descartes's physiology of the mind-body union. If that union is truly a substantial union, on the model of Scholastic physics, then neither mind nor body can be taken for granted as always already given in their mature form, requiring only an account of how they interact. Rather, to grasp the nature of the mind and body, as well as the physiology of their union, one must begin with an account of how each of these three substances is generated. In this chapter, I will investigate the birth of minds, bodies, and their composite—the substantial union—in Descartes's work as well as the implications of this paradigm for later race thinking. The reader will find that the possibility of a substantial union of mind and body in Descartes's work hinges on a significant, though often overlooked, passage from the *Passions of the Soul*. Here, Descartes writes,

> [I]t seems to me that when our soul began to be joined to our body, its first passions must have arisen on some occasion when the blood, or some other juice entering the heart, was a more suitable fuel than usual for maintaining the heat of the heart, which is the principle of life: this caused the soul to join itself to this aliment and love it.[14]

The notion that the soul bonds with a particular accommodation in the body at birth is hardly inaugurated by Descartes. He follows a number of significant precedents, not the least of which is the sixteenth-century French physician Jean Fernel. Contrasting Descartes's thoughts on the generation of the union at birth to those of Fernel will not only afford a first look into the importance of sexual reproduction to the mind-body problem; it will also aid in the recognition of how Descartes's understanding of sexual reproduction makes the initial union of mind and body at birth impossible. This impossibility emerges not from the purported interaction of heterogeneous substances in a mature human being, but rather from a genealogical dualism, which posits distinct causes for mind and body. This perspective has the effect of drawing one's attention away from a divine system of correlations, the pineal gland, and Descartes's thoughts on sensation toward what must be recognized as the foundation of Descartes's mind-body problem: sex.

I will trace the contours of this problem along three steps. First, I will study Descartes's mind-body dualism as primarily a dualism of causes, a position rigorously established in *Meditation III*. Once one sees how every human being is a product of both God and the parents, one is led to investigate *why* a divinely created mind would unite with a mundane body on the basis of certain accommodations or dispositions innate to the body. In the second section of the chapter, I contrast Descartes's views on the initial union at birth with those of Fernel and William Harvey to clarify the nature of Descartes's problem. Emphasis will be placed on the fact that the problem of sex is not merely another problem alongside the problem of interaction often cited as the precursor to the twentieth-century mind-body problem. Rather, it is the more basic and primary issue, since it calls into question how the mind was ever received by the body at birth, a precondition for their supposed interaction or correlation. Finally, I examine the legacy of Cartesian dualism in the writings of two French race theorists from the eighteenth and nineteenth centuries, Georges-Louis Leclerc, Comte de Buffon, and Joseph Arthur, Comte de Gobineau.

The history of the mind-body problem as it is traced to Descartes, which focuses so intently on the interaction of mind and brain, sets philosophers on a path that not only overlooks the life of a racialized non-being; it also fails to properly trace Descartes's thinking. These mistakes stem from the systematic neglect of the basic problem of why mind and body unite at birth. Commentators overlook the fact that Descartes's mind-body problem should be framed in terms of sexual reproduction and the action of the seminal fluids. Blind to the problem of sex at the root of the mind-body problem, philosophers fail to see the problem develop along the axis of sexual reproduction and regeneration in the works of thinkers in Descartes's wake. As a problem of sex, this mind-body problem is ultimately solved by a theory of sex. As I will demonstrate in chapter 3, that theory of sex is Kant's concept of race, a solution that opens onto what is a radically other mind-body problem specifically addressed to a racial non-being.

In this chapter, I only intend to demonstrate that the problem often assumed to be both Descartes's mind-body problem and a precursor to philosophy's modern-day problem deserves neither title. Of course, readers can certainly find evidence of a problem based on the pineal gland, but so much has to be taken for granted in order to even reach the point where that problem can be posed. Namely, one must assume that a human being—composed of mind and body—was generated in the first place. This is not so much a problem of *how* mind and body interact, but rather *why* they come into proximity at birth. This is where Descartes's problem truly begins.

THE DISTINCT ORIGINS OF MIND AND BODY

As nearly every philosopher is aware, Descartes begins his *Meditations* with the process of hyperbolic doubt. This exercise has the effect of razing the empirical fields of physics, astronomy, and medicine as well as the a priori fields of arithmetic and geometry. As a result of this doubt, in *Meditation II* Descartes famously discovers the *cogito* as the first indubitable certainty in the series of certainties to follow. Descartes argues that in order to think, doubt, or be deceived, a thinking thing, the *ego*, must exist. In this way, thinking defines the *ego*, since any attempt to doubt the essential connection between the *ego* and thought only reaffirms that the *ego* is a thinking substance: "The only thing that cannot be separated from me [. . .] is that I am a thinking thing."[15] In this way, through doubt, *Meditation II* discovers a substance, the *res cogitans*.

However, this preliminary discovery is not sufficient to guarantee the objective existence of the thinking substance. At this point in the *Meditations*, the *res* exists only precariously, since the possibility of the evil genius still intervenes and annuls its existence when the meditator does not actively perceive himself. Thought alone is not sufficient to establish the *ego* as a substance existing independently even when it is not held in thought, since the *ego* only exists if and when thought is fixed on it: "I exist—this is certain. But for how long? For as long as I am thinking; for perhaps it could come to pass that if I were to cease all thinking I would then utterly cease to exist."[16] Or as he states elsewhere, "The proposition 'I am, I exist' is necessarily true every time that I refer to it or that I conceive it in my mind."[17] The progress of *Meditation II* is limited such that once thought turns to other matters, such as science, the *ego* does not go along with it. No longer present, it becomes merely a memory. To guarantee the objective existence of the *res cogitans* as a scientific truth, Descartes will turn to a higher rule, one that will establish the existence of a mind independent of whether the subject is thinking it. While the certainty of the existence of the meditator's essence as thought is initiated in *Meditation II*, it is not ultimately secured until Descartes establishes its existence on the basis of its cause.

Although the *ego* is first discovered in thought, it, like all beings, only achieves objective existence once it is determined as an effect. As Descartes explains,

> The light of nature established that if anything exists, we may also ask why it exists; that is, we may inquire into its efficient

cause, or, if it does not have one, we may demand why it does not need one.[18]

As I discuss in chapter 2, this is not quite what Leibniz means in announcing 'nothing is without reason.' Nevertheless, this axiom does govern the being of beings in Descartes's philosophy insofar as causation not only serves as the necessary and sufficient proof for existence; it is fundamental to every being, even God.[19] As a thinking thing, a *res*, the essence of the human being falls under this rule, and as such, it can only be rendered real once an efficient cause is found to provide a reason for its existence. In other words, while all thoughts depend on a thinking substance, this substance is itself an effect, and, like all beings, its own existence is null without a demonstration of the grounds upon which its own existence depends. Accordingly, once the *res cogitans* is discovered, Descartes immediately investigates its existence through an analysis of efficient causality.[20]

This is the project of *Meditation III*, where Descartes furnishes the genealogy of the *ego*, and in so doing, fully establishes its existence. Through this proof, the *ego* will be essentially defined in its relation to God, or as Descartes says to Burman in defining the human essence, "God is the cause of me, and I am an effect of him."[21] The proofs of God in *Meditation III* are well documented. I do understand that some of this is old hat to certain readers, but I only rehearse what is essential to a thorough reading of Article 107 of the *Passions*. This background allows an opening to Descartes's own peculiar mind-body problem. *Meditation III* features two proofs for the existence of God. The first proceeds on the basis of the meditator's idea of God and inquires into the possible origins of that specific idea, while the second asks into the cause of the *res cogitans* as a whole. At the start of the second proof Descartes writes,

And I ask, from whom do I derive my existence? Perhaps from myself or my parents, or from some other source less perfect than God; for we can imagine nothing more perfect than God, or even as perfect as he is.[22]

In answering this question, Descartes establishes that the *res cogitans* could not exist with the idea of God if God did not also exist. I now review Descartes's proof for this claim.

He begins by asking if he might be the source of his own mind given that his mind possesses this idea of God. This is absurd, since if the meditator had the power to create his own substance, then he would have the power to accomplish the easier tasks of creating his own attributes. Unfortunately, he cannot generate and attribute properties to himself at will, and hence, because he cannot do the easier thing (creating attributes), he also cannot then accomplish the harder task of creating himself (a substance). Since the meditator cannot have caused himself *ex nihilo*, then the *res cogitans*, and its idea of perfection, must be defined according to an external cause. However, whatever might be the cause of the *cogito* and its idea of the perfect, that cause must have at least as much reality as its effect.[23] As a thinking thing with a certain idea of God, "it must be granted that what caused me is also a thinking thing and it too has an idea of all the perfections which I attribute to God."[24] This entity is God himself, upon whom the meditator's existence stands as an effect. Descartes summarizes the ancestry of the *cogito* in stating,

> [W]e should now go on to inquire into the source of our being, given that we have within us an idea of the supreme perfections of God. Now it is certainly very evident by the natural light that a thing which recognizes something more perfect than itself is not the source of its own being; for if so, it would have given itself all the perfection of which it has an idea. Hence the source of its being can only be something which possesses within itself all these perfections—that is, God.[25]

He reiterates this conclusion in his 1648 *Notae in Programma Quoddam*, where one finds Descartes's most succinct statement on the gene-alogy of the mind:

> Since the mind is a substance which is newly created in the process of generation, the correct view seems to be that the rational soul is brought into existence by God during this process, through an immediate act of creation.[26]

What is significant here is that in *Meditation III* 'my existence' is not secured simply through thought. Rather, once the meditator discovers himself as a thinking thing, the being of that substance is defined on the basis of this analysis of causality. Without establishing this cause, the 'I am,' developed so rigorously in *Meditation II*, is put in peril, since a being without a cause is not a being at all. Descartes emphasizes the *ego*'s dependence on God as its cause when he writes, "The whole force of the argument rests on the fact that I recognize that it would be impos-sible for me to exist, being of such a nature as I am [. . .], unless God did in fact exist."[27] Thus, to boil all this down in a summary, suffice it to say that while *Meditation II* discovers the *ego* as a *res cogitans*, the *ego* risks slipping into non-being until the being of that substance is deter-mined by the reason for its existence, understood as an efficient cause. That reason is God.

   Furthermore, as *Meditation III* makes clear, the parents have abso-lutely no role in determining the being of the *cogito*. While Descartes devoted considerable attention to the processes of sexual reproduction, this science does not address the being under consideration in *Meditation III*, since here Descartes is limited by the order of reasons to the *cogito* alone. The body itself, to say nothing of its ancestry, has not yet been recovered from the realm of the doubtful. For this reason Descartes does not need to refute the parents' role in generating a soul, yet he devotes several lines to the possibility:

Finally, so far as my parents [from whom it appears I have sprung] are concerned, although all that I have ever been able to believe of them were true, that does not make it follow that it is they who conserve me, nor are they even the authors of my being in any sense, insofar as I am a thinking thing; since what they did was merely to implant certain dispositions in that matter in which the self—i.e. the mind, which alone I at present identify with myself—is deemed by me to exist.[28]

As readers will see, the nature of these dispositions generated by the parents is crucial to a substantial union, since "for this [union] there is required a natural disposition of the body."[29] For now, I only emphasize the parents are neither the efficient cause nor are they responsible for conserving the *cogito* through the duration of time. God alone is the cause of the *cogito* in both senses. The parents participate in merely establishing the existence of a body, but they do not generate a human being in the strict sense.

On the basis of this analysis of causation in *Meditation III*, the dualism of *Meditation II* is rigorously reestablished. Whereas *Meditation II* demonstrates that the mind is distinct from the body because it is better known, *Meditation III* takes up this dualism of substances and grounds it in a dualism of genealogies. The distinction of mind and body is hereby founded on a distinction of causes. Of course, the body, like all extended substances, relies on God and God created its matter at some distant historical point.[30] Nevertheless, Descartes is clear in *Meditation III* that the mind is not generated the way a human body is. Moreover, because the very existence of each substance depends on a demonstration of its cause, this causal dualism is more primordial than the dualism established on the basis of certainty and dubitability in *Meditation II*. Thus, it is true to say that Descartes's philosophy features a dualism of substances, thought and extension. Yet without a cause, these substances are ontologically groundless and cannot be certain to exist at all until the substance takes the form of an effect. For this reason, when one looks at Descartes's person as composed of two substances, this dualism is primarily a doctrine of efficient causality, ancestry, origins, or genealogy.

THE DISPOSITION OF THE BLOOD AND
THE SEXUAL GENERATION OF THE UNION

In declaring that God creates the mind while the parents generate the body, Descartes follows a long-established tradition of granting the human being two efficient causes. The problem of how two really distinct things, mind and body or form and matter, with distinct genealogies, could generate a human being is a problem not only for Descartes but his predecessors as well. It is perhaps Francisco Suarez who most clearly recognizes that if mind and body are designated separate causes, then the complete human being will require a third act of generation—the generation of the union. In contrast to all other forms, which he thinks are educed from matter, Suarez explains,

> [T]he rational soul comes to be in itself, at least by priority of nature, and receives its own being independent of matter, and afterward, it is united to matter by *another action* by which the whole composite is generated.[31]

Suarez, like other Scholastics, explains the physiology of this initial union of mind and body at birth in terms of 'dispositions' or 'accommodations' on the side of matter. Descartes is no different on this account, as evidenced by the aforementioned passage where he asserts that the parents 'merely implant certain dispositions in which the self, i.e. the mind [...] is deemed by me to exist.' In 1649 he elaborates on the body's primary disposition to accommodate the soul, identifying it as the blood producing a vital heat in the walls of the heart. Allow me to repeat his statement from the *Passions*, for it is of vital importance to any understanding of the significance of sex to Descartes's mind-body problem:

> [I]t seems to me that when our soul began to be joined to our body, its first passions must have arisen on some occasion when the blood, or some other juice entering the heart, was a more suitable fuel than usual for maintaining the heat of the heart, which is the principle of life: this caused the soul to join itself to this aliment and love it.[32]

This position finds inspiration in authors Descartes acknowledges, particularly the medical texts of Jean Fernel and William Harvey. These thinkers offer a complex picture of the blood and the body's vital heat that grant a celestial or divine status to these aspects of the body. Because they believe the spirit or blood to be celestial bodies, these substances serve as the ideal intermediary joining a soul born from the heavens to a mundane body.

In this section, readers will find that despite these parallels with his predecessors, Descartes fails to coherently explain how the distinct ancestries of mind and body can unite to create a whole person. His notion of the human being ultimately can be understood neither as a substantial union nor a causal interaction because the accommodation found in the heat of the heart has no particular relation to the soul. Instead, in Descartes's work, this accommodation is neither particularly 'divine' nor is it even living. It has no unique character to receive the soul from God, and it cannot be distinguished from other mundane processes found outside the human body. That is, because no part of the body is generated for the sake of the soul, Descartes lacks any explanation *why* the soul might bond to a human body. Thus, there is no explanation as to how the mind enters the body in the first place, something universally taken for granted by commentators on Descartes's mind-body problem. Because Descartes believes this conjunction occurs on the basis of a certain disposition of the blood, my reading of the passage from the *Passions* will reveal the extent to which the mind-body problem is in part owed to Descartes's characterization of the blood in the human heart, which in turn is a problem fundamentally grounded in Descartes's hypotheses on sexual reproduction and the nature of the semen.

I begin with an introduction to Fernel's thinking on substantial union. Upon establishing that the human being derives from two efficient causes in his work, I pose two questions. First, what is the physiological condition for the possibility of the body's reception of the mind? Second, what distinguishes this disposition from other body parts, granting it a unique relationship to the mind? Fernel is clear that this disposition is a certain spirit, and its unique nature is found in its quasi-divine or celestial status. This quality not only provides a unique affinity to the mind; it also carries the body's vital heat and directs the generation of the body. I then address the question of why Descartes asserts that the mind joins itself not to a divine spirit, but rather an 'aliment' responsible for the body's vital heat, which is the blood. Recognizing Descartes's extensive interest in Harvey's work on circulation, one also finds that Harvey attributes each and every characteristic of Fernel's celestial spirit to the blood itself. This furnishes Descartes with an important precedent in prioritizing the blood in relation to the vital heat, corporeal generation, and the soul. Finally, to see the critical connection between sex and the mind-body problem, one must understand how the nature of the body's disposition to receive the mind is derived from sexual generation. For this reason, I conclude by contrasting Descartes's account of generation with that of Fernel to better grasp the nature of the vital heat and its origins. In exploring these themes one will discover why not only the attention heaped on the pineal gland is deeply misguided, but also why Descartes's mind-body problem cannot be resolved by invoking a substantial union. When readers of Descartes argue that he offers no explanation as to how an immaterial mind interacts with an extended body and thereby include him as a canonical thinker in a traditional history of the mind-body problem, they assume that the mind managed to find its way into the body to begin with. Approaching mind and body from the perspective of generation permits philosophers to understand that this initial bond is where the problem truly begins.

Jean Fernel was one of the leading proponents of Galenism in the Renaissance period. He was physician to his king, Louis De Bourges, just as Galen was to Marcus Aurelius. His *Physiologia* from 1567 is considered the first systematic treatment of physiology in the West. The full extent of Descartes's familiarity with Fernel is not entirely clear.[33] Descartes is likely introduced to Fernel through his Jesuit education, where the Coimbrian commentary on the *Parva naturalia* repeatedly cites Fernel as a contemporary authority on anatomy and medicine.[34] Descartes himself cites Fernel as a respected medical expert in a letter to Plempius from February 15, 1638.[35] From that date, it is certain that Descartes is familiar with Fernel's writings before penning any of his thoughts on the mind-body union or the human mind as a substantial form. Nevertheless, I do not claim that Descartes necessarily worked through Fernel's texts in the level of detail offered in the following discussion, and Descartes could have learned similar ideas through various other sources.[36] Suffice it to say, Fernel is a common point of reference for both Descartes and Scholastic physiology, and as such, a close reading of his work provides a helpful point of contrast to aid an evaluation of Descartes's mind-body problem. Specifically, Fernel's work provides a useful backdrop to Descartes's thoughts on concepts such as spirit, the origin of the soul, and the role of sexual reproduction, all relevant to his writings on the substantial union. On the question of the mind-body union, two of Fernel's texts are essential: his *Physiologia* from 1567 and *De abditis rerum causis* from 1584.[37]

Regarding the origins of body and soul, Fernel too believes that the human being derives from two distinct efficient causes. He writes, "A human being and the sun beget a human being."[38] That is to say, the rational soul derives from the sun, while the body is created by the parents.[39] Fernel indicates in the *Physiologia* that only the rational soul has this celestial origin, while natural and sentient souls are educed from matter.[40] Fernel makes the transcendent origin of the mind clear when he writes, "[I]t is mind pure and simple [*mens illa simplex*] alone, neither provided with nor in need of the earthy bulk of the body, that accrues from outside."[41] The body and its dispositions are inherited from the parents in the act of sexual generation, but the mind or rational soul derives from an eternal or immortal source, an inheritance not from sex, but from the celestial bodies, specifically the Sun.[42]

Addressing the union of form and matter in *De abditis rerum causis*, Fernel first confronts the problem of how a human body, composed of diverse materials including flesh, bones, and fluids, can possibly be a simple 'this'—a human being. Fernel must demonstrate "that the form of a composite body is simple and similar, and also dispersed through the parts,"[43] a concern Descartes addresses in his *Responses* through the analogy of heaviness.[44] If the form is simple, how can a simple and uniform soul unite with all the diverse parts of the body? What relates this matter to create *a* body to which the mind can join itself? Fernel writes,

> If you are prepared to think straight about this resemblance
> of parts, what needs to be reckoned is, as I said before, not the
> temperament or thickness of the substance, but its own special
> property, and the spirit that makes it ready in a special way for
> the arrival of form.[45]

But what is this 'special property' or 'spirit'? Fernel devotes much of his attention to this question not only in book 1 of *De abditis rerum causis* but also throughout his *Physiologia*. However, before turning to that question, what is most important to comprehend from the outset, and it is implicated in the previous quote, is that matter is not strictly passive. Instead, it has an inherent force that readies it to receive its appropriate form. This force is not the essence of the being, nor is it completely uniform throughout all of nature. The matter of each organism, be it a dog, a mule, or a human, has a particular disposition or amenability to receive an appropriate form, and this amenability preexists the form that is said to differentiate the material. The union of the two is made possible by the dispositions that 'predispose' matter to receive a certain form.

Regarding these predispositions, Fernel explains, "In the bodies of all living things, at least three preparations must be in place for the reception of form."[46] The first is "a proper and suitable temperament,"[47] while the second is "a harmonious combining, accord, and adaption" of each organic part.[48] As the preceding quote indicates, these are not as essential as the third, which Fernel states is "a spirit pervading the whole, in which the salutary vital heat resides."[49] In Fernel's works there are several different kinds of spirit, each of which plays a specific role in organic processes. Natural spirits are formed in the liver and mediate the functions of the nutritive and vegetative soul. Vital spirits are formed in the left part of the heart out of blood and air in order to distribute heat throughout the body. Animal spirits are formed out of the vital spirits, and, as for Descartes, they travel through the nervous system to facilitate motion and sensation. In addition, there is a fourth, more fundamental spirit, which Fernel calls the divine or celestial spirit. Not only is celestial spirit the source of all vital functions; it is the essential prerequisite for the soul's unification with the body, since it is nearest in nature to the rational soul. The effects of this spirit are in large part due to the vital heat it carries, a heat distinct from that found in inorganic nature, and Fernel argues at length that "this heat is above the nature of elements,"[50] featuring a divine aspect.

Because the spirit's vital heat is a celestial body but nevertheless already present in the fetus, it serves as an ideal mediator to bond soul and body at birth. In Fernel's words,

> [I]t is exceedingly intimate with both [mind and body], and not being devoid of body, can be placed in a coarse body. But being more rarefied and bright it can be linked to the mind. Sharing thus in both after a fashion, it bonds a nature without body to corporeal nature, the immortal to the mortal, the pure to the impure, the divine to the earthly.[51]

That is to say, the soul only bonds to the body through this 'third term,' the celestial spirit. This spirit is not itself a body part, but rather it is that which readies the body parts as a unified living being. This is the essential disposition for the reception of the soul, making its union with the body possible.

While none of this passes for science by today's standards, Fernel does formulate a coherent doctrine of the genealogical difference between mind and body as well as their union at birth. The latter is entirely made possible by the supra-elemental heat of the body. Descartes also insists on the distinct origins of mind and body, and while he does believe the soul bonds to a particular aliment producing the vital heat, he considers this to be the blood.

Although Fernel has much to say about the body's vital heat, when Descartes discusses the matter it is almost always with the work of William Harvey in mind. Harvey appears in several of Descartes's letters and texts, but perhaps he is most notable in Section V of the *Discours*, which Descartes devotes almost entirely to the functioning of the heart and Harvey's anatomical methods. Although Harvey makes several key breakthroughs in anatomy, his ideas on the body still reside in the Scholastic world, relying heavily on material tendencies and substantial forms.[52] However, despite this discrepancy with Descartes, his work is important insofar as he identifies the blood, not the spirit, as the source of the body's vital heat. In contrast to thinkers like Fernel, the heat and spirits unique to the blood are actually identical to the blood, making any divine or celestial spirit redundant. Harvey writes,

> There is, in fact, no occasion for searching after spirits foreign to, or distinct from, the blood; to evoke heat from another source; to bring gods upon the scene and to encumber philosophy with any fanciful conceits; what we are wont to derive from the stars is in truth produced at home: the blood is the only *calidum innatum*, or first engendered animal heat; a fact which so clearly appears from our observations on animal

reproduction, particularly of the chick from the egg, that it seems superfluous to multiply illustrations.[53]

In *De generatione*, Harvey further clarifies that it is blood and not spirit that acts on account of its own immanent, spiritual nature:

> The tenuity, subtlety, mobility, etc. of the spirits, therefore, bring no kind of advantage more than the blood, which it seems they constantly accompany, and already possess. The blood consequently suffices, and is adequate to be the immediate instrument of the soul, inasmuch as it is everywhere present, and moves hither and thither with the greatest rapidity.[54]

Harvey is certainly not the first to claim the blood is the initial site of the mind-body union. For instance, Akan philosophers had submitted the hypotheses far in advance of Harvey's time.[55] At any rate, Harvey believes the blood, a corporeal substance, acts in a way that cannot be explained by the mere interaction of the four elements. In other words, the blood is a kind of material, but an active material with its own spiritual nature. That spiritual quality allows the blood to effectively replace Fernel's celestial spirits, a notion that finds no role in Harvey's work.

Descartes reads *De motu cordis* in 1632[56] and he studies Harvey's work as he writes his *Traité de l'homme*, one of his most prolonged engagements with human anatomy. Although Harvey's *De generatione* is not published until 1651, a year after Descartes's death, the *De motu cordis* addresses the body's vital heat and the blood on several occasions. Reference to the blood's celestial and spiritual nature is quite explicit in Harvey's appropriation of Aristotle's circular metaphors. To Harvey, the circulation of the blood mirrors the circulation of the heavens, granting the heart and blood a unique divinity. Harvey writes in *De motu cordis*,

> So the heart is the center of life, the sun of the Microcosm, as the sun itself might be called the heart of the world. The blood

is moved, invigorated, and kept from decaying by the power and pulse of the heart. It is that intimate shrine whose function is the nourishing and arming of the whole body, the basis and source of all life.[57]

This makes the blood not only the principle of life but also a material featuring an aspect analogous to the divine and immortal realm of heavenly bodies. Although Descartes devotes a full paragraph of Section V of the *Discourse* to a summary and conditional approval of Harvey's theory of the circulation of the blood and his methods of demonstration,[58] he nevertheless strongly criticizes Harvey's characterizations of the blood and the heart several times in his written correspondence.[59] Just what does this point of disagreement consist of? Both agree that the heart and the blood in conjunction produce the body's heat. Yet, while Harvey believes that the blood is the source of vital heat on account of its celestial power, Descartes insists that the heat found in the heart's blood is due to strictly mechanical causes, a phenomenon he calls the *feu sans lumière*.

It is well documented, and as the concluding remarks of *Le Monde* make clear,[60] Descartes believes the body, *qua* body, is known strictly on the basis of extension and the movement of its particles.[61] For this reason, the blood and the heat in the heart are not anything peculiar to living beings, but rather the 'principle of life' is the same phenomenon that is found in any fire. Descartes details how this *feu sans lumière* functions in the walls of the heart in arguing that neither the blood, the spirits, nor the vital heat have any divine properties, and instead it is owed to a kind of combustion through fermentation. Attempting to explain this, he writes that this heat is not "at all of another nature than that which heats hay, when we have stored it before it was dry, or that boils new wines when we leave them to rest on the grate."[62] Similarly, in the *Description*, he makes another reference to inanimate processes of fermentation, writing,

We cannot doubt that there is a heat in the heart, because we can even feel it with our hand when we open the body of a living animal. And it is not necessary to imagine that this heat is of another nature than is generally all those that are caused by the mixing of a liqueur or agent of fermentation . . .[63]

In the *Discourse*, he repeats this claim, writing,

[God] excited in its heart one of these fires without light which I had already explained, and which I conceived to be of the same nature as that which heats grain, when we store it before it is dry, or which makes new wines boil, when we leave them to ferment in the pulp.[64]

In his *Principles*, Descartes gives a detailed explanation of how a *feu sans lumière* is created in inorganic matter, again using the example of wet hay.[65] Of course, all of this stands in stark contrast to statements by Fernel arguing that the vital heat is *not* an elemental fire and is carried by a certain divine spirit. In Descartes's work the heat is carried by nothing other than the motion of the blood itself. As Descartes claims in the Section V of the *Discourse*, the blood is "used to feed the fire in the heart," and just as the liquid in wet hay facilitates the production of heat, so it is with blood, as tiny particles agitate the pores in the walls of the heart.

This is the background to Article 107 of the *Passions* when he writes, "the blood, or some other juice entering the heart, was a more suitable fuel than usual for maintaining the heat which is the principle of life."[66] In this regard, Descartes is aligned with Harvey, who positions the blood as the basis of the vital heat as well as the mediator between soul and body. However, Descartes believes that this 'vital' heat is not unique to the organic world at all. It is nothing more than the inorganic movement of particles, and ultimately Descartes's 'principle of life' is not an organic principle. Life's 'organic' distinction becomes a casualty of the mechanical view of nature, as the heart and its heat are merely an instance of a process of fermentation found in various inorganic materials.[67] This is crucial to Descartes's mind-body problem, yet its full significance is only appreciated through a consideration of the sexual generation of this 'vital' disposition, to which I now turn.

Descartes's corpus provides significant evidence that he feels it necessary to give an account of sexual reproduction on the basis of his mechanical physics. In fact, as Descartes writes his *Description* and *Traité*, he is immersed in the embryological treatises of his contemporaries, hypothesizing the nature of the seed, how the organs are formed, and the role of God. There are four places in Descartes's oeuvre that address generation directly: *Primae Cogitationes circa generationem animalium*, first published in 1692; the *Excerpta anatomica* and *Remedia et vires medicamentorum*, which both survive thanks to Leibniz, who recopied them into his notebooks; and finally the *Description* itself, published in 1664 by Claude Clerselier.[68] Add to this the previous discussion from *Meditation III*, and one finds a rather extensive body of work on the topic of sex. Here, I focus on the *Description*, which is arguably Descartes's most polished writing on the question of corporeal generation.

Descartes believes that as the site of the vital heat, life can only be said to begin once the heart is formed.[69] His challenge is to describe its formation without recourse to final causes, Aristotelean souls, or Galenic faculties as had his predecessors. He decides that during intercourse, males and females exchange fluids. These fluids interact to generate heat, and that heat in turn drives unformed matter to create the organs. Descartes explains the action of the semen and the formation of the heart and other organs as follows:

> It suffices to say that [the particles of the seed] of plants, being hard and solid, can have its parts arranged and situated in a certain way [...] but it is not the same with the particles of animal semen, which are completely fluid, and ordinarily produced by the conjunction of the two sexes, and which seem only to be a confused mix of two liquids which serve as a leaven for each other, heating each other in such way that some of their particles acquire the same agitation as fire, dilate and press

upon the others, and in this way arrange [*disposent*] the particles little by little in the way required to form the organs.[70]

This heat produced in the womb is of the same nature as the heat in the heart. That is, the heat produced by the mixture of semen ferments and creates an identical *feu sans lumière*, which results in the formation of the heart. Descartes again invokes the familiar metaphors of wet hay and fermenting wines when he writes,

> I believe that the first thing to appear in the mixture of semen, and which makes all of its droplets stop from being the same, is that the heat is excited here, and acts in the same way as in new wines when they boil, or in hay when it has been shut away before dry, and here it dilates, they press the others that surround them and begin to form the heart.[71]

According to Descartes, once these particles press on each other enough to form a solid substance, their continued dilation forces some particles to expand outward. Following the principle of rectilinear inertia, these particles begin to move in a straight line, but they do not travel far until they encounter resistance and are pushed back the way they came. This point of resistance is nothing other than what will become the walls of the heart. As the heat pushes particles outward to the wall, and the particles circulate back toward the heat, a circle of movement is formed. As the particles continue in this circular movement, they expand each time and move away, following the same path. With each circulation the particles move away from the heat a little farther until bit by bit the walls of the heart are pushed out and all of its cavities are formed. In this way, Descartes believes it is a process of growth without a final cause much like nutrition whereby particles of matter are carried farther away by a steady flow of liquid, be it blood or first element particles.[72]

I would not go so far as to say that Descartes's embryology is easy to understand or that it all adds up in the end, but the basic idea is that the male and female semens combine to create heat, heat creates the heart, the heart is the first organ formed, and it becomes the source of heat for the animal throughout the course of its life.[73] Again, note that this heat, a *feu sans lumière*, is always of the same nature because the heat of the heart is a product of the semen's heat. Descartes even invokes the same metaphors of fermentation to explain the heat that propels generation as well as that which resides in the fully formed heart.

In his writings on generation, Descartes is at once close to and distant from what one finds in Fernel's work. Fernel's explanation of generation begins with the assertion that the celestial spirit is responsible for all generation:

> [T]his spirit, the regulator of heat and all the faculties and the originator of procreation, gathers into the center of the semen. It does not vanish or fly off from the semen, although many people take Aristotle this way, but continues in it as the craftsman fashioning all the parts, is utterly and fundamentally imbedded in them, and becomes their original nature.[74]

Yet, even though the spirit and the vital heat it carries are embedded in the whole body, it is most concentrated in the heart. This is due to the fact that the semen itself is not uniform; rather, the celestial spirit, which is responsible for accommodating the mind into the body, is concentrated in the center of the semen. Each organ that develops takes on the particular character of that part of the semen from which it derives. As Fernel explains,

> First of all, swelling with much spirit, [the semen] spreads itself out, and pervading everything, it separates off the different parts in the semen (which looks simple and uniform, yet is not so), the hot from the cold, the thin from the thick and earthy, so that individual parts end up adopting their own nature, and are assembled for the fashioning of the parts from which in the past they withdrew.[75]

The heart develops out of the hottest, most spirituous, and most divine bit of semen, and this is how Fernel accounts for the heart as the final residence of this heat and divine spirit.

Anticipating Descartes's view, Fernel believes that as the soul unites with the body, the bond will occur on the basis of this spirituous heat in the heart. It is crucial to note here how the fundamental possibility of this union is ultimately derived not from the nature of the heart but the semen that forms the heart out of its dense accumulation of divine spirit. This leads to a preliminary conclusion that I wish to emphasize: According to Fernel, the primary accommodation for the reception of the rational soul is founded upon this specific account of the semen and sexual reproduction. This point is fundamental to his science of the substantial union of mind and body.

Elements of Fernel's doctrine are reflected in Descartes's understanding of the mind-body union at conception, as he adopts a similar position. The heat driving fetal development first generates the heart and then remains there, fueled by the blood, which in turn serves as the body's disposition to receive the mind. Yet, his account does not permit the accommodations provided by a celestial spirit. In its place, the formation of the heart and its resident heat are composed of strictly corpuscular motion. These accommodations are in no way celestial or divine. As I have underscored, Descartes describes the semen as mechanical and inorganic, and the same is true of the semen's heat driving the process of generation. Accordingly, the heat of the heart is no more organic, as it is the first product of the movement of the semen's particles. Descartes takes care to emphasize this position in the *Description*, when he claims, "And I do not know of any fire or heat in the heart other than this agitation of the particles of the blood . . . ," or "this movement of the diastole has been caused from the beginning by heat, or by the action of fire, which, following what I explained in my *Principes*, is not able to consist of anything other than the first Element."[76] This is just to say that the body's purported disposition to receive the soul is the concentrated residue of the materials and processes responsible for fetal development.

The way Descartes characterizes the heat of the heart, which supposedly accommodates the soul, joining it to the body, is an extension of his explanations of sexual reproduction. This is equally true of Fernel's account, and one finds both thinkers agreeing on the homogeneity of the materials responsible for fetal development, the body's vital heat, and the disposition charged with the reception of the soul. Clearly, the way Descartes and Fernel each theorize fetal development ultimately determines their respective characterizations of the disposition responsible for joining soul and body.

However, that is where the similarities end. In Fernel's work, the celestial spirit accounts for sexual generation while also serving as the source of vital heat. Beyond these duties, celestial spirits make the union of mind and body possible insofar as their Janus-faced nature serves as the accommodation necessary for the reception of the soul. This quality of celestial spirit allows Fernel to say, "The body of each living thing, and especially the human body, is constructed for the sake of the soul."[77] As I have explained, Descartes will have no part in this physiology of the substantial union. Not only is there an explicit rejection of a physiology based on final causes; there is no intermediary substance present in the body to accommodate the soul. Thus, despite Descartes's repeated references to substantial forms and unions, he systematically dismantles the physiological foundation of that doctrine. While he does state in Article 107 that the soul, at birth, 'loves' the blood responsible for the heat in the heart, there is no explanation of what makes this disposition uniquely human or what makes this heat particularly attractive to the soul.[78] If this disposition is no different from fermenting wine or decomposing hay, why does the soul not love those materials as well? In other words, preceding the customary question of *how* mind and body interact, Descartes must reckon with the primordial problem of *why* they unite in the first place. Why does the soul love *my* body when this body presents no distinct accommodation for the soul? Descartes claims this 'joining' is a kind of love, but what guides the soul's love to human bodies? This question of *Why?*, ultimately rooted in Descartes's account of sex, cannot be answered within the parameters of his metaphysics, since no third term, or mediating accommodation, can distinguish the human body as the uniquely appropriate residence for the divinely created human soul. Thus, despite his invocation of certain Scholastic terminology, the sexual physiology required for the generation of a substantial union is entirely absent.

All of this leaves one rather removed from the usual understanding of the problem as it is laid out by Searle and other philosophers of mind. Moreover, this problem of sex is not particularly easy to see. Even Descartes seems to think he has coherently explained how God generates the mind, the parents generate an appropriately disposed body, and the two unite to create the whole person. Presumably, this is why he goes on to tackle the questions of mind-body relations in the mature human being. Paradoxically, the obscurity of the problem of sex stems from the problem's primacy. What makes the problem both disguised and primordial is that it must be discovered by approaching the mind-body union from the perspective of generation. When one presses Descartes on how the initial mind-body union is generated, the results can be summarized as follows:

1. The mind is generated by God, while the parents generate the body.
2. Descartes follows Scholastic precedents in asserting that the initial conjunction of mind and body occurs on the basis of certain corporeal dispositions or accommodations.
3. He believes this disposition is the blood, specifically, the blood responsible for generating the heat in the walls of the heart.
4. The nature of this disposition derives from the process of sexual reproduction that generates it.
5. Because sex is but a mundane process of matter and motion, so are its products, namely, the disposition charged with accommodating the mind.
6. The blood, and the heat it produces, has no unique disposition to attract the soul's love and the initial mind-body union is foiled.

This difficulty should be recognized as a problem of blood and, ultimately, sex.

I do not deny how tempting it is to draw a direct line from Descartes's work to today's mind-body problem as it is framed by many esteemed philosophers of mind. Yet, the notion that the twentieth-century formulation of a problem concerning "how it is possible for the mental to exercise causal influences in the physical world"[79] is just a "souped-up version"[80] of Descartes's problem is simply a fantasy. Not only is this history of the mind-body problem not historically accurate; it buries a more basic problem of sex. This question should be seen as primordial because, again, without an account of *why* the mind ever enters the body at birth, any discussion of *how* mind and body, or mind and brain, interact in a mature adult is rendered moot. In other words, if one is ever going to approach the problem of how heterogeneous substances interact in the brain, then one must be able to explain how Descartes's mind and body came to form a person in the first place. Moreover, if the contemporary mind-body industry is grounded in a problem of interaction, relation, or association between mind and body in a mature adult, then Descartes's most primordial and rudimentary problem is not part of this enterprise. His is a problem of sex, and it is the account of sex—not the pineal gland—that leaves the union without explanation.

However, one cannot overstate the difference. Even though Descartes's problem and the premises from which it develops, including God's generation of the soul and the supposed generation of the body's accommodations, is not part of philosophy's contemporary mainstream mind-body debate, it nevertheless cannot truly earn the title of 'another mind-body problem.' Although my emphasis here is on problems of sexual reproduction and not the anatomy of the brain and nervous system often highlighted in Descartes's work, I am still dealing with the question of the union of mind and body. Merely following Article 107 of the *Passions* to the point of repositioning the problem of the union on the terrain of sex does not go far enough to encounter the problem of a racial non-being, since, as I noted in the introduction, the contemporary discussion, in its broadest terms, is defined by this very question of 'relations' and 'associations.' Descartes too struggles with these questions in Article 107, though it is a problem of how the mind relates to the blood or, ultimately, the semen.

Going forward, I will continue to press several authors on these themes until I arrive at a race concept from which another mind-body problem emerges. For now, it is sufficient to note the crucial importance of sex to Descartes's problem. As the reader will discover in the following chapters, Descartes's problem of sex will mutate significantly until it reaches the point where it can be solved by the theory of sex Kant calls 'race.' It is only at that point that the problem of a racial nothingness can emerge, and philosophy can begin to reckon with the contours of a problem that has nothing to do with interaction or the relation between consciousness and brain states and everything to do with a racist violence.

THE RACIAL LEGACY OF
A GENEALOGICAL MIND-BODY DUALISM

A range of authors have argued that Cartesian dualism cannot possibly support a theory of race and thus stands as a metaphysical barricade against racism. Voegelin himself advances a version of this position in writing that with the Cartesian division of body and soul,

> race speculations of the sort we are familiar with today are still impossible; those require a basic reciprocal spiritualization of the body and the embodiment of the spirit into the union of earthly-human existence as their foundation.[81]

Ivan Hannaford echoes Voegelin in noting dualism's effect on delaying the emergence of the race concept in Early Modern Europe, stating that

> attempts to establish anatomical, physiological, geographical, and astrological relationships between man and man, and

man and beast, did not develop a fully developed idea of race, since there was no proper anthropology, natural history, or biology to support it.[82]

More recently, Justin E. H. Smith has joined this tradition in writing,

an important feature of Cartesian mind-body dualism and its corollary, Cartesian human-animal dualism [is] that in such an ontology there is simply no space for finer gradations of race, where race is understood as marking out physical differences between different human groups that in turn correspond to differences of mental capacity.[83]

These claims are anything but baseless. Indeed, a study of Descartes's work indicates there is reason to think dualism precludes a science of human difference and thereby stands as a bulwark against racism. Specifically, the key question is how human difference is possible if the essence of each and every human being is universally determined by a cause that transcends the effects of sex. In concluding this chapter I survey how through the eighteenth-century writings of Georges-Louis Leclerc, Comte de Buffon, one does glimpse why Cartesian dualism could stand as a bulwark against a scientific doctrine of human races, even while it permits a racialization of the body. However, in the mid-nineteenth-century work of Arthur de Gobineau one discovers the total cooptation of this genealogical dualism in the service of not only 'race' thinking but, more specifically, Aryanism. This leads me to conclude that rather than following Voegelin, Hannaford, and Smith in citing Descartes's dualism as a concept simply in favor of human equality, the more interesting point for those who want to understand racism's historical development is that the metaphysics of an archetypal White supremacist can be favorably compared to ideas at one point known as a metaphysics of human equality. Thus, while it is tempting to turn to history in order to identify a metaphysics of mind and body immune to racism, the fact that racism is neither uniform nor static undermines any such attempt. It is more productive to reckon with the changing historical contexts within which racism, anti-racism, and the metaphysics of mind and body have been assembled in order to grasp the interchangeable nature of racism and a presumed antiracist mantra such as 'human equality.' Furthermore, I do not mean to sidetrack my investigation into the history of the mind-body problem with this debate. However, it is helpful for readers to see that these questions of sexual reproduction, the mind's origin and relation to God, the mind's relation to sex and the sex organs, as well as the birth of the mind-body union are never far removed from theories of race and human difference. In the chapters to follow, readers will see these overlaps become only more pronounced.

In my discussion of the *Meditations*, I mentioned how once the thinking substance is discovered, Descartes turns to a more rigorous determination of its existence on the basis of an analysis of efficient causes. This leads Descartes to claim the essence of the human being is not only synonymous with thought and a capacity to reason; it is more essentially defined by a certain relationship to God. Insofar as all existence is rooted in a determination of efficient causality, the *cogito*, above all else, exists as an effect of God and bears his distinctive mark. Accordingly, *Meditation III* not only fulfills an epistemological duty of dispelling the threat of the evil deceiver; it simultaneously establishes the cause, and thus the objective existence, of the thinking substance.

However, the author of the *Second Objection* (probably Marin Mersenne) discovers a possible exception to the doctrines presented in *Meditation III* when he wonders if the idea of God is universally innate given that certain non-Europeans must be taught the idea: "But that this idea [of God] comes from previously conceived notions seems to be established by the fact that indigenous people of Canada—Hurons and other primitive men—entertain no such idea."[84] This comment implies a series of questions one can unfold. If a human being lacks the idea of God, the "mark of the craftsman,"[85] does this being stand in the same relation to God? Is the pagan mind a *cogito* in the same sense as the meditator's, made "in [God's] image and likeness"?[86] Or is his or her whole being produced sexually, like that of an animal? How might the 'Huron,' as the French called them, demonstrate his cause and thereby confirm his or her human existence?[87]

In response to this dilemma, Descartes explains that there are no people so primitive as to lack the idea of God, and those who lack knowledge of 'God' simply do not recognize the name. In Descartes's words, "[T]hose who deny they have an idea of God, but in place of it form some image [idolum], and so on, deny the name but concede the fact."[88] The full significance of this statement is best understood in the context of Descartes's ontology. If the idea of a perfect being were not innate for certain non-Europeans, then these people would lack the idea of the perfect altogether since they could neither produce it themselves nor receive it from their parents. Because every cause must have at least as much reality as its effect, a Huron intellect that concedes the fact of a perfect being must recognize that the idol or idea must have been created by a being with equal reality and perfection. Although Descartes believes the Hurons are wrong not to recognize this idea as 'God,' they nevertheless 'concede the fact' of their conscious experience of a perfect being. This conscious experience is nothing other than what Descartes had called in *Meditation III* the "mark of the craftsman." It is only on the basis of 'the reality' of this idea that one can demonstrate the unique relationship to God that distinguishes one's intellectual nature from other merely corporeal animal beings. Implied in Descartes's comment is that through this idea 'primitive men' too can discover an essence not determined as a product of the parents, but of God. Thus, the Huron's existence rises above mere animality, rooted in the divine, a belief consistent with his assertion from the *Discourse on Method* where he writes, "that all those who have opinions that are entirely at variance with ours, are not therefore barbarians or savages, but several of them use their faculty of reason as well as or better than we."[89]

Of course, none of this should distract from the fact that in the case of the Huron, just as with any human being, there remains a basic problem of how the mind-body union is generated at birth. Nevertheless, without distracting from that overriding question, I fill in these blanks simply because Descartes does not entirely do so himself, adding to his relative silence on questions of human difference.[90] One might argue that his allusion to the Hurons raises more questions than it answers. Nevertheless, despite these silences, throughout Descartes's writings one finds a fundamental homogeneity characterizing the mind. That is, each and every person who has the capacity to reason has the ability completely, naturally, and without degrees, or as he writes in the *Discourse*, "Reason is complete in each person."[91] However, it deserves mention that the 'equality' of intellects should not be taken too far. The *cogito*, as a pure intelligence, is in a certain sense an abstract and potential being, but it is only the 'intellectual nature in general' that is complete in each person, regardless of what it thinks, true or false. The principle of individual difference lies elsewhere, specifically in the way in which one directs one's native intelligence, a task Descartes addresses most explicitly in the *Rules for the Direction of the Mind*.[92]

Nevertheless, however it is put to use, difference is never found in the *cogito* as such, understood as a potential to reason generated by God. Descartes emphasizes and reiterates this intellectual homogeneity in several passages. Consider, for example, where he writes,

> The power of forming a good judgment and of distinguishing the true from the false, which is properly what is called good sense or reason, is *by nature* equal in all men. Hence too it will show that the diversity of our opinions does not proceed from some men being more rational than others, but solely from the fact that our thoughts pass through diverse channels and the same objects are not considered by all.[93]

Moreover, human equality is *naturellement* or as it must be heard according to its Latin root (*natio*), by birth. As I have discussed, God produces the *ego*, making him an efficient cause that transcends the local influence of climate, parental ancestry, physiology, and the like. As such, considered strictly according to its ancestry or cause, the *cogito* is necessarily "whole in each of us." This definition is univocal across the species, despite whether each and every mind achieves wisdom through the order of reasons, or even if, as in the case of the so-called Hurons, they lack knowledge altogether of a Christian God *per se*. I emphasize all this in part because it sheds light on Descartes's lack of a theory of human difference, but also because the status of the Hurons is of no small significance to the history of the mind-body problem, and in chapter 2 I will discuss how Charles Bonnet radically reinvents the Huron on the basis of a newly conceived mind-body union.

Descartes is certainly not alone in his assertion of human unity and equality on religious grounds. Arguments for the abolition of slavery at this time were driven by religious appeals that had less to do with physical or mundane equality and everything to do with equality in relation to God.[94] This discourse is further buttressed by Descartes's works and it is apparent in Descartes's immediate legacy. In a related context, these principles formed the basis of François Poullain de la Barre's feminism of the late seventeenth century. This author takes Cartesianism's uniformity of the mind and its distinction from the body as the basis for an attack on sexual inequality. For Poullain de la Barre, the distinct causes of mind and body played a fundamental role in his argument for an essential human sameness. He argues that since 'sex' refers to those aspects of the human being used in reproduction, sexual difference concerns only the body. According to Cartesian philosophy, the mind is not involved in sexual reproduction, and hence has no sex. In other words, the mind is not defined by sex, since it is not an effect of sex. Rather, the mind arrives in the human body as an effect of God, and its being is defined spiritually rather than sexually. Writing in 1673 he states,

> It is easy to see that the difference between the two sexes is limited to the body, since that is the only part used in the reproduction of mankind. Since the mind merely gives its consent,

and does so in exactly the same way in everyone, we can conclude that it has no sex [. . .]. A woman's mind is joined to her
body, like a man's, by God himself, and according to the same
laws. Feelings, passions, and the will maintain this union, and
since the mind functions no differently in one sex than in the
other, it is capable of the same thing in both.[95]

Beyond Poullain de la Barre, of the thinkers working in the Cartesian tradition, it is George-Louis Leclerc, Comte de Buffon, the foremost natural
historian of the French Enlightenment, who best demonstrates how this
ontology might be said to hold out against a science of human races.

Writing in the mid-eighteenth century, Buffon's study of the human
being pivots on a profound dualism. Following Descartes in the order
of knowledge, the human being is primarily and essentially a mind. The
distinction of mind and body is established once the mind is known with
certainty while the body's existence remains subject to doubt:

To exist and to think are for us the same thing—this truth is
intimate and more than intuitive, it is independent of the senses,
of our memory and of all related faculties [. . .].The existence
of our body and of all external objects is doubtful for anyone
who reasons without prejudice.[96]

However, as in *Meditation III*, this division of the person is further
grounded in a genealogical theory positing two distinct causes for mind
and body. I will examine Buffon's causal ontology in two steps. First,
Buffon follows Descartes in appealing to distinct genealogies for body
and mind because it is demanded by both his methodology of natural
history as well as his views on embryology and sexual reproduction.
This leads him to follow the historical precedents I have been tracing in
positing a transcendent, divine ancestry of the mind, one that is analogous to the sun's emanation of light. Second, despite appearances, Buffon
does not and cannot articulate a coherent theory of human races, since

the lineage of characteristics that defines a race is isolated from the metaphysical ancestry that produces the essence of every human being regardless of body type. Through this study, one will see most clearly what in a Cartesian approach to mind and body are obstacles to race thinking, obstacles that, oddly enough, form the basis of Gobineau's Aryanism a century later.

Buffon's genealogical approach to racial and species classification emerges against the backdrop of Linnaeus's *Systema Naturae*, which had ordered nature on the basis of resemblances between supposedly essential characters.[97] This taxonomy, based on a static and atemporal analysis of individuals, created unified groups by highlighting certain similarities and ignoring others, a method Buffon considers totally arbitrary. In contrast to Linnaeus's taxonomy Buffon writes,

> It is neither the number nor the collectivity of similar individuals that makes the species; it is the constant succession and the uninterrupted renewal of these individuals that constitute it [...]. Species is, therefore, an abstract and general word, which describes something that exists only by considering Nature in the succession of time and the constant destruction and equally constant renewal of beings.[98]

This approach not only makes the species synonymous with its history; it opens the possibility for the study of lineages subordinate to the species. On the basis of his study of reproduction and offspring, Buffon can classify variations within the species as subordinate historical lineages produced in response to local environmental conditions. As he explains in *De la dégénération des animaux*, as generations of the human species spread out from Europe around the globe and are subjected to various climates, the body 'degenerates' as the skin color, hair texture, and other characteristics are molded by the surroundings. These racial degenerations are not ephemeral or random, but rather display the constancy and relative permanence necessary to be studied lawfully. In fact, it is precisely the constancy of these traits across time that invites Buffon to demarcate sub-special groups: "These impressions do not occur suddenly or in the space of a few years; [they are] perpetuated by generation [and] have become general and constant characters in which we recognize the races and even the different nations composing the human species."[99] These regularly reproduced differences can thereby be classified on the basis of their permanency across time. In other words, on the basis of this historical methodology, 'race' can be seen as a meaningful and necessary category insofar as it specifies relatively constant characteristics transmitted through sexual reproduction.

Given these innovations, it is in a way true what Claude-Olivier Doron has recently written about a "genealogical depth" to Buffon's thinking, on the basis of which races can be studied as a relative constancy of characteristics across generations "between the quasi-anomic accidental variety and the quasi-absolute constancy of species."[100] As Buffon defines it, "The races in each species of animal are only constant varieties which perpetuate themselves by generation."[101] I will return to these themes in detail in chapter 3, since the constancy and permanence of certain alterations is absolutely crucial to Kant's race concept. Suffice it to say that through these developments one may be tempted, with Doron, to claim that Buffon invents the science of human races because he inaugurates a genealogical approach to classification that treats intraspecial differences as objects of science. That is to say, Buffon treats them as characteristics that are constant and, to some degree, law-abiding.[102]

However, against the backdrop of Cartesian philosophy it is necessary to circumscribe the dimensions of this accomplishment in the history of race thinking. While Buffon does develop a new and rigorous idea of race, one that strongly influences the eighteenth century, his notion of race does not, and cannot, properly be applied to human beings. Because the essence of the human being—thought—is defined by a divine cause under which everyone stands as an effect, the concept of 'race' cannot be applied to the person as such. However, the races Buffon's writing does produce, the raced animal body, is only made possible because of this dual ancestry of mind and body. For this reason, one must first recognize how the Cartesian dualism of causes is a condition for the possibility of a concept of race in order to then see how this very possibility is simultaneously the condition for the impossibility of its application to the human species.

It is not by accident that the dualism of mind and body dominates Buffon's natural history. Buffon believes the opportunity to study human beings' natural history only emerges once the body has been isolated and the uniquely human aspect of the being has been left behind:

> When we compare man with animal creation, we find in both a material, organized body, senses, flesh and blood, motion and many other striking resemblances. But all these analogies are external, and authorize us not to pronounce that the nature of man is similar to that of the brute.[103]

The mind is not included in the natural history of humans. Rather, it is addressed in a separate chapter devoted to the 'internal' being of the human, situated just before Buffon goes on to "give the history of his body."[104] On the basis of this dualism, Buffon believes he can study the human body as a part of the animal world without sacrificing the dignity of the human essence. For this reason, the history of the body that serves as the foundation of Buffon's concepts of species and race is thereby not a history of human beings as such. Nor can it be, since the mind, defined as a *partless* substance, cannot be accounted for by Buffon's theory of sexual reproduction, which, as he explains, occurs entirely through the organization of physical particles.[105]

To account for the generation of the human essence, Buffon must invoke a separate explanation, one that transcends the corporeal series. Following the tradition I have traced throughout this chapter, the mind is not generated by the parents, but rather it is "a gift from the Almighty."[106] When Buffon discusses the mind, he is never far from Descartes's precedent, and while he does distinguish mind and body on the order of knowledge, that difference is ultimately established through a distinction of origins. Buffon's clearest statement on the efficient cause of the mind comes in *Les animales domestiques* from 1753:

> [T]he ray of divinity with which man is animated ennobles and elevates him above every material existence. This spiritual substance, so far from being subject to matter, is entitled to govern it; and though mind cannot command the whole of Nature, she rules over individual beings. *God, the source of all light and of all intelligence*, governs the universe, and every species, with infinite power: Man, who possesses only a ray of his intelligence, enjoys, accordingly, a power limited to individuals, and to small portions of matter.[107]

Here, one finds an unambiguous dualism of causes in Buffon's description of the human being. Not only is the human being defined as a thinking substance, and thus "above every material existence," but the thinking substance is further specified as an effect of God. God is not only the efficient cause of the thinking substance ('the source of all [...] intelligence'), but, through an analogy with the sun, one finds that the mind bears the mark of its cause insofar as it too is a ray of light, able to shine on beings. As with Descartes, the significance of the soul lies not merely in the capacity to think, but moreover it is that which grants the human being an existence that is more than merely animal. To have a soul is, most importantly, to have an exclusive relationship with God as his immediate effect. This formulation of the mind as an effect of God makes no reference to Buffon's internal mold, organic particles, the successive generation of individuals, the succession of time, or reproduction, all of which are essential to his study of species and race. As an effect of God, the mind has no place in those concepts, or as Descartes writes, the parents are not "the authors of my being in any sense insofar as I am a thinking thing."[108]

While Buffon follows a long tradition in claiming that the soul arrives on the fortieth day of gestation, he never clarifies exactly how the lineages of mind and body unite at birth.[109] Yet, his reticence might be expected if one keeps in mind that Buffon never claims to address the natural history of the person considered as the unity of mind and body. In fact, he believes natural history can only address humans at all on account of this dualism that allows one to divide the person along the lines of a spiritual and sexual ancestry. If the generation of the human body could not be abstracted and studied along with other animals, the language of natural history, with its vocabulary of 'species' and 'variety,' could not be applied to humans at all. These concepts organize the person's 'external' being, the aspects that resemble animals and can be studied as a part of the physical world. Only once the body is abstracted from the whole is the study of raced bodies made possible. Dualism, that is, the dualism of genealogies, is in this way the condition for the possibility of the racial studies found in *Variétés dans l'espèce humaine*, since the body alone can be studied as the effect of particular local causes without reference to God.

However, this very condition for the possibility of a science of race makes a Buffonian science of human races impossible. In Buffon's natural history, there are no human races, only raced animal bodies, since a raced human being would have to account for the physical generation and subsequent degenerations of the mind. Yet when addressing the methodology of natural history regarding human differences, Buffon takes care to leave this element aside:

> Men differ from white to black in terms of color, size, [weight], strength, and in terms of their mind, but this last characteristic, which does not belong to the material world, should not be considered, while the others are ordinary variations produced by the influences of climate and food.[110]

Insofar as the human being exists as a thinking thing, this existence is extra-racial and transcendent to any hereditary difference, it being derived from a wholly distinct order from that of the raced body. This is why the very mind-body dualism that makes Buffon's science of (animal) races possible is precisely the very structure that makes a Buffonian theory of human races impossible. Defined as a thinking thing inherited from God, human beings, no matter which corporeal race they belong to, are born of the same divine ancestry, and the various environmental causes generating a diversity of bodies simply do not apply to the essence of the person, which transcends that lineage. Therefore, when Doron argues that Buffon invents a science of race, I can conditionally agree, while asking just what is included in this particular concept of 'race.' One must see that when Buffon claims the people of Malacca and Sumatra "originate from India,"[111] or all the Americans "come from the same stem,"[112] these statements can only be directed to the racial ancestry of bodies alone, and they do not bear on the origin of a spiritual essence. In this way, just as one finds in Descartes's writing, the dual genealogies of mind and body preclude any possibilities for differences between human beings, although one may speak of differences regarding human bodies.

As noted previously, certain Cartesians exploited the divine origins of the mind to argue for an essential human sameness. Descartes himself seems sympathetic to this possibility when he seems to refuse to exclude the Hurons from participating in the *Meditations*. Buffon, however, overlooks the implications of his genealogical dualism as he at times fails to isolate the material and spiritual realms in his catalog of human varieties. Despite the neat division of mind and body I am underscoring, his works are littered with transgressions against the strict exclusion of psychic characteristics from natural history. A striking example is found in his evaluation of the Caribbeans, where he writes, "All these savages seem to be dreaming, and though *they never think about anything* they have sad faces and seem to be melancholy."[113] Not only does Buffon forget that the mind should be immune from racial degeneration; he does not even question what this evaluation means to the being of the Caribbeans, who think of nothing and yet are human. Are the Caribbeans capable of thought? If 'To exist and to think are for us the same thing,' in what sense do the Caribbeans exist? Do they have an essential relation to God without knowing it as such, as Descartes believed of the Hurons? Do they not govern material objects by way of a higher spiritual nature, or are they mere bodies left to be dominated? Here, it seems as if Buffon abruptly breaks with the transcendent and divine determination of the human being in order to redefine both mind and body on the basis of mundane, sexual causes. Or, to put it more straightforwardly, he forgoes all the implications of his methodology and helps himself to what can only be seen as a racist denigration.

This difficulty is further complicated when one considers that Buffon is not entirely recognized by his contemporaries as an advocate of this Cartesian construction. As Gurdon Wattles has argued at length, Buffon was suspected by some to be an atheist materialist on topics such as cosmogony, sexual reproduction, innate ideas, and even intelligence. Wattles argues that Buffon afforded animals a high degree of intelligence and accorded most of humanity's intellectual capacity a material basis. On Wattles's account, Buffon's *Homo-duplex* is a calculated and disingenuous doctrine, since the immaterial mind is ultimately defined by the body.[114] In the next chapter, readers will find Charles Bonnet take up a vaguely similar approach, albeit with no claims whatsoever to materialism nor atheism.

Regarding Wattles's interpretation, it may be tempting to believe that Buffon is a disingenuous Cartesian, and, in that case, his estimation of the Caribbeans' minds could be explained on the basis of physical differences. Yet, one has to wonder why Buffon never develops this line of thought in the context of his claims against the Caribbeans and other non-Europeans. Certainly by the middle of the eighteenth century a scientific account of human difference is in high demand, and yet Buffon displays a consistent reluctance to submit the whole person, body and mind, to a materialist science. His hesitancy is perhaps best witnessed by his refusal to provide plates illustrating the varieties of the human species as he does with nearly every other organism.[115] This absence seems to afford a supernatural place to the essence of the human species such that humans are defined less by their physical form than by their soul, an emanation of God, which does not admit to variation. As Thierry Hoquet has written on this point,

> Every man is a unique individuality that is impossible to represent: it is not the mask of leather and wool that accounts for the face of the Hottentot, but this incomprehensible light that radically separates him from all the pongos and jockos of the earth.[116]

Nevertheless, this is only what Buffon ought to say given the tradition he adopts. It is equally certain that he cannot help but transgress his own boundaries of psychic and somatic traits when it comes to describing 'exotic' human types. Yet, in order to coherently accomplish the racialization of the whole person, the differentiation of effects demands a differentiation of causes. Buffon particularizes the causes of the body in his account of degeneration, but the cause of the mind remains universally an effect of God. This makes any claims on his part to racial psyches nothing more than baseless stipulations.[117]

This glance at Buffon's thoughts on mind and body opens onto several themes I will revisit in later chapters. For now it is enough to acknowledge the difficulties in constructing a theory of human races when the lineage of the mind is isolated from that of the body. Because Buffon borrows a Cartesian framework in excluding the specifically human aspect of the raced being from the processes that produce the raced body, one cannot cite him as the inventor of the race concept, even though his documentation of human varieties was incredibly influential. The radical separation of soul and body permits one to study each lineage in its distinct register and without reference to the other. While this ontology could permit a study of races within the human species, those races would classify only an inessential corporeal being, while reserving a universal relation to God, of whom each and every individual is an effect.

Over a century later, Francis Galton, the infamous proponent of eugenics and half-cousin of Charles Darwin, will explicitly reject this ontology as a folktale when he writes,

> Most persons seem to have a vague idea that a new element, specifically fashioned in heaven, and not transmitted by simple descent, is introduced into the body of every new-born infant. Such a notion is unfitted to stand upon any scientific basis with which we are acquainted.[118]

Galton clearly recognizes that his eugenics program, which hopes to breed intelligence through an enforced policy of sexual selection, could not accept a transcendent origin for the mind. One might even be tempted to conclude that the race concept is only relevant to human beings as such once the divine and universal cause of the mind is replaced by particular and mundane causes found in the climate or the environment. This transition certainly occurs and it has a profound role in facilitating the sciences of race and racism in the late eighteenth century.

However, it would not be accurate to conclude that the modern race concept is necessarily predicated on a total immersion of body and mind into nature and the processes of generation that define it. One crucial exception appears in the nineteenth-century writing of Joseph Arthur, Comte de Gobineau. In his work one finds the very metaphysics of human equality I have been excavating transformed into a 'science' of Aryanism. This occurs not because Gobineau attacks the notion of 'equality,' but rather because he uses many of the elements of Cartesian dualism to redefine the domain of the 'human.' The result is such that Gobineau can subscribe to the genealogical dualism of mind and body exemplified by Descartes, Buffon, and others while still advocating a doctrine of race and racism. For this reason, his work stands as an important historical counterexample to those arguing that mind-body dualism precludes a doctrine of race. In concluding my survey of the mind-body dualism's place in the history of the race debate, I now turn briefly to Gobineau's ideas on White supremacy and the distinct ancestries of mind and body.

A basic claim of Gobineau's multivolume *Essai sur l'inégalité des races humaines* (1853–1855) is that every great civilization is initiated by the White race, including those of the Indians, Egyptians, Assyrians, Chinese, Greeks, and Germans.[119] Gobineau believes the White race distinguishes itself in various ways, but its origin is most noteworthy. The Aryan family constituting the purest stock of the White race originated in a barren landscape Gobineau describes as "a series of plateaus that seem isolated from the rest of the universe, bordered by mountains of incomparable height on the one side, a desert of snow and a sea of ice,"[120] migrating from there. What did this original White family, the Aryans, gain from such a brutal environment to make them the author of all civilizations to come? Gobineau makes plain that he should not be included in the tradition of thinkers who agree that a difficult climate pushed the White race to a position of intellectual and cultural supremacy. He devotes an entire chapter to argue that civilizations emerge and decline independently of climate or global region.[121] However, as Gobineau reveals in the conclusion of the *Essai*, the White race's remote point of origin was not entirely isolated from the rest of the universe. Rather, in passages similar to Fernel, Descartes, and Buffon, who argue that the intellect or soul is an effect of a supernatural cause distinct from that of the body, Gobineau states that a specific soul was passed on to the White race by a certain transcendent or 'cosmic' source. Reminiscent of Aristotelean philosophers who believed a substantial form unites matter to create a discrete entity, this *grande âme*, as he calls it, molds individuals such that they form a unified society. Gobineau attempts to articulate the singular ancestry of the White intellect when he writes,

> It is, in the order of material things, a sovereign milieu where active forces move. Life-giving principles are in communication with the individual as well as the group, of which respective intelligences contain certain parts identical to the nature of

the forces. The mind of the people is in this way prepared and
eternally disposed to receive the impetus of these principles.[122]

On the basis of its exclusive relationship to a transcendent realm, Gobineau
believes that the White race is marked less by physical characteristics
than by a certain homogeneity of thought, a uniformity inspired by their
unique relationship to the intellect's transcendent source. Influenced
by these causes, each individual comes under the rule of a certain set
of common principles or values. Insofar as Gobineau is concerned with
the rise and fall of civilizations throughout history, this 'discovery' of
the origins of the mind is of crucial importance.[123]

While historians are often led to study the history of civilization by
looking at the actions of individuals or the various forms of government,
Gobineau argues these approaches reveal nothing essential. A civilization
persists despite the comings and goings of individuals or the displacement of political regimes. In order to comprehend the endurance of a
people, historians must study "the different modes of intelligence allot-
ted to the different races and their combinations."[124] Thus, the principle
of Gobineau's science of history is a common soul or mind granted to
White people at birth that compels them to unite and form a people.[125]
This is effectively the underlying cause found at the origin of all great
civilizations.[126] According to Gobineau, it is no accident that those civilizations are White, since only White people are united in their ways
of thinking while others remain scattered and asocial. In chapter after
chapter, he explains how the uniformity of thought and discourse allows
White people "the same grasp of their civilization."[127]

What is most significant in this is that Gobineau's ideas on race and
White supremacy emerge not in spite of his belief in the mind's transcendent ancestry, but precisely because of it. What made Descartes's
or Buffon's doctrines of an essential human sameness possible becomes
the foundation of racial inequality once Gobineau limits and particularizes humanity's relationship to the intellect's cause. How can it be that
one of the most infamous racists of the nineteenth century deploys a

conceptual scheme that at one point served to deny a coherent doctrine of human races? Can it be that in the seventeenth and eighteenth centuries dualism did stand as a bulwark against racism while also serving as precedent for a nineteenth-century racist ideology? Where might this leave Voegelin, Hannaford, or Smith in their evaluations of Cartesian dualism and racism? More importantly, what, if anything, might philosophers learn about racism and antiracism in all this?

Whether one is studying Descartes's Huron, Buffon's Caribbean, Gobineau's Aryan, or Fanon's *homme total*, no race concept is simple. Every concept has its components. For instance, Descartes's 'Huron' is a concept built of a certain combination of elements. The Huron is constituted by the mind, a 'mark of the craftsman,' the axiom of the cause, the cause of the mind, a body, the cause of the body, and so on. As I have argued, Descartes's Huron features much of the same conceptual apparatus constituting the European or the meditator carrying out the project of the *Meditations*. In theory, Buffon's Caribbean displays the same conceptual apparatus insofar as the Caribbean is composed of a combination of elements including a sexually generated body, a mind born from a divine source, and, in short, the same genealogical dualism comprising the Cartesian human. I write 'in theory' because, as I have noted, Buffon is not terribly motivated to consider Jamaicans and others as essentially his equal. At any rate, Gobineau's 'Aryan' deserves to be situated in this conceptual lineage because it too combines the key elements making up Descartes's 'Huron' or Buffon's 'Caribbean.' These elements include a sexually generated body and an intellect derived from a transcendent cause. That is to say, Gobineau is a 'dualist' insofar as his concept of the Aryan is composed of two substances derived from two divergent sources.

All concepts, including the 'Huron,' the 'Jamaican,' and the 'Aryan,' are connected to problems. If the concept is detached from the problem from which it was derived, it ceases to have meaning. This is the failure behind the claim that mind-body dualism is an inherently antiracist position that precludes any doctrine of human racial difference: the claim is only possible once the philosopher detaches the concept 'mind-body dualism' from the various problems the concept has been called upon to solve. Only once the concept is reunited with its problem can one begin to evaluate whether mind-body dualism stands as a bulwark against racism. Consider Descartes's 'Huron,' composed of its two substances and their unique genealogies. What problem is this concept designed to solve? From the *Second Objection*, one problem concerns how some humans have minds yet seem to lack the 'mark of the craftsman,' and thus appear to be a without cause. Yet, 'to be' and not have an efficient cause is a contradiction according to Descartes. Of course, Descartes could clear this up by denying that the Huron has a mind and is entirely an effect of the parents like any animal, but instead he constructs the Huron in such a way that the Huron too bears the mark of the craftsman albeit in a different guise. This means that the being of the Huron is grounded in its cause— God—the same cause as the meditator. Writing over two centuries later, Gobineau is not faced with the problem of non-Europeans that do not recognize 'God.' His is a nineteenth-century European problem of just what exactly is being lost in miscegenation. His response is, in a word, the homogeneity of thought granted by Aryan purity. Unlike Descartes, Gobineau deploys the dual ancestry of mind and body to provide a metaphysical validation for White supremacy. The elements of the concept are nearly the same, but the historical context and the problem to which the concept responds has changed so radically that the 'Huron' and the 'Aryan' become virtually unrecognizable to each other. This is to say that it is not the case that Descartes lacks the conceptual apparatus necessary to support a racial hierarchy. Rather, he does not have a racist problem for which his metaphysics could serve as the solution.

Of course, this is not to say Descartes is racist. In fact, as I am sure the careful reader has noticed, even though Gobineau helps himself to most of Descartes's conceptual schematic, I cannot even provide a citation to where Gobineau credits Descartes for these ideas. Yet, at the same time one must not go so far as to declare that Descartes's dualism cannot be racialized or put in the service of racism. Gobineau proves otherwise when he constructs the Aryan from a genealogical dualism, but then simply circumscribes the relation to the intellect's transcendent source. Whereas Descartes had drawn a line between humans and animals so as to include non-Europeans, Gobineau excludes all non-White beings from a relation to the intellect's cause. In other words, despite the title of his book, Gobineau still operates with an idea of 'human equality' present throughout other manifestations of mind-body dualism, but he delimits the domain of the human so as to respond to what he sees is the overriding question of his time, which is the metaphysical foundations of Aryan supremacy. Accordingly, 'human equality' is no more a bulwark against racism than mind-body dualism until one studies the historical and conceptual context to grasp how the human is defined and what might be the cause of the human essence.[128]

This is all just to say that Cartesian dualism is antiracist in some contexts while still standing as a precursor to nineteenth-century Aryanism. This only becomes clear if one ceases to focus on whether Descartes himself believed racist things and begins wondering if certain experiences or explicit doctrines of racism make use of Cartesian concepts. For those more concerned with the relentless and ubiquitous machinations of racism, this genealogical approach has the advantage in this case of offering useful insights into racism. Namely, while racism often survives in the form of new iterations of old racist ideologies, racism is equally content to dress itself up in the garb of what was once an antiracist doctrine. And that is just to say that the antiracist commonplaces of today, including the language of 'equality' and 'diversity,' could very well be the instruments of racism of tomorrow.

Be that as it may, it is time I get back on track with the study. My primary question was never whether Descartes is racist or even whether mind-body dualism could be a permanent bulwark against racism. While it is helpful that readers become aware of the ways in which racist doctrines have been formulated as theories of mind, body, their ancestry, and the generation of their union, the foremost aim of this chapter has been to better understand Descartes's mind-body problem. While not immediately bearing out a concept of race, Descartes's primary mind-body problem is, at bottom, unequivocally a problem of sex. Going forward, I will continue to trace the mind-body problem along the contours of various theories of sexual reproduction. My pursuit will encounter not only new mind-body problems but also other concepts of the mind-body union, sexual regeneration, race, and racisms. Ultimately, in pursuing the development of the mind-body problem along the axis of sex, I will reckon with Kant's theory of race insofar as it furnishes a theory of sex that effectively solves the problem of how mind and body unite over generations. With this solution in hand, philosophy can at last pivot with Kant to another mind-body problem that ignores neither the insights nor the professional qualifications of a racial non-being.

Chapter Two

A Thing Not-Yet Human

Bonnet's Problem of the Egg

A commonplace holds that racial segregation occurs in space. For instance, one might argue that racism operates through unequal proximity and access to job centers, commercial services, financial capital, schools, grocers, and the like, all brought about by distancing or corralling a minority group in space.[1] In the colonial context, racial segregation in space is evidenced by a number of authors, including Fanon, who writes extensively on the compartmentalization of the colony, an arrangement of space maintained by barracks, police stations, soldiers, and police.[2] However, racial segregation does not only occur in space. Racism can also divide time. Fanon himself writes that he experiences White supremacy in terms of a belatedness, or the feeling of being "too late." In chapter 5 of *Black Skin, White Masks* he writes, "You come too late, much too late. There will always be a world—a white world—between you and us."[3] Homi Bhabha interprets this as Fanon's identification of a brand of racism based on a certain conception of time and history. This temporality positions White people in modernity while all others are not-yet modern, not-yet White, and ultimately, not-yet fully human. Alternatively known as 'developmentalism' or 'historicism,' this racism has been widely documented over the past several decades. It posits White culture as the norm and telos of all 'primitive' peoples who are excluded from the vanguard of cultural progress by a time lag that holds them in a supposedly infantile state. 'Modernity' thus becomes both a time and a place—Europe. Thus, Fanon's exclusion from the White world is in a sense territorial insofar as there are certain areas of space he is not permitted. Yet, insofar as Fanon is 'too late,' he is fundamentally barred from the present, relegated to

Europe's past. Bhabha calls this "the problem of the ambivalent temporality of modernity," not because the time of 'modernity' is undecided.[4]
On the contrary, it is 'ambivalent' because this racism preys on the multiple meanings of the word 'presence.' Fanon, as a 'not-yet human,' is
'present' in the sense that he is available and accounted for. However, he
is not present in the sense of being 'of this time.' He is present only in
representing the past, which is to say, Europe's past. Present as Europe's
past, Fanon is 'too late.'

Writing in 1952, Fanon has good reason to speak of a temporal
prohibition from Whiteness. By the mid-twentieth century, historicism
had become a dominant interpretation of time. For example, the twentieth-century mind-body discourse takes recourse to a racial theory of
time when an author needs a living example of Europe's first attempts
at addressing the mystery of consciousness. The esteemed philosopher
of mind Mario Bunge writes that although,

> nothing is known with certainty about the philosophy of mind
> of primitive man [...] we do know something about the beliefs
> of contemporary primitives, such as Australian aborigines, the
> Amazonian Indians, and the Eskimos: they believe in spirits of
> humans and animals, inhabiting them while alive, and wan-
> dering about disembodied after death.[5]

Here the non-European makes an appearance only to serve as evidence
in favor of determining substance dualism as an outdated theory. It is
the first theory, but for that very reason, primitive and the least progressed. Furthermore, only eight years after Fanon's comments in *Black
Skin, White Masks*, the American economist Walt Whitman Rostow
will publish his *Stages of Economic Growth*, which still stands as one of
historicism's high-water marks. In this work Rostow argues that every
society can be plotted somewhere along his five stages of economic
growth. These stages progress from a 'traditional' tribal or clan-based
social arrangement and terminate with the 'age of mass-consumption,'

modeled by the United States. Regarding the belatedness of non-White peoples, it is interesting what examples Rostow uses to describe the first stage of history: "In terms of history then, with the phrase 'traditional society' we are grouping the whole pre-Newtonian world: the dynasties of China; the civilization of the Middle East and Mediterranean; the world of medieval Europe."[6] Reading between the lines one can see that, as 'traditional societies,' the present-day Middle Eastern society exists in the same historical time as medieval Europe. Some thousand years behind Europe, the Arab is 'not-yet' European. Rostow himself would rely on this theory of time as the justification for organizations such as USAID, The Alliance for Progress, and the Peace Corps, all projects originally designed to 'modernize' belated peoples.[7]

Rostow and other twentieth-century economic theorists such as Talcott Parsons or Seymour Martin Lipset are hardly original in describing non-Europeans as a kind of living past. Dipesh Chakrabarty, Johannes Fabian, and others have gone to great lengths demonstrating the ubiquity of historicism in the nineteenth century. John Stuart Mill, for instance, writes of bringing primitive peoples "to a higher stage of improvement," and, through colonization, "training the people in what is specifically wanting to render them capable of a higher civilization."[8] Marx also makes clear that Europe is the model all others are imitating when he writes, for example, the "country that is more developed industrially only shows, to the less developed, the image of its own future."[9]

Although the rise of historicism is often attributed to nineteenth-century political theorists and philosophers, thinkers such as Mill and Marx are drawing from what was already an established tradition that views non-White peoples as following more or less closely in Europe's wake. In this chapter, I examine one early precedent found in the works of the eighteenth-century Genevan naturalist Charles Bonnet. In Bonnet's sprawling work, one finds an early iteration of the racism to which Fanon and others testify. Moreover, Bonnet's formulation is relevant to my study because he articulates this racist temporality in terms of a mind-body union developing over generations. Bonnet's theory of generational development is rooted in a new theory of sex—preformation—that declares bodies are not generated anew at birth, but are rather preformed in miniature. Because the contents of the mind are furnished by sensations and experience, the degree to which the mind is developed depends on the body's development. Taking the European body as the norm and *telos* for all of nature, Bonnet ranks all other bodies (and the minds they interact with) on a descending scale of 'primativity.' This situates the mind-body union in a long generational history such that terms like 'progressed' or 'backward' refer neither to political arrangements nor economic models but to the sophistication of the mind-body union.

Bonnet's hypotheses are not without grave shortcomings in addition to his racism. As I will detail in the following pages, one notable flaw is his inability to completely reconcile preformation with the mind-body union. Although Bonnet's thinking contrasts with that of Descartes in so many ways, he too fails to formulate a theory of sex that accounts for the mind-body union at birth and across generations. In chapter 3 I will detail how Kant, citing Bonnet by name, will reject his approach to mind-body interaction and go on to reinvent both the mind-body union and the racism to which that union gives rise. In this chapter, I illustrate how Fanon's experience of being "too late" is already being devised in the mid-eighteenth century as a theory of the temporality of the mind-body union. When Bhabha asks, "What is this 'now' of modernity?" Bonnet responds with a science of sex and the mind-body union's historical development.[10]

Last chapter I discussed how Descartes believes the fetus is formed. On his view, the male and female semens, both understood as homogeneous matter lacking spirit or soul, ferment to create a heat that then produces the body. As Jacques Roger details, this idea held by Descartes, but perhaps more notably at the time by William Harvey, is thought by many to be incoherent. While the Scholastics had understood nature as synonymous with birth, once final causes, substantial forms, and Galenic faculties had been banished from science, generation must be explained by the laws of motion alone. As such, it seems nature, conceived as a conglomerate of machines, is powerless to form an organized, living body, since machines cannot build themselves.[11] Additionally, Cartesian physics fails to account for spontaneous generation, a problem that particularly concerns seventeenth-century chemists such as Jean-Baptiste van Helmont and Jean-Baptiste Morin. On Roger's account, these seventeenth-century authors contribute significantly to the rise of a new theory of sexual reproduction known as preformation. However, by nearly all accounts, the formal doctrine of preformation is first officially formulated by the Dutch microscopist Jan Swammerdam in 1669. His description of generation diverges from that of the Cartesians in that the living being is not formed from some mysterious action of the seminal fluids. Swammerdam believes that the organism was created by God at the beginning of the world, and the parents actually generate nothing at all, rather serving only as a kind of temporary abode until a microscopic preformed seed reaches its proper time to develop.[12]

Although preformation marks a sharp departure from Descartes's explanation of generation, it is no less mechanistic. Its advocates still believe that the birth of the animal can be accounted for on the basis of matter and motion, but its birth is nothing more than the enlargement of a tiny machine that was only truly generated by God himself at creation. By recasting generation as enlargement and development, preformation reconciles the mechanistic view of nature with the fact that birth cannot be studied mechanistically. This is to say that aside from God's creation, generation is not a natural phenomenon. While authors like Claude Perrault found it inconceivable that an animal might generate itself out of homogeneous matter, it is considered entirely plausible that God generated the body through his infinite power and wisdom. Because preformation can so elegantly reconcile Descartes's mechanistic physics with God's omnipotence and perfection, it quickly came to dominate the scientific study of animal generation.

Because this book is concerned with the current situation of racism in relation to the mind-body problem, the rise of preformation in the seventeenth and eighteenth centuries bears significantly on my study, since it marks a radically new understanding of how minds and bodies relate across generations and throughout history. The study of the human being at this time, along with the development of anthropology as a scientific discourse, coincides with a broadening of the meaning of 'preformation' that can later be seen in the works of Kant, Herder, and Blumenbach. Peter J. Bowler,[13] Robert Bernasconi,[14] and John Zammito[15] agree that Bonnet was often seen as responsible for this more robust notion of preformation. However, with the possible exception of Lorin Anderson's 1982 work, *Charles Bonnet and the Order of the Known*, Bonnet's specific innovations are not well understood in this context. Regarding the significance of Bonnet's role, Zammito writes,

> [T]he germs [. . .] for all organisms were not only preformed, but they had within them the capacity for growth and even, within sharply circumscribed limits, for adaptation. This was a far hardier form of preformation, and, at the level of species, it persisted even into the early forms of epigenetic theory of Johann Friedrich Blumenbach and Immanuel Kant.[16]

This is true insofar as it refers to Bonnet's early text, the *Corps organisés*, which he wrote for Albrecht von Haller in 1762. However, if one follows Bonnet's philosophical development, it turns out that this text is but an introduction to his later metaphysical work, namely, *La palingénésie philosophique* from 1769. This text takes the notion of preformation far beyond the parameters of physiology, inserting it in a wide-ranging philosophy of history, progress, salvation, immortality, and the mind-body union. I will bring Bonnet's innovations into focus by contrasting his work with that of Leibniz, an author whose work Bonnet both greatly admired and deeply criticized. The reader will see that Bonnet develops the meaning of 'preformation' such that it becomes a brazenly historicist theory of sexual reproduction and development.

Bonnet's expansion of the concept of preformation is threefold. The first development is his 'natural' explanation for the origin of the rational soul. Against Leibniz and others who resorted to God's intervention, Bonnet develops a physical science of the organs, sensation, and the nervous system to explain how the soul progresses from sentience to reason. This then motivates Bonnet's second innovation, which is based on the gradual perfection of the organic world, and centers on the idea that the perfection of the soul is parallel to and dependent on that of the body. Here, Bonnet transforms the notion of the preformed egg itself, arguing that the egg and the union of soul and body are but one and the same thing. That is, within the mysterious point of contact between the soul and body, Bonnet's *siège de l'âme*, lies all future iterations of the body. Finally, the union of soul and body allows Bonnet to infer mental characteristics on the basis of the body to which it is united, creating a natural hierarchy not only of bodies but also minds, something the Cartesians had rejected. Through these three maneuvers Bonnet expands the domain of preformation in a way that bears heavily on the historical development of the mind and its specific characteristics. The end result is a science of the mind-body union that defines non-European peoples as not yet fully developed, marking Bonnet's philosophy as an early manifestation of the temporal segregation that demotes Fanon and others to "the waiting room of history,"[17] to borrow Chakrabarty's phrase.

Bonnet, unlike Descartes or Buffon, approaches the mind from the perspective of the history of the species. History, of course, is never an innocent recounting of what was. What one discovers in Bonnet's writings is a theory of the mind-body union that invents some peoples as not merely behind the times or 'backward' (as opposed to 'progressed' or 'advanced') but necessarily, permanently, and essentially so. Through all the archival minutiae to follow, it is important for the reader to keep in mind that this characterization is not only ontological and metaphysical, but also imperial and colonial. Having decided that non-European people's inferiority is owed to a temporal deficit, putting them on the path to modernity but perpetually not yet there, Bonnet distances himself from non-Europeans in both space and time. In another place, living in another time, Bonnet studies these people not as fellow subjects, but as objects. As

Johannes Fabian has demonstrated, this strategy fixing non-Europeans in the past will later enable anthropologists and ethnologists to deploy terms such as 'primitive' or 'savage.' This construes the object of the investigation as something less than human—a *thing* not-yet human.

Bonnet's history of the human being, understood as a mind-body union, will be in service of colonialist and imperialist agendas preying on a temporality that denigrates non-Europeans as objects or tools. To illustrate the connection between those that are 'not-yet' and those that are 'inferior,' I refer the reader to European representations of Palestine in the nineteenth century. Recall that various European explorers portrayed Arabs as "brutally ignorant, fanatical, and above all, inveterate liars," and "disgustingly incapable as most other savages." Palestine in particular was picked out as "perhaps the most unprogressive country on the face of the earth."[18] Given their purported backwardness, in 1879 the British traveler Claude Reignier Conder could recognize the Palestinians' potential to serve as instruments in the hands of a colonial power, writing, "[Palestinians] have qualities which would, if developed, render them a useful population."[19] This plan to develop 'inferior' or 'unprogressed' peoples into tools is later famously encapsulated in Aimé Césaire's formula, "Colonization = 'thingification.' "[20] Of course, these authors do not need to consciously invoke Bonnet to work through a tradition he helps establish. To better understand the dynamics of this phenomenon I turn now to Bonnet's history of the mind-body union that supports a 'thingification' of the not-yet human.

LEIBNIZ'S HISTORY OF MIND AND BODY

Bonnet's philosophy, an amalgamation of metaphysics and his studies of microscopic life, is exceedingly complicated. This, coupled with the fact that he is, at best, a peripheral figure in philosophy's Modern canon, leads me to seek assistance in the form of some preliminary context. Because Bonnet sees himself working in the Leibnizian tradition, I begin with

Leibniz's ideas on the history of mind and body. In recent decades a number of philosophers have published tremendously detailed and sophisticated studies of Leibniz's adoption of preformation and its significance to his notions of substance, history, and theology.[21] This brief summary is not intended as an in-depth study of Leibniz's philosophy. I only aim to sketch the necessary backdrop to approach Bonnet's thought with some context more familiar to philosophers today who likely are unacquainted with his work. Picking up the discussion from last chapter, my main interest lies in Leibniz's explanation of the origins of the rational soul. Although this is hardly Bonnet's only point of engagement with Leibniz's thinking, it serves as a helpful point of entry into Bonnet's system.

Leibniz's place in the history of racism is complex. As I have written elsewhere, his importance to the institution of orientalism in the nineteenth century is beyond doubt.[22] However, orientalist racism is directed at Arab peoples to exclude them entirely from the historical processes that define Europe.[23] By contrast Bonnet's racism defining others as not-yet European is of a different stripe insofar as non-Europeans are included in the same historical process but are further behind Europe's development. In this context Leibniz's writings on language and philology are less important than his thoughts on the history of the organism.

While Descartes and others consider souls freshly minted at each birth, for Leibniz the soul and body unfold according to a long history. Following Swammerdam and others, his doctrine of preformation holds that both souls and bodies come into existence at Creation. Regarding the development of the body, Leibniz writes,

> Today, when exact investigations made on plants, insects and animals have shown that the organic bodies of nature are never produced from chaos or putrefaction, but always through seeds in which there is undoubtedly some preformation, it has been concluded not only that the organic body was already there before conception but also that there was a soul in this body and in a word that the animal itself was there, so

that conception is merely the means by which the animal is
prepared for a great transformation by which it becomes an
animal of another kind.[24]

Leibniz did not arrive at this insight straight away, and his ultimate
understanding of generation develops along with new ideas presented
by the scientific community mentioned previously, including not only
the work of Swammerdam but also Marcello Malpighi and Antoine
van Leeuwenhoek. Leibniz's spermist preformation holds that the future
body already exists in miniature within the sperm. Because of this, only
a process of 'intussusception' (the absorption of material and growth) is
required for the emergence of a full-grown organism. If this organism is
male, his sperm also carries a miniature body that needs only to fertil-
ize an ovary to then begin its career as a mature organism. Conversely,
just as no organism is ever truly generated (its 'birth' is actually just
an enlargement), Leibniz also contends that the being never perishes.
Rather, 'death' is merely a metamorphosis as the organism transitions
to a future life, or as Leibniz writes in the *Monadology*, "[W]hat we call
death is enfolding and diminution."[25]

   As a result, Leibniz's study of the body must reckon with its history
over the course of an infinite series of envelopments and developments.
Moreover, this history bears not only on bodies, but souls as well, since
Leibniz's doctrine of concomitance holds that no souls are ever detached
from these preformed bodies, and "everything that happens through
itself [*per se*] in the one corresponds perfectly to everything that happens
in the other, just as if something passed from me to the other."[26] This is
to say there is one soul appropriate to each body, and these pairs originate at Creation, making this concomitant relation of soul and body
an important aspect of Leibniz's preformationism insofar as it offers a
hypothesis on the origin of both bodies and souls. These doctrines of
preformation, metamorphosis, and concomitance introduce significant
innovations over the ideas discussed last chapter, such that all the questions of how God generates the soul, how the soul bonds with the newly
generated body, when this bond occurs, and a host of other questions

become entirely irrelevant. If the soul exists along with a preformed concomitant body in the sperm of the father, then there is no need to appeal to a supernatural account of the generation of souls that must then bond with a mechanical body.

In fact, if one fully grasps the implications of this long history of soul and body throughout its infinite metamorphoses, it would seem that Leibniz offers an exceedingly elegant solution to the relationship between minds and bodies across generations: both are generated by God at Creation to unfold in a harmonious unity. Moreover, if one takes Leibniz at his word and understands the development of mind and body as 'spontaneous' such that "its subsequent state is the result [...] of its preceding state, as if there were only God and itself in the world,"[27] then he should offer an equally clear explanation of how new rational souls emerge in the course of nature. That is, Leibniz might argue that a rational human being spontaneously develops out of a series of metamorphoses at a moment that was divinely preestablished long ago with God's creation of nature. Following his dictum, "We ought not to multiply miracles beyond necessity,"[28] this hypothesis evades the miracle of the soul's creation *ex nihilo*, the generation of animals from seminal liquids, as well as the mysterious interactions of mind and body—all problems that plague the Cartesian system. This conceptual schematic would seem a sufficient and coherent explanation for the generation and history of reason in relation to a concomitant body.

However, as Bonnet is well aware, Leibniz does not embrace this possibility, instead appealing to 'transcreation' as the most likely account of the mind's origin. On this view, rational souls preexist, but only as sentient or animal souls. Their elevation to the realm of rational souls occurs only "through some special operation"[29] requiring God's intervention. In the *Theodicy*, a work that holds tremendous influence over Bonnet's metaphysics, Leibniz expresses this idea in writing that sentient souls, devoid of reason,

> remained in this state up to the time of the generation of the
> man to whom they were to belong, but that then they received

reason, whether there be a natural means of raising a sentient soul to the degree of a reasoning soul (a thing I find difficult to imagine) or whether God may have given reason to this soul through some special operation, or (if you will) by a kind of transcreation. This latter is easier to admit, inasmuch as revelation teaches much about other forms of immediate operation by God upon our souls.[30]

Because God must intervene in the course of nature, transcreation is not a mechanical or 'natural' process, a point Leibniz emphasizes in his correspondence with Des Bosses, the *Monadology*, *The Principles of Nature and Grace*, and the *Theodicy*. Transcreation brings Leibniz back into the Cartesian paradigm to some extent insofar as the rational soul does not preexist as such, but is instead miraculously contributed by God at conception.

Leibniz recognizes this process as hypothetical and somewhat unsatisfying, but with a natural explanation seemingly unavailable he is forced to appeal to God's interference in the natural order in this case.[31] Cognizant of this shortcoming, Leibniz attempts to clarify his position in his *Causa Dei*, appended to the *Theodicy*. Here he explains that rational souls do not preexist as such, but instead lie in a state of potentiality within certain monads that have been preestablished to attain reason:

> [I]t is apparent that I have not asserted that there is preexistent rationality. However, it can be held that in preexistent things not only the human organism but also rationality itself is now divinely preestablished and prepared *signato*, so that I would thus say that it is exercised by a prevenient act.[32]

As Daniel Fouke has detailed, this means that God decided in advance which spermatozoa will develop reason, such that certain sentient souls have the potential for reason while others actualize their potential as merely sentient beings. However, this "prevenient act" only establishes the potential for reason, the actualization of which requires a divine intervention.[33] This gives rise to a contradiction that is perhaps best expressed by Bonnet himself:

> Why take recourse, with [Leibniz], to a particular operation of God or a kind of transcreation, which is the most obscure thing in the world? He said himself that it does not appear reasonable that everything regarding the soul is done by a miracle in Man.[34]

For all the explanatory power of preformation, and for all his efforts to limit God's interventions in the workings of nature, Leibniz still finds himself resorting to miracles when it comes to the generation of the rational soul. At least on this point his preestablished harmony and ideas on preformation have no advantage over the approaches to constructing the human being I examined in chapter 1.

This is not to say that Leibniz opposes a natural explanation for the origin of the rational soul. Yet, without an account of how nature can promote a sentient soul to reason over the course of an infinite series of metamorphoses, Leibniz is left with what Bonnet saw as a *deus ex machina*. As I turn to Bonnet's work, one must understand that for him, Leibniz represents both a thinker ahead of his time and one utterly confused on the crucial points. On the issue of preformation, Bonnet is quite pleased with Leibniz's willingness to side with the evidence presented by the microscopists. Adopting Leibniz's position, Bonnet no longer needs to explain why the soul and body unite at each and every birth, and it is enough for him to cite Leibniz's authority in arguing that soul and body have been united since Creation, and they will remain united for eternity or until God annihilates them. This framework allows him to study the union of souls and bodies over the course of multiple generations, affording him a long history of the mind-body union. However, regarding the origins of the rational soul, Bonnet accepts no recourse to miracle, and he believes Leibniz's doctrine of concomitance led him to overlook a clear solution to the problem of how the capacity to reason develops naturally. After all, it was Leibniz himself who wrote, "If rationality is not added miraculously to a preformed soul, then it follows automatically from this that it appears by virtue of a natural evolution."[35] In his explanation of how reason does come about through a natural evolution, Bonnet presents a radical reformulation of preformation based on the union of mind and body that permits a thorough reinterpretation of envelopment, preformation, and future life.

THE NOT-YET HUMAN:
BONNET'S HISTORY OF THE MIND-BODY UNION

Leibniz's writings on preexistence and metamorphosis bring a historical perspective to the mind-body union, but not one that is necessarily historicist. In this section I will detail the ways in which Bonnet repositions Leibniz's metaphysics such that the doctrines of preformation, metamorphosis, and above all historicism have a material and physical foundation. These amendments ultimately furnish a new theory of the unity of the human being throughout his or her historical development.

Bonnet combines several ideas crucial to certain elements of historicism and a 'science' of racial inferiority, including theories of progress, sex, and comparative anatomy. Bonnet's inventiveness is clear when contrasted with certain themes from chapter 1, where I demonstrated how, with the notable exception of Arthur de Gobineau, a race concept can struggle to apply to human beings when the genealogies of mind and body remain distinct. To the extent that 'race' is a concept that applies to the ancestry of the person as a whole, generally understood in the Modern period as a mind-body unity, this construction divorces the raced body from the mind such that the historical ancestry of one has no relation to that of the other. Drawing on Leibniz, Locke, and others, Bonnet will be among those in the eighteenth century who overcome this obstacle and open the possibility of a genuinely physiological evaluation of the mind, while maintaining a conventional mind-body dualism. As I will explain at the close of this chapter, Bonnet's mind-body union is not without its own problems, but it represents a significant development away from the ideas present in, for example, Buffon's writing, and most importantly, it offers perhaps the best approach to understanding Kant's dramatic innovations.

Malebranche's *Récherche de la vérité* first introduced Bonnet to the ideas of preformation and matter's infinite divisibility. With the observations of his close correspondent Albrecht von Haller, Bonnet is confident in asserting "that there is no true generation in nature; but we improperly call 'generation' the beginning of a development that makes visible to us what we previously had been unable to perceive."[36] From these thinkers as well as his own experiments, Bonnet is convinced of the basic principle of preformation: nature, insofar as it is a machine, simply cannot create a body, and thus all organisms were generated by God at Creation, a position he elaborates in his 1762 *Considerations sur le corps organisé*.[37] This makes Leibniz a natural ally, and in the winter of 1748 he reads the 1720 edition of the *Theodicy* quite closely.[38] By the time Bonnet writes the *Palingénésie philosophique* in 1769, which devotes a full chapter to analyses of Leibniz's work, he has access to the *New Essays on Human Understanding* published by Rudolph Eric Raspe in 1765, as well as Louis Dutens's *Opera omnia* from 1768.[39] In the *Palingénésie*, Bonnet acknowledges his debt to Leibniz, writing, "I drew the majority of my ideas on the past and future states of animals from this great man."[40], [41] Had he done even the most cursory reading of the *New Essays*, given his interests, Bonnet would surely have noticed Leibniz's claims that soul and body are permanently united, and moreover,

> These souls are destined always to preserve *persona*, which they
> have been given in the city of God, and hence to retain their
> memories, so they may be more susceptible to punishments
> and rewards. I further add that in general no disruption of
> its visible organs can reduce an animal to total confusion, or

destroy all the organs and deprive the soul of its entire organic body and of the ineradicable vestiges of its previous traces.[42]

To comprehend how Bonnet broadens and deepens the concept of preformation, it will be crucial to see how he engages these themes of preservation, transformation, *persona*, and memory. When Leibniz compares the preservation of the animal to the "transformation of a caterpillar into a butterfly,"[43] Bonnet, whose first published work is on insects,[44] will interpret this quite literally, such that all 'preservation' is in fact metamorphosis, and, due to God's benevolence, all metamorphosis is progress.

By the mid-eighteenth century 'progress' had become a popular interpretation of history, such that human history was seen as an incessant accumulation of knowledge and experience. Bonnet couples this understanding of time with a Lockean empiricism, such that the soul is not concomitant with a body but is rather directly affected by the surrounding world. Bonnet calls the point of the body that constantly accumulates sensations from the surrounding atmosphere and remains permanently attached to the soul the *siège de l'âme*. This 'seat of the soul,' presumably located somewhere in the brain at the terminus of the nerve fibers, is much more than the point of interaction between mind and body. It is the physical site of memory, responsible for preserving an accumulation of sensations and experiences from the beginning of time. In this section I will unravel and retie these threads together, always aiming to grasp how Bonnet merges the mind-body union with a historicist theory of progress. Since Bonnet presents an incredibly sophisticated history of minds and bodies, my study is broken down into four closely related questions: 1) *How is progress guaranteed?* 2) *What is the efficient cause of reason?* 3) *How does preformation promote the thingification of the not-yet human?* and 4) *What is the purpose of the not-yet humans and why do they exist?* In answering these questions much of the edifice constructed in chapter 1 is demolished and a new landscape emerges. Above all stands a historicist racism of inferiority built on a metaphysics of sexual reproduction and the mind-body union. This union, which grants the environment and the body an overriding importance in determining the essence of the being has the effect of generating what one might call a 'new Huron,' such that minds are no longer universally defined as effects of God but instead result from particular, more or less stimulating environments.

How is progress guaranteed?

Because Leibniz's notion of preformation is simultaneously a theory of generation and metamorphosis, and the organism is neither created at birth nor annihilated at death, the history of mind and body must take a much longer view than that taken by Descartes. Of course, in Descartes's work the history of the rational intellect is quite recent, dating only to birth. In the Leibnizian tradition within which Bonnet works, the relationship of minds and bodies in time requires a general theory of history, since the animal is metamorphosed an indefinite number of times. Without a statement on the trajectory of time it is entirely possible that metamorphosis yields a degenerated organism, a repetition of the same life, or it could even be that the future states of the organism are entirely random. Bonnet's understanding of the movement of the time within which bodies and minds develop is a progressive history. Certainly Bonnet is not entirely original in this regard, as his approach to history receives its impetus from several precedents.[45]

Regarding the meaning of 'progress' in the eighteenth century, those authors interpreting the history of nature through an analogy with the life of a single individual are of particular interest. These thinkers, including the likes of Pascal and Fontenelle, construe the history of humanity as a kind of growth that begins in infancy and develops to maturity, marking off stages of history analogous to grades in school. This creates an inversion of 'old' and 'young,' such that what seems old, namely, the Ancients, are in fact the youth of the species. Juvenile as they were, the Ancients were full of spirit and energy, but not necessarily wisdom, and in modernity's mature age they have long been surpassed in this regard.[46] Since it is human nature to have experiences, historical progress becomes a necessary outcome of human affairs, and, depending on the author, perhaps nature in general. Furthermore, for these Moderns, the development from youth to maturity never reaches old age or a point of decline. Rather the accumulation of experiences continues indefinitely, resulting in an increasingly rational, wise, and thus, happy human being.[47] Confidence in progress depends on the accumulation of experience across generations. If knowledge and experience do not accumulate, then the species might make progress over the course of individual, solitary lives. However, there could be no progress across generations, since the experiences would then die with the person. Accordingly, as appealing as the analogy of youth and old age might be, certain Moderns cannot deny the possibility that nature amounts to nothing more than a constant cycle of birth and decay from generation to generation with each individual compelled to start anew.

This is the problem to which a young Parisian economist named Anne-Robert-Jacques Turgot addresses himself in three important works: *Recherches sur les causes des progrès et de la décadence des sciences et des arts ou réflexions sur l'histoire des progrès de l'esprit humain* (1748), the *Tableau philosophique des progrès successifs de l'esprit humain* (1750), and finally, the *Plan de deux 'Discours sur l'histoire universelle'* (1751). Turgot agrees that the accumulation of experience is the foundation of historical progress, but for him this capacity is unique to human beings insofar as humans alone use language and, most significantly, write. Turgot explains the importance of writing as the medium for progress when he states,

> The arbitrary symbols of speech and writing, in presenting men with the means of reinforcing possession of their thoughts and of communicating them to their fellows, have created a treasure house of all individuals' knowledge, which one generation contributes to the next, a heritage constantly increased by the discoveries of each age.[48]

This effectively creates two relationships to time, one human, the other brute. On the one hand, there is a time appropriate to those beings who do not use language and cannot write, and thus have no means to accumulate discoveries or experiences. For these creatures, "time does no more than restore continuously."[49] Life without writing is a constant repetition of the same. Without going into detail here, it is at least worth noticing this is roughly the temporality within which Kant will imprison non-White people such that they regenerate without reason. For Kant, this is not 'brute' time, but rather the time of a racial nothingness. However, according to Turgot, literacy grants all of humanity a fundamentally different relation to time, since it permits a preservation and accumulation of ideas. This produces a linear, rather than circular, history. While body and mind decay and are swept up by the cycle of nature, writing,

> rescues from the power of death the memory of great men and models of virtue, unites places and times, arrests fugitive thoughts and guarantees them a lasting existence by means of which the creations, opinions, experiences and discoveries of all ages are accumulated, to serve as a foundation and foothold for posterity in raising itself ever higher.[50]

For Turgot, writing is the ultimate technique of survival, allowing great minds to live on, be remembered, and then eventually be surpassed by future generations. To answer the question with which I started, progress is not only possible but necessary on the basis of the residue of marks and traces that serve as the condition for the possibility of accumulation, which, in turn, is the condition for the possibility of humanity's continuously increasing knowledge.

Readers should not have the impression that Turgot is the only proponent of this view—theodicies of nature could be found in the works of many authors, including that of the Archbishop William King, Lady Anne Conway, William Whiston, or F. M. van Helmont.[51] Nevertheless, Bonnet reads Turgot and even repeatedly boasts that he knows him personally in his correspondence.[52] He will assimilate Turgot's theory of a necessary, continuous, linear, cumulative, irreversible, and indefinite[53] advancement of knowledge and experience to a physiology of mind and body that makes the accumulation of sensations and experience inevitable for all organisms, not just the human. In this way, nature as a whole will participate in a history whose progress toward rational thought and beyond is inevitable, although some achieve the age of reason later than others.

What is the efficient cause of reason?

In the *Palingénésie* Bonnet explains his project as a double critique of Leibnizian preformation, which he thinks postulates only the *conservation* of *souls* at the expense of understanding the *progress* of *both* soul and body. He attempts to distinguish his project from that of Leibniz in writing, "I will observe here, that in my ideas it is not a matter of the simple conservation of souls, but it is above all a question of the perfectibility and future perfection of all mixed beings."[54] Rather than a constant recycling of souls, Bonnet attempts to articulate the constant improvement of organisms, understood as a 'mixed being' or mind-body whole, without resorting to miracles. In addressing this hypothesis, one confronts Bonnet's thoughts on the origin of ideas, the union of mind and body, the role of memory, and the inevitable progress of all organisms. This will amount to my study's first encounter with a physical and historical account of the origin of reason, a development that has important implications both for a philosophical understanding of not only the mind-body problem, but also a racism that segregates and hierarchizes in time.

Of course, when Leibniz wrote in the *New Essays* that no soul is ever entirely without a body, he was alluding to his notion of concomitance, by which mind and body were united through a preestablished harmony. This idea is perhaps best known for its rejection of any causal interaction between mind and body, referring all causation to a substance's effect on itself as it unfolds. This doctrine achieves widespread influence in the first half of the 1700s, but, as I will detail more extensively in the next chapter, it had fallen into decline by the time the likes of Bonnet and Kant were writing in the middle and second half of the century. Like many of his contemporaries, Bonnet assumes a real causal interaction between mind and body, such that mental states are the effect of bodily states. Jacques Marx reports that in this regard Bonnet is particularly indebted to Locke,[55] who argues in his *Essay on Human Understanding* that the mind could not be understood without reference to effects of the body and the experience of sensation.[56], [57]

Convinced that all contents of the mind derive from the outside, Bonnet is led to look at the mind not only in its relation to the body and its ability to experience, but also in its relation to the climate and atmosphere responsible for producing sensations. Bonnet writes,

> An idea is only present to your soul as the result of a movement made in your brain: you know that all of your ideas derive from the senses: this movement itself depends on another movement, linked to others that preceded it, and the result of all these impulsions constitutes intellectual life.[58]

This is to say that psychology is a science that cannot be isolated from a general theory of the globe as a whole, since every idea refers to the body, which is then impacted by various events developing outside of it. Even the simple idea of a mountain stream is necessarily connected to a chain of events that includes the mountain, its formation, its erosion, precipitation, evaporation, and so on.

The effect of this approach is such that Buffon's study of the human being, for example, loses relevance. In his *Homo-duplex* from 1753, Buffon claims, "Man is double. He is composed of two principles different in nature and contrary by their action."[59] For Bonnet, a psychology that neglects the body would be left with a mind utterly devoid of content. That is why when Bonnet studies the mind, he is immediately led beyond it to investigate a climate's potential to stimulate the body and the body's potential to receive sensations. Physiology and psychology share identical subject matter, and although the soul is distinct from the body, it is nevertheless permanently enmeshed in the material world, and it must be studied in this way:

> Psychology and Physiology shed light on each other. They have a number of commonalities since man is the principal object of both. If everything is directly connected in man, if he is a marvelous system of relations, it is certainly also necessary that the sciences that attend to man are themselves linked together. It is without doubt a consequence of this natural connection that I was called to meditate successively on two of the great mysteries of nature, the mechanism of the operations of the soul and the origin of organized beings.[60]

It should then come as no surprise that Bonnet introduces his historicist theory of development with successive summaries of his *Considérations sur les corps organisés*, a book on the development of the body, and his *Essai analytique sur les facultés de l'âme*, a text addressing the mind. Any metamorphoses of the body will simultaneously serve as advances of the mind, since each body part offers a unique opportunity for sensation and experience.

This is one reason why Bonnet is a significant figure to a history of the mind-body problem that properly acknowledges its overlap with various doctrines of race and racism: he so intensely pursues the union of mind and body, while simultaneously thinking the relative developments and progress of that union across generations. Although Bonnet ultimately lacks an explicit theory of race, one finds the achievement of one of the race concept's most significant elements, which is the simultaneous psychologization, or spiritualization, of the body, accompanied conversely by the study of a being's mental capacity on the basis of its body as it develops in time.[61] This can be seen in Bonnet's work once he adopts a Lockean empiricism, which reorients the development of the mind and its ideas away from God and toward the particular circumstances of the organism's surroundings and the constitution of its sense organs. In what immediately follows, I only intend to emphasize Bonnet's naturalist approach to psychology, leaving a more extensive discussion of his role in the maturation of historicism to the following segment.

In Bonnet's oeuvre, an *être-mixte*, or 'mixed being,' is the soul-body compound characteristic of every organism. That every soul is immortal and eternally paired with an organic body is considered a permanent accomplishment of Leibniz's philosophy. However, the soul does not unite to the body as a whole, but rather one specific part. Again, he calls this site where soul and body interact the *siège de l'âme* or 'seat of the soul,' which Bonnet stipulates is the point where all nerve fibers terminate in the soul. How this happens or what exactly it may look like are consistent points of trouble for Bonnet, but he insists conscious awareness of sensation is sufficient to prove its existence. Although the *siège de l'âme* is corporeal, it must be differentiated from the rest of the physical organism for two reasons: not only is it the lone organ that communicates with the immaterial soul; it is also the only part of the body that eternally remains with the soul throughout all its metamorphoses. Whereas Bonnet takes Leibniz to have argued that the soul is permanently united to a body that is never constant, Bonnet argues that most of the body disintegrates at death, while the soul will rest permanently bonded to its seat. Thus, as the soul is immortal, it will experience multiple cycles of development and envelopment, just as Leibniz thought, but it will always maintain an immortal bit of indestructible matter along with it.

Because the nerve fibers that terminate at the seat of the soul retain traces of the impressions transmitted to the soul, the memories captured in these traces are also permanent. That is to say, not only does the soul remain united to the same bit of matter for eternity; this matter eternally retains the requisite physiological conditions for memory.[62] This means that the *siège de l'âme*, the site of the mind's union with the rest of the body, is also the point where experiences accumulate to make historical progress possible. Excluded from the cycle of life and death that affect other parts of the body and retaining the traces of experience accumulated since Creation, this organ performs the function that Turgot had reserved for writing. Moreover, because every organism, and not just the human, is united by its own *siège de l'âme*, every organism participates in the accumulation necessary to progress. This means that every *être-mixte* is constructed at Creation to achieve a continual, necessary, linear, cumulative, and incessant increase in its ideas, wisdom, and happiness.[63] As such, the *siège de l'âme* not only unites mind and body anatomically, in space, it also unites the organism historically, in time.

On the basis of this twofold unity, Bonnet attempts to explain how the sentient being progresses to the quality of a rational being. Though it is a topic of the 1769 *Palingénésie*, the specifics of this process are developed a decade earlier in his *Essai analytique sur les facultés de l'âme*.[64] Since the perfection of the soul is directly proportionate to that of the body, this development will occur through the increased complexity of the organs and the stimuli they receive. The question becomes, how can a merely sentient animal attain reason through the perfection of its organs?

On Bonnet's account, a sentient soul, unlike a rational soul, can only be what it feels at a certain instant: a pleasant sensation makes for a pleasant being; a painful sensation results in a pained being. There is no ability to reflect or awareness of a transcendent 'I' that exists beyond the incessant flux of sensations. Mired in sensation and unaware of itself, the animal lacks the capacities to reflect on itself and willfully order its sensations by directing its attention to one idea or another. Never the subject, always a predicate, the animal simply experiences itself as 'warmth,' 'hunger,' 'fatigue,' and so on. However, since each of these thoughts depend upon sensations received through the sense organs, as the body develops, particularly the nervous system, the animal receives new sensations. As Bonnet explains, this diversity of feelings provides the organism with a more robust experience of its existence:

> The organism thus has a more lively sentiment of its Being with variety than with uniformity: a thousand identical

nerve fibers only produce the same feeling: a thousand different nerve fibers produce a thousand diverse feelings, which
are a thousand ways of being that the soul distinguishes
from itself.[65]

The diversity of sensations may be multiplied by a more stimulating
climate, or, just as well, the growth and maturation of new preexistent
sense receptors. In either case, Bonnet believes the result is an activa-
tion of dormant nerve fibers, supplying the soul with a broader range
of feelings and ideas.

Within the diversity of sensations, there remain those feelings that
are most pleasurable, and thus most common and familiar, to the animal.
When, among the endless chain of sensations, the animal experiences
one sensation repeatedly, Bonnet believes the soul finally recognizes it
as a repetition. The experience of repetition, a memory, provides the
foundation for reflection of the fact that it is 'I' who experience these sensations. Upon recognizing that the stream of sensations consists simply
of modifications of a selfsame 'I,' the soul is no longer mired in the body,
but has now raised itself to a position outside the stream of sensations.
Again, in Bonnet's own words:

Reminiscence thus teaches the soul that it has already been as
it is. But the soul is conscious of all its manners of being: the
soul recognizes that it is itself that has already been as it is.
And voila, the sentient being has the feeling of its proper per-
sonality, of its 'I.'[66]

Self-awareness is the necessary and sufficient condition for reason
insofar as a being with a notion of itself outside of its current sensations
can then supervise these feelings and memories, more or less ordering
them as it pleases. This activity gives way to generalizations, categories,
deductions, inferences, idealizations, and all the higher order functions
associated with reason.

It is important to recognize that the ability to recognize oneself occurs not through a divine intervention, but only once the organism has experienced a sufficient range of sensations, a condition met only on the basis of highly developed sense organs. In contrast to transcreation, Bonnet emphasizes the lack of miracles in his account of this process in writing,

> [T]he development of the soul is the result of its varied modifications; and these modifications are the necessary effect of the play of organs and the circumstances that determine it [...]. The number, variety and type of modifications determine the degree of the soul's perfection.[67]

That is to say, if the body and its surroundings do not provide the necessary stimulations, then the soul could never be incited to self-awareness and thereby order its thoughts in a logical, rational fashion. As a result, the mind, and its capacity to reason, is again understood as an effect, just as Descartes demonstrates in *Meditation III*. Here, however, it is an effect of the body and sensation, since a sufficient diversity of feeling coupled with the repetition of one experience allows the sentient being to awaken to the fact that 'I' have experienced this before:

> How simple this is! How obvious it is! A sentient soul, as Leibniz calls it, is a soul that has but pure sensations: a rational soul operates on these sensations and, through reflexion, deduces from them notions of every sort.[68]

In this way, Bonnet believes he has incorporated the origin of reason into a broader theory of nature based on bodies, sensation, memories, and the development of the nervous system, thereby making Leibniz's hypothesis of transcreation wholly unnecessary.

In sum, Bonnet does not oppose the sentient to the rational. Rather, sentient life is the foundation of reason, and everything necessary to the latter is found in the former, though to an insufficient degree.[69] This is a key element of Bonnet's 'scientific' representation of non-Europeans as mentally inferior and underdeveloped. Since their bodies and surroundings have not provided adequate stimulation, some peoples are merely sentient and not-yet rational. In other words, by reinventing reason such that its efficient cause is geographic and physiological rather than divine, Bonnet can grade various capacities for reason according to his estimation of global environments. With a typically European hubris, Bonnet situates his cohort at the vanguard of historical progress, forcing all others back into both a place and time that is not-yet 'modern.' In this way the question of where a people live is transformed into one of when they live, allowing places to be hierarchized in time.[70]

How does preformation promote the thingification of the not-yet human?

The experience of self-reflection and the development of reason is a possibility, and even an inevitability, for every organism. However, this is unlikely to occur in most organisms' present life. This is due to the fact that an organism's body can only develop so much in the course of a single life, and because of this limitation, sensations and experiences will be equally circumscribed. Bonnet recognizes that if every organism is created by God, such that it perpetually progresses to new levels of thought, reason, wisdom, and happiness, then the body responsible for communicating new sensations to the soul must develop such that through each metamorphosis it achieves new capacities to be affected. The soul itself, considered in isolation, would not accomplish this progress, since, according to Bonnet, its nature is static and unchanging, a passive receptor of sensations. This could only occur through the development of increasingly nuanced and sensitive body parts in each of the organism's future lives.

Whence this body of higher perfection? It cannot preexist in the soul, since this substance is, of course, immaterial. Yet, it cannot preexist in any part of the body that disintegrates and detaches from the soul at metamorphosis (what is mistakenly called 'death'), since this would make the soul's progress discontinuous. Bonnet recognizes that if the soul cannot transmigrate, but is instead permanently united to its *siège de l'âme*, then the future body must be preformed within this microscopic body. And here one finds Bonnet integrating a theory of how organisms sexually regenerate in time with his doctrine of the mind-body union:

> This small organic body through which the soul grasps the larger body, already contains, in an infinitely small body, the elements of all the parts that will compose this new body under which the animal will rise in its future state.[71]

On the basis of an imperceptible, immortal body, the *siège de l'âme*, God has presumably implanted all the organs and senses necessary for the soul to eventually rise to continual degrees of perfection. What the ape or elephant lacks, preventing it from reflecting and reasoning, is presumably found encased in the *siège de l'âme*, albeit in a miniature, still undeveloped state. In fact, what appears to be an ape or elephant is truly the egg of future humans and other more complex forms. And what of humans? Are humans too not called to a higher perfection? Or as Bonnet asks, "Is man really what he appears to be? Would the death of man not be a preparation for a kind of metamorphosis that would bring along the pleasures of a new life?"[72] Within each *siège de l'âme* lies innumerable bodies waiting to present themselves, as if each human being were an egg predestined to give birth to yet unseen organic forms.

However, progress is not to be confused with evolution in the sense in which that word is used today. The continual perfection of every organism is set out along a predetermined path and this path is nothing other than nature itself, understood as a chain of beings. Bonnet, like most of his contemporaries, understands nature as a hierarchical structure, ordered according to the complexity of each organism. The path to perfection along which each organism progresses is strictly demarcated by this hierarchy. For this reason, the preexistent body latent in the caterpillar is not a mystery or an accident. It is determined from Creation by God and every variation is predetermined by this primordial act. In this way the hierarchy of beings is not merely a taxonomy, but rather it represents either the past or the future of every being, depending on where it stands in the chain. For the caterpillar, the butterfly represents its future life, for the butterfly, the caterpillar is the present incarnation of its past—the not-yet butterfly.

With each step occupied in the progress to perfection, the elevation of one organism will require a displacement at the next highest point on the chain. This creates a taxonomy that is not only spatially arranged as a hierarchy, but also temporally progressing as each step in the hierarchy advances. Anachronistically, one might picture nature as an escalator insofar as each step remains below the next, but all the steps progress higher up the ladder. Bonnet speaks to this progression when he writes:

[T]here will be a constant and more or less continual progression of all species toward a higher perfection, so that all the degrees of the scale will be continually variable within a fixed and constant relation [...]. Man, once transported to an abode better suited to the eminence of his faculties, will leave to the ape or elephant that preeminent place which he formerly occupied among the animals of our planet. In this universal restoration of animals, therefore, it will be possible to find Leibnitzes [sic] and Newtons among the apes or elephants, Perraults and Vaubans among the beavers and so on. In this new hierarchy, inferior species, such as oysters and polyps, will stand in the same relation to higher species as birds and quadrupeds do to man in the present hierarchy.[73]

When Bonnet speaks of the Perraults and Vaubans[74] among the beavers, he is addressing the preformed bodies that lie latently within them. Of course, with the maturation of a more complex body comes greater mental capacities, which is why Bonnet speaks not just of humans in general preformed within the ape or beaver, but he uses the example of what he considers to be the great minds of the present day.

Furthermore, the notion of a preformed germ containing infinite bodies of greater perfection bears not only on the future. Again, if the butterfly could self-reflect, it could see the caterpillar as its past, just as the caterpillar could see it as its future. As humans who can use language, reason, self-reflect, and perform every kind of abstract thought, the 'great minds of Europe' such as Newton or Leibniz, or even Bonnet himself, might be tempted to see the subhuman world of insects, reptiles, birds, and so forth, as ineradicably other to themselves. However, similar to the way Rostow, writing in the 1960s, positions the modern-day Middle East and medieval Europe at the same stage of historical development, Bonnet sees the world outside Europe as Europe's past. In this way, 'history' and the 'Other' become synonyms such that to study the Other is to study European history. Moreover, just as the non-European, sentient, vegetative, and mineral realms stand as living monuments to Bonnet's past, he can study their future just by looking at himself and his cohort. This is effectively the amplification of a sentiment held by Turgot and others whereby the history of the European is manifested by those societies that only developed the ability to write relatively recently and, hence, got a delayed start on the path of progress.[75]

When Zammito, Bowler, and Bernasconi credit Bonnet with introducing a richer notion of preformation to Modern European science, this claim must be understood specifically. By defining preformation as a theory of development wherein some bodies are more or less progressed, Bonnet invents an early version of the not-yet human. This allows him to study every non-European organism as a kind of living fossil.[76] His concept of preformation does this by positing the European climate and body as norms toward which all non-Europeans are approaching but have not yet reached. Upon the development of this body at the appropriate historical moment, the non-European will at last access the sensations, experiences, and thoughts that gave birth to the 'great European minds.' However, they will still remain 'primitive' and 'backward,' since the European will by then have progressed to even greater heights.

This is clearly not an innocent or 'objective' science of sexual regeneration and the mind-body union. Bonnet's expansion of the concept of preformation is profoundly political, a fact best witnessed through later writings on colonial and imperial development throughout the eighteenth and nineteenth centuries. As I wrote at the opening of this chapter, the narrative positioning non-Europeans in both another place and another time remains deeply influential long after Bonnet. Consider for example John Stuart Mill's words from 1861:

> [Those societies not-yet fit for representative government], must be governed by the dominant country, or by persons delegated for that purpose by it. This mode of government is as legitimate as any other, if it is one which in the existing state of civilization of the subject people, most facilitates their transition to a higher stage of improvement. There are [...] conditions of society in which a vigorous despotism is in itself the best mode of government for training the people in what is specifically wanting to render them capable of higher civilization.[77]

As a people behind the times, Europeans eagerly nominate themselves to show 'primitives' the way forward. And there is only one way forward and that is to mimic Europe. Of course, in this mimicry, the mime or copy always comes after the model. This makes Fanon's experience of being 'too late' a permanent condition. Thus, the escalator of progress bringing 'primitives' to 'a higher civilization' becomes a tool of oppression.[78] This particular invention of the not-yet human is not fully appreciated until one sees how the 'primitive' is not only necessarily and permanently 'too late,' but also essentially inferior like an animal, a tool, or a thing. For this, one must reckon with the principle of reason.

What is the purpose of the not-yet humans?
Why do they exist?

In chapter 1 I wrote that Descartes defined the essence of the human, the intellect, as an effect of God. This is best understood through his axiom of the cause, which states every being has a cause, or, every being is an effect. Given Descartes's near-total rejection of final causes, when he seeks the cause of the *res cogitans* this cause is an efficient cause. Bonnet too thinks the human intellect has an efficient cause, although this is not at all what Descartes imagines it to be. As I have explained, Bonnet offers a radically different account of the efficient cause responsible for bringing about the capacity to reason, one rooted in a psychological evaluation of the body. That is, in Bonnet's explanations for the origin of the rational intellect, the complexity of the mind's faculties are the effects of the body and the impressions received from its surroundings.

Bonnet argues that the efficient cause of reason is mundane, and the diversity of surroundings serves to introduce a radical heterogeneity into the species. Although Bonnet acknowledges that all minds are identical at Creation, since the actual capacities of minds are effects of the body and its environment, the variety of causes results in a diversity of effects. As Bonnet explains, "when we suppose this perfect resemblance between all human souls, it suffices that there is a difference between bodies."[79] While Descartes and Bonnet would agree that the intellect can and should be studied on the basis of its efficient cause, Bonnet's account of the origin of reason allows him to introduce a difference within the species where Descartes or Buffon saw only a difference between humans and animals. He emphasizes this point of contrast in writing, "In this way, were all the souls to be exactly identical, it would suffice that God had varied the brains, in order to vary all the souls."[80] As I have explained, because the intellect is causally determined by the physical world in this way, Bonnet's *siège de l'âme* effectively furnishes a way to not only posit a 'variety' of intellects but actually hierarchize minds on the basis of each organism's capacity to feel. And he makes this possibility explicit whether he is contrasting Leibniz with an Iroquois:

> What then is the essential difference between an Iroquois and Leibnitz? For one, the intellectual fibers are nearly all paralyzed. In the other, they have been put in play and their infinitely varied movements follow each other in the most beautiful order.[81]

Or if he is opposing Montesquieu to a Huron:

> If the brain is modeled in a way on objects, and if there are fibers appropriated to every type of perception, if these fibers retain the determinations that objects imprinted on them, if such is the law of the union of soul and body, that to certain fibers and to a certain state of fibers, corresponds certain sentiments of the soul, certain perceptions, then it will be necessary to agree that the soul of a Huron Indian, lodged in the brain of a Montesquieu, would here feel the same sensations, the same perceptions as the soul of Montesquieu.[82]

Although, in the abstract, the intellect as such transcends the diversity of bodies, in reality, there are no intellects as such—every soul or mind is permanently joined with its *siège de l'âme*. On this condition, the capacity to reason is precluded from any theological evaluation of the sort witnessed last chapter. Given the repositioning of the intellect's efficient cause, reason must now be studied according to the laws of nature. Accordingly, due to the alleged paucity of certain environments, the corresponding inactivity or insensitivity of the nervous system, the variety of sensations necessary to bring a sentient soul to reason, Bonnet believes there is no trouble accounting for the existence of non-Europeans lacking the capacity for rational thought altogether. His philosophy of the mind-body union now subjects everyone, including the Huron, to a comparative anatomy that defines them according to variations of the body and climate. This serves to ground a comparative anatomy of the mind, such that the degree of intellectual faculties is proportionate to the complexity of the brain and nervous system.

The study of efficient causes thus provides an answer as to *how* the Huron and other non-Europeans come to be 'backward.' Yet that does not explain *why* the Huron, as a 'backward' and 'inferior' being, ought to exist in the first place. In stark contrast to Cartesian thinking, Bonnet's study goes beyond the efficient cause of the human being to ultimately ground each person's existence in a final cause, or reason. While it is true that the seventeenth and eighteenth centuries are commonly remarked on for the rejection of final causes, and the likes of Descartes, Spinoza, or Bacon had no place for them, teleology did not face a unanimous rejection. Nearly everyone does scrap final causes taken as the actualization of a form. However, several authors reinterpret the idea in the context of nature as a whole, produced by a divine artificer. While Leibniz is perhaps best known in this regard, he had company in the writings of Gassendi, Boyle, Newton, and Bonnet.[83] It should not be surprising to find Bonnet in this camp considering how much of his metaphysics is appropriated from Leibniz. The German's influence is quite pronounced on this point insofar as when Bonnet seeks the reason for the Huron, the Iroquois, the African, or the Hottentot, he does not rest with the science of efficient causes detailed earlier, but rather he gives an account as to why their belatedness and inferiority is necessary for the sake of the totality and unity of nature.

Recall that Leibniz's *New Essay* and *Theodicy* had a profound impact on Bonnet's thinking. In his studies Bonnet must have noticed not only the harmonies of nature and grace, body and mind, but also Leibniz's harmony of efficient and final causes. For Leibniz, both causes serve to explain nature, although the realm of efficient causes, which pertains to bodies, remains heterogeneous to that of final causes, which bears on minds.[84] Although it is not clear that Bonnet read it, one of Leibniz's clearest statements on this point comes in his *Tentamen Anagogicum*:

> I usually say that there are, so to speak, two kingdoms even in corporeal nature, which interpenetrate without confusing or interfering with each other—the realm of power, according to which everything can be explained mechanically by efficient causes when we have sufficiently penetrated into its interior, and the realm of wisdom, according to which everything can be explained architectonically, so to speak, or by final causes when we understand its ways sufficiently.[85]

This second kingdom is necessary because the first, based solely on the study of matter and motion, cannot supply the reason why this matter and these motions are necessary.[86] In Leibniz's philosophy, when one asks into the reason for the existence of a being, one cannot, like Descartes, rest with the efficient cause. Instead, the final cause, being 'intentional,' stands as the reason *par excellence*.

In a passage from the *New Essays* Bonnet surely does read, Leibniz reiterates this bond between the kingdom of final causes and the reason for a being: "A cause in the realm of things corresponds to a reason in the realm of truths, which is why causes themselves, and especially final ones—are often called 'reasons.' "[87] This prioritization of final causes has to be understood in the context of Leibniz's *principium magnum, grande et nobilissimum*: the principle of reason. This principle reads, 'nothing is without reason,' or as Bonnet reads in the *Theodicy*,

> [N]othing ever comes to pass without there being a cause or at least a reason determining it, that is, something to give an a priori reason why it is existent rather than non-existent, and in this way rather than any other.[88]

This cannot be confused with Descartes's axiom of the cause, which guided the inquiry into the being of the Huron last chapter. Here, the 'reason' must be heard as the Huron's final cause, that is, what it is for the sake of in the architectonic of nature. While today's literature offers myriad interpretations of Leibniz's principle of reason,[89] there can be no doubt that Bonnet hears it as a demand to render an account of what each organism is for the sake of, an explanation not given through efficient causes.

If nothing is without reason, and Hurons, Africans, and the like, are beings (inferior beings, but beings nonetheless), what is the reason grounding the existence of these peoples? Bonnet's governing statement on the matter appears in the *Palingénésie*:

> As nothing could exist without a sufficient reason, it is a necessary consequence of this great principle that everything would be linked or harmonic in the universe. In this way, *nothing is solitary or separated*, since if there was a being absolutely isolated, it would be impossible to assign a sufficient reason for the existence of such a being.[90]

In this passage, one encounters two statements on non-being: 'nothing exists without reason' and 'nothing is solitary.' The a priori principle uniting the two statements is, 'Solitary existence is without reason' or, stated positively, 'Linked existence has a reason.' This is not a statement on efficient causes, which is amply clear if I reformulate it as 'Everything is for the sake of the harmony of the universe.' Moreover, 'harmony' in this context refers to a kind of ordering or taxonomy of beings. Again, Bonnet's taxonomy is modeled on the chain of being, which organizes all beings along a vertical, infinitely divided hierarchy.[91, 92] The universal harmony must be understood as a result of all the particular harmonies that result from the exact ways in which each and every being was created. Thus, the reason for each and every being is found in its completion of this "unique whole" that is characteristic of the most harmonic collection of entities, the universe. In this kind of thinking one finds an intimate connection between unity and being such that unity is the ground of being. That is, every being exists for the sake of unity, or, in other words, all parts exist for the whole. Any part that violates this principle would have no reason, and thus would not be a being.

As the reader can see straightaway, the ultimate reason for the Hurons, the Iroquois, the Laplanders, the Hottentots, and others will be to fill in these gaps that would otherwise exist between the European and the ape. Of course, this is the well-documented idea of the 'missing link,' which Bonnet frames in terms certain people's paucity of experiences and sensations.[93] The influence of Bonnet's hierarchal taxonomy, grounded in an anatomy of the mind-body union, can be seen in various attempts in the late eighteenth century to develop a science of reason and a scale of intellects on the basis of a comparative anatomy.

The goal of demonstrating a perfectly smooth gradation of minds and bodies from the Simian to the European reaches its climax in Josiah Nott and George Gliddon's *Types of Mankind* in 1854.[94] However, the debt this tradition of racism owes to Bonnet is apparent in works such as Charles White's 1795 *An Account of the Regular Gradation of Man*. This short text, written by a self-proclaimed amateur and composed mostly of quotes, details the gradation of not only minds, but also nearly every body part, from the elephant through to the European. Devoting two full pages to diagram Bonnet's theories, White works to demonstrate a union between the sizes of the skull and brain on the one hand, and the ability to think on the other, in order to ultimately conclude "that, generally speaking, those animals which have a greater quantity of brain have also more reason or sagacity."[95] However, White claims that this relationship is only tenuous, since, in his extensive survey of the literature, so little is known of the brain and nerves that no one can state with any certainty how the hierarchy of body types is anatomically united to, and determinate of, the purported hierarchy of intellects.

Nevertheless, even without an account as to how the purported differences of the nervous system are linked with those of the mind, the logic of Bonnet's philosophy demands inferior humans. Without the Hurons and other inferior people, nature would suffer an irremediable interruption, its unity would be sundered, and it would fail to be perfect. In this way, the Huron body, which purportedly renders these people incapable of so many philosophical and abstract ideas, is nevertheless perfect, if perfection is taken to mean 'complete.' This body, and the soul it carries, is perfect and necessary for its place in nature, and thus every 'stupid' Huron and every 'filthy' Hottentot is absolutely perfect in their stupidity and complete in their filth:

> As there are two general classes of substances, bodies and souls, there are also two classes of perfection; corporeal perfection or that which is proper to the body, and spiritual perfection, or that which is proper to the soul. These two perfections are reunited in every organized-animated being and the one corresponds to the other.[96]

This is certainly small consolation to the Huron. However, it is important to anticipate the alternative, which would be to state that indigenous people actually play no role in nature, and thus their existence is contingent, or without reason. This will be Kant's evaluation of the Tahitian. For Bonnet, the nonexistence of the Huron is totally illogical, representing an affront to the order of nature on par with the notion that the Hurons are somehow innately equal to or essentially identical to the European. Grounded in the principle of reason, the logic of Bonnet's philosophy dictates that some people must exist and even be preserved as inferiors, and thus cannot be exterminated without radically violating both the principle of reason and the divine order of nature. This is all to say that, given Bonnet's rationale, non-Europeans must be recognized as not only 'too late,' but because of that belatedness, non-Europeans are necessarily inferior. Segregated in time and akin to animals, the Other is recognized as an object or a tool. The result is the thingification of the not-yet human, a status demanded by the harmony of nature.

This reasoning is not lost on those adopting the instrumental ideology of colonial racism, which, as Pierre-Andre Taguieff states, amounts to a practice of "domination and exploitation that strives to conserve the life of the Other—an inferior, of course, but a source of profit."[97] Nowhere is this metaphysical strategy more apparent than in Edward Long's 1774 *History of Jamaica*, a veritable handbook of Caribbean plantation life and a sustained justification of slavery. In this work one finds the nexus of several ideas covered in this chapter, including the hierarchy of nature, the principle of reason, and the inferiority of mind and body put directly into the service of the plantation colony.

Part of Long's goal is to argue that the genuine reason for the existence of the African is to be enslaved. To recognize this purpose, he claims the African must be studied as part of "a regular order and gradation, from inanimate to animated matter."[98] Vertically arranged as a system of subordination, the chain of being governs the being of the African in both body and mind. For Long, the inferiority of the Africans' physical characteristics is indubitable, and their proximity to subhuman animals is made clear simply by pointing to certain features such as the hair ("a covering of wool, like a bestial fleece"[99]), the odor (a "bestial and fetid smell"[100]), their table manners ("they tear the meat with their talons"[101]), their senses ("their hearing is remarkably quick; their faculties of smell and taste are truly bestial"[102]), and their copulation ("in these acts they are shameless as monkies, or baboons"[103]). The inferiority of the intellect is also nearly as obvious to Long, so much so that he can simply 'observe'

> the like gradations of the intellectual faculty from the first rudiments perceived in the monkey kind, to the more advanced stages of it in the apes, in the *orang-outang*, that type of man, and the Guiney Negro; and ascending from the varieties of this class to the lighter castes, until we mark its utmost limit of perfection in the pure white.[104]

Again, this natural inferiority in both mind and body is, for Long, demanded by the harmonious unity of nature, a product of God's infinite wisdom.

Without question, the invocation of nature and divine omniscience as the justification for human inferiority received strong opposition from precisely those Christian precepts covered in the previous chapter, namely, the doctrines of innately homogeneous capacities to reason with an impassable gulf separating the human and brute.[105] In this regard, Long is particularly aware of the challenge presented by Buffon, even though he tries to cite him and marshal the *Histoire Naturelle* as his ally whenever possible. However, in declaring the inferiority of the African intellect, Long clearly encounters a roadblock. As I mentioned in the previous chapter, Buffon defines the mind in relation to God in such a way that it should be immune to any sort of racial hierarchy, the very hierarchy of minds and bodies Long is at pains to establish to legitimate the plantation colony. In chapter 1, I cited a key passage from Buffon pertaining to the uniformity of minds:

> Men differ from white to black in terms of color, size, [weight], strength, and in terms of their mind, but this last characteristic, which does not belong to the material world, should not be considered […].[106]

Long's refutation of this claim to an essential human sameness is laughably unsophisticated. He simply doctors the quote and declares Buffon's support for the necessary inferiority of the African in both body and mind. His citation of Buffon reads,

> Men differ from white to black, from compound to simple, by the height of stature, size, activity, strength, and other bodily characteristics; and from the genius to the dolt, from the greatest to the least, by the measure of the intellect.[107]

With the professed approval of the most influential naturalist of eighteenth-century Europe, Long is at liberty to declare slavery a condition not only in line with but actually upholding the vertical hierarchy of nature:

> The Negro race (consisting of varieties) will then appear rising progressively in the scale of the intellect, the further they mount above the Orang-outang and brute creation. The system of man [i.e., slavery] will seem more consistent, and the measure of it more complete, and analogous to the harmony and order that are visible in every other line of the world's stupendous fabric.[108]

According to Long, the system of slavery is demanded by nature not only because it is in harmony with the chain of being, but to the degree that it preserves the inferiority of the African it also preserves the very order of nature. While this is clearly an oppressive tactic aimed at denying the equality of the African, Long argues that without the slave trade and the plantation colony to preserve the African, it is possible that they disappear, and, again it must be emphasized, the elimination of a people is the greatest transgression against this reasoning. The imperative to preserve the Other as an object is thus deployed as a bulwark against extermination or genocide.

Of course, one has to be cognizant of the fact that Long is really spinning his own fairy tale here. The facts of the slave trade and the Caribbean plantations make his metaphysical justifications hard to see in practice. I count at least nine instances of a person beaten to death or near-death among all the violence in James Williams's short narrative of part of his time as a slave in Jamaica written in 1837.[109] By contrast, Long's fantasy is on display in those passages where he portrays slavery as a 'life-saving activity' that actualizes the reason for the existence of the African, one they cannot realize if they are simply left to die in a 'savage' land. As he argues, more Africans being shipped to Jamaica

> would [result in] so many lives saved, and rendered useful to the community; which advantages would be wholly lost, were the slave trade universally given up; [...] the breaking up of the slave trade might indeed alter the punishment to that of death. [...] To abolish this trade, is therefore no other than

to resign them up to those diabolical butcheries, cruelty, and carnage which ravaged their provinces before the European commerce with them began.[110]

The debt this brand of racism owes not just to the chain of being but, more fundamentally, the principle of reason is difficult to overstate. It can be summarized by the following chain of reasoning: As Bonnet states, "The author of nature left nothing without a use,"[111] or as one might say, nothing is without reason, or alternately, every being has a reason. The Huron, or the African, is a being. The reason for these beings, like all beings, is to uphold the unity of nature. The unity of nature is expressed as a hierarchy or vertical chain, and the reason for the Africans and Hurons of the world is to complete this chain. According to this hierarchy, these types are inferior to some and superior to others. However, given their 'primitivity' and the fact that they are not-yet European, they are 'behind' and hence inferior to the White European. As such, their reason for existence is to be a link or bridge uniting the White European to brute creation. Because the being of each being is grounded in its reason for existence, and the reason for these types is, in a word, to be inferior, one must recognize the Hurons and Africans as *essentially inferior*. From Long's vantage point this inferiority is that of an animal, or even a tool, and as such it can be justifiably put to use in other ways aside from their ultimate, 'natural' purpose.

In the introduction, I mentioned Marcus Garvey's definition of the 'Negro' as a person without utility. This is not that kind of racism. Bonnet's Huron or Long's African is not a 'Negro' in Garvey's or Malcolm X's sense. Rather, Long understands the rationale of the metaphysics underlying colonial exploitation only too well when he coolly explains that the African "is wisely fitted and adapted to certain uses, and confined within certain bounds, to which it was ordained by the Divine Fabricator."[112]

'Nothing is without reason,' Leibniz writes. Some philosophers know this as a principle of logic. Others identify it as a precept of metaphysics or ontology. Still others recognize it as a principle of epistemology. For

Bonnet, it grounds the hierarchy of nature. Long, going a step further, understands it as a principle of colonial slavery and the economy of the sugar plantation.

To summarize these ideas on being, unity, and time, allow me to retrace my steps. Bonnet believes that every human being, a union of mind and body, metamorphizes an infinite number of times. The being of the human, and every organism, is grounded in its purpose or reason, which is none other than to complete the perfect harmony of God's creation. Each being's place on the chain is determined by its degree of complexity in both mind and body, a measure calculated according to the being's capacity to receive sense stimuli and communicate those experiences to the soul through the nervous system. This account of the being of the human being is predicated on the union of mind and body, since the abundance or paucity of sense stimuli communicated to the soul presumes a certain point of interaction where a cluster of more or less complex nerve fibers end and the soul begins. Moreover, this point, the *siège de l'âme*, not only accounts for the spatial or anatomical union of mind and body; Bonnet also calls on it to unite the organism to its past and future iterations. This grants Bonnet's *siège de l'âme* both an anatomical and historical role. This history is one of progress, a trajectory made possible by the increasing complexity of each organism's sense receptors and nerve fibers across each of its metamorphoses. Because only the *siège de l'âme* remains united with the soul from generation to generation, Bonnet declares that every preformed body must exist within this tiny point of interaction. This makes the union of mind and body itself an egg holding within it the possibility of the progress of this mind-body union. This is what allows Bonnet to argue that not only preformation, but, if one thinks along with Bonnet on these themes, the union of the person is an idea about historical progress, a project in which every being necessarily participates simply on account of their anatomy. Again, what makes Bonnet's writings important to this study is not only that he illustrates an early formulation of a widely documented form of racism, but he also attempts to think the history and unity of the being simultaneously through his concept of the *siège de l'âme*. Bonnet's entire philosophy is based on this concept, including his thoughts on the being of the being, the union of the being, and the history of the being. I now turn to more judiciously interrogate this union/egg Bonnet calls 'the *siège de l'âme*.'

A PROBLEM OF THE EGG

It should now be clear that Bonnet's theory of preformation bears as much on the development of souls as it does on bodies. As I detailed above, this development is owed to his idea of the *siège de l'âme*, which is of profound importance not only to his understanding of the organism's development and progress toward perfection but also his account of the mind-body union. Bonnet's attempt to think sex and the mind-body union simultaneously puts him in conversation with the likes of Descartes and, later, Kant. However, like Descartes, Bonnet never quite manages to reconcile a coherent theory of sex with an account of the mind-body union. Even though he stipulates that the union of mind and body regenerates endlessly, accumulating experiences and thereby furnishing the conditions for a physiology of historical progress, because this history is based on a spatial anatomy, Bonnet only finds himself in deeper confusion on the problem of the mind-body union. That is, without a coherent account of *where* the *siège de l'âme* stands in relation to the organs of sexual reproduction, his entire philosophical project falls apart.

The crucial significance of the *siège de l'âme* as the intersection of his thinking on sex and the mind-body union is evident in Bonnet's repeated references to this point as a 'germ' or 'seed.' Again, to substantiate his belief in historical progress, Bonnet argues that the outside world leaves its traces on the body through the nervous system, and these effects accumulate in the *siège de l'âme*. As the storehouse of these traces, the *siège* is responsible for preserving the continuity between this and a future life. It must be emphasized again that this point is unique insofar as it remains with the soul while the rest of the body disintegrates and is cast off. This is why Bonnet refers to it as an 'egg': if the future body is preformed, where could it be, except in this tiny body that will remain with the soul through all its metamorphoses? This characterization of the *siège de l'âme* is apparent in the *Palingénésie* when he claims,

> This small organic body [the *siège de l'âme*] through which the soul grasps the larger body, already contains, in an infinitely small body, the elements of all the parts that will compose this new body through which the animal will rise in its future state.[113]

In other places he contrasts his ideas against those of Leibniz, writing, "My hypothesis admits, as we know, no kind of envelopment. It supposes that the future body, lodged from the beginning in the larger terrestrial body, is the true *siège de l'âme*."[114] A lot rides on these claims if one takes them in the context of Bonnet's broader philosophy. If the *siège de l'âme* does not house the future body, where is that body? Does another organ also persist with the soul throughout the organism's regenerations? To avoid these questions Bonnet hypothesizes a perfect overlap of the unity and history of the organism. Unfortunately, this theory and all that rests on it is foiled by Bonnet's total inability to locate this "small ethereal body" in the brain and the sex organs simultaneously.

At one point in the *Contemplation de la nature* Bonnet seems fairly certain that the *siège* should be identified with the corpus callosum. Yet, because his theory of experience, accumulation, and progress applies not just to those organisms with brains but also those that are "entirely gelatinous and yet very sensitive,"[115] he is led to momentarily consider the *siège de l'âme* as a kind of liquid in the brain or even a kind of fire in the brain. Perhaps at an impasse, Bonnet shortly thereafter drops these hypotheses to reside with the stipulation that there simply is a point in the brain closest to the soul where the nerve fibers end. He even goes so far as to say that the solution to the mind-body problem, understood as a problem of where an interaction between two substances occurs, is of no significance to his research so long as one simply knows that any modification of the nerve fibers results in a corresponding modification of the soul. He writes,

> It was indifferent to the goal of my research to discuss the different hypotheses that have been imagined for making sense of the union of soul and body, since all these hypotheses equally presume a constant relation between the modifications of the soul and the body.[116]

However, he could never have been truly indifferent to the problem. In his correspondence and published works, Bonnet repeatedly worries over the location of this point. For instance in a letter to the Italian anatomist Vincenzo Malacarne that highlights how essential this problem is to his history of the organism, he states, "You see that this Palingénésie that you like relies a bit on this *siège de l'âme* that so troubles your studies in anatomy."[117] Bonnet hopes, and it will remain throughout only a hope, that this location will someday be discovered, perhaps with improved microscopes, thereby confirming all his writings on the mind-body union and the future life of the organism.

The repercussions of his inability to locate this point are amplified when one tries to reconcile his writings on corporeal generation with those on the palingenesis of the soul-body union. One discovers anything but an identity of the preformed body and the *siège de l'âme*, as Bonnet consistently refers the preformed body to the ovaries with no attempt to reconcile the location of the ovaries with the terminus of the nerve fibers. For instance, in his early work on animal generation from 1762, *Considérations sur le corps organisés*, Bonnet identifies the preformed seed with the ovaries wherein successive generations are encapsulated one inside the other. This idea, known as *emboîtement*, is referred to again in his 1769 *Contemplation de la nature*, a text previously cited regarding the location of the *siège de l'âme* in the brain. Here he discusses the relative merits of *emboîtement*, wherein "the germs of all organized bodies of the same species are enclosed, one inside the other and are developed successively," over and against the rival doctrine of dissemination, which holds that preformed bodies are scattered throughout nature only to develop once they find their way into a suitable womb. In deciding between these options Bonnet faces a dilemma: clearly the sexual organs are somehow essential to the reproduction of the body, making *emboîtement* an appealing theory, but if the *siège de l'âme* is in the brain and must then somehow find its way into the womb, perhaps dissemination is the proper account. In a move that gives the lie to his fundamental inability to reconcile the mind-body union with his understanding of sexual reproduction, in the *Contemplation* Bonnet chooses both options. He believes the *emboîtement* of the ovaries is empirically verified insofar as nature shows us "ossified parts of a fetus enclosed in another fetus, an egg enclosed in another egg, a fruit inside another fruit, a fetus inside another fetus, etc."[118] From these passages one would be led to believe that the preformed body is located in the seed, which in the case of human beings, would be the ovaries. Nevertheless, in a later chapter dedicated to the metamorphosis and successive passage of every substance through the kingdoms of minerals, plants, insects, reptiles, fish, birds, quadrupeds, and humans, he states that this is only made possible by a process of dissemination:

> By a law to which we do not pay enough attention, all organized bodies decompose and are imperceptibly changed into earth. While they undergo this dissolution, their most volatile parts pass into the air, which transports them everywhere. In this way, animals are buried in the atmosphere [...]. All of these particles are dispersed here and there and soon return to new organic wholes, themselves called to the same revolution.[119]

On this account, the animal, a soul-body unity, is not encapsulated but dispersed throughout nature. Meanwhile, in the very same text, one reads that the *siège de l'âme*, which "links the present being to the future being," is found at the extreme end of the nerves. Therefore, from this text alone, the *siège de l'âme* is simultaneously in the ovaries, dispersed throughout nature, and somewhere in the brain.

A charitable reading might attempt to help Bonnet out of this predicament by positing two distinct lineages in each person. This is Peter Bowler's interpretation, as he tries to explain the sequence of bodies contained in the ovary as parallel to that contained in the *siège de l'âme*. He writes,

> The relationship between these speculations [on the *siège de l'âme* in the *Palingénésie*] and the original theory of generation is quite complex. Bonnet now held that there were two types of germ sequence. Any female would contain within her ovaries the normal germs destined to reproduce the series in that particular geological period. She would also contain another series, centered upon the seat of the soul within the brain, which would represent the future sequence of bodies which her soul would inhabit. Obviously the new system is in addition to, rather than a direct development of, the original emboitment theory, but the similarity between the two seems obvious.[120]

However, without a citation to where Bonnet distinguishes the sequences, nothing is quite so obvious. Max Grober presents an interpretation similar to Bowler's when he writes that the development of the seat of the soul is "a process analogous to ordinary generation."[121] However, if these sequences are truly analogous, then 'ordinary generation' transcends, and is distinct from, the development of the seat of the soul, thus defining every person as two sequences without any account of their union. In fact, the introduction of two parallel germ sequences not only contradicts Bonnet's claims that the future body is located in the *siège de l'âme*; it would also introduce an irremediable hiatus into the being of every person. That is, every person is a unity and yet they develop along two radically unrelated germ sequences, a theory that would violate the very first principle of growth, which according to Bonnet is *il n'est point de sauts dans la nature*, or nature does not make leaps.[122]

That is not to say that Bowler or Grober are necessarily wrong in this interpretation. The point is that one simply does not know where the mind-body union stands vis-à-vis the reproductive organs because Bonnet effectively gave up trying to locate the point of interaction that would serve as the *siège de l'âme*. Since Bonnet decides that the union is a location, once he tries to look at the union generationally he necessarily stumbles on this question of where the soul is located not only in relation to the brain, but also the ovaries. Is the *siège de l'âme* identical to the ovaries that encapsulate all future bodies? Or is it as Bowler imagines, distinct but analogous? Either answer is possible, but since Bonnet cannot and will not find the *siège de l'âme*, he remains lost on this essential question.

To philosophers today, it may seem that Bonnet's work is riddled with shortcomings, fantasies, and 'armchair' talk of metamorphosis, progress, and the like. However, Bonnet spent more time in the laboratory than many scientists today, and, although his vision failed him at an early age, he had a strong commitment to empirical studies. One could only pass this sort of judgment if one selectively forgets his historical context and the logical steps he takes to solve the mysteries of his time. Namely, in the mid-eighteenth century there is the recalcitrant difficulty of the sexual generation of organisms, making preformation and metamorphosis appealing hypotheses. In addition, nearly everyone agrees that somehow the body has a real causal influence on the mind. Bonnet's mind-body problem, a problem of the egg, simply emerges from the confluence of these two discourses. In adopting Leibniz's framework, he answers the question of *Why?* explored in the previous chapter insofar as he posits a complete preformed soul-body union joined at Creation. He never has to explain why the soul bonds with the body at birth, since 'birth' is merely an enlargement. Bonnet's question is then where this union is located in generation and the processes of sexual reproduction. As I have noted, he never succeeds in answering this, since he could never find the point where the soul interacts with the world and then situate this point along the trajectory of subsequent and previous generations.

This is certainly not the only problem in Bonnet's work, and the modern-day reader will be quick to point out the others. However, I am tracing the moments facilitating the development of another mind-body problem, and to that end I am focused on the ontological constructions of the human being that permit one to grasp the person, understood as a mind-body whole, as a raced being. In this regard, Bonnet finds a place in this narrative, since he tries to think the relationship between the unity of the being and the movement of that unity in time. Yet, in stumbling on the fundamental problem of the place of the egg, he fails to reconcile his theory of sex with that of the mind-body union. Bonnet does manage to account for the being of every organism on the basis of the principle of reason and the chain of beings, a theory contributing to a vicious and denigrating form of racism. However, this account of being does not explain the unity of the being. That leaves Bonnet with a mind-body problem understood as a being that lacks a unity. On account of this, even though Bonnet's thinking introduces a number of important innovations in contrast to the framework elaborated in chapter 1, it remains only a variant of the problem studied there, one which is more or less familiar to philosophers of mind today. That problem is one of relations, interactions, or, simply, unity: How can *a* being be *one*? Accordingly, this study has not yet pushed the mind-body problem to its point of transformation. Nor have I encountered an understanding of sexual regeneration that accounts for the mind-body union, nor a coherent philosophy of human races. For that I move beyond Bonnet's struggles with the location of the *siège de l'âme*. In reading Kant's philosophy I will distinguish a doctrine of race that approaches the unity of mind and body in time, without deference to place. While Descartes or Bonnet stumble over a theory of sexual reproduction that accommodates the union of mind and body, Kant makes their relation synonymous by formulating a theory of sex that is itself a veritable union of mind and body. Kant calls this theory of sex and the mind-body union 'race.' Yet, in accomplishing this, he will simultaneously generate the deepest and most unsettling mind-body problem hitherto. I now turn to see how Kant manages the synthesis of sexual reproduction and the mind-body union in order to forge a truly unprecedented problem, one that genuinely deserves to be recognized as philosophy's mind-body problem.

Chapter Three

"All races will be extinguished . . . only not that of the Whites"

A Mind-Body Problem in the Kantian Tradition

I am examining the development of a racial non-being as it came to be imagined in Modern Europe as a theory of minds and bodies. As a guiding thread, I have been following Eric Voegelin's claim, "The race concept is a part of the body-soul problem; the former requires for its adequate understanding complete clarity about the latter and therefore about the nature of man."[1] This has led me to consider the mind-body union from the perspective of sexual regeneration while tracing the emergence of theories of human difference. As a result, I have exposed two preliminary mind-body problems, both of which emerge from two distinct understandings of sexual reproduction. To review, I first encountered Descartes's problem of *why* minds and bodies unite at birth, and then, in the previous chapter, I considered the problem of *where* mind and body unite in relation to the preformed egg. Clearly, these two snapshots could not claim to represent a comprehensive history of this discourse in Modern Europe. Yet, for those intrigued by Voegelin's hypothesis, these moments are instructive insofar as they introduce a nexus of ideas, including theories of sex, the mind-body union, and human difference, or race. In this chapter my study will realize what the first two chapters failed to accomplish—a theory of sex that accounts for the mind-body union. Although some Moderns try to study the unity as an 'interaction' and others name it 'harmony' or 'concomitance,' Kant's singular concept of 'race' serves as the union of mind and body. Upon establishing the precise relationship between Kant's race concept and the mind-body union, the second part of the chapter attends to the being of this unity. While Descartes, Bonnet, and many others run aground on the problem of a mind-body unity, Kant only manages to solve this problem in a way that generates what properly deserves to be understood as another mind-body problem. This problem then opens onto not only a new landscape of concepts that may serve as solutions, but also a new field of experts on philosophy's mind-body problem.

RACIAL MIND-BODY UNIONS

In the course of demonstrating "how the modern race idea gradually grew out of the problem of body and mind in the eighteenth century,"[2] Voegelin sets Kant's contribution above nearly all others. Passages from both the precritical and critical works are marshaled as instances of particular relevance and acuity regarding the race idea. Voegelin consistently argues that Kant best understands what is at stake in the concept, and this supremacy holds not only over Kant's contemporaries, but Voegelin's as well. For instance, consider his evaluation of Kant's racial categories:

> Though Blumenbach's and Kant's [racial] subdivisions are primitive compared to our knowledge of the subject matter, the Kantian one in particular has two decisive advantages over *all* modern systems: (1) its methodology is clear and neat; and (2) it takes into consideration *all* inevitable questions of race theory.[3]

Voegelin holds Kant as one of "the essential sources for an understanding of the mind-body-spirit relationship,"[4] and Kant's authority is cited in a variety of contexts.

Were he writing today, Voegelin would no doubt find himself among a growing chorus of philosophers declaring Kant's historical significance in the development of the modern science of race and racism. However, he would be rather lonely in his estimation of Kant's importance to the mind-body discourse.[5] In fact, Kant explicitly and repeatedly rejects the basic terms of the problem as it is formulated by his contemporaries. The eighteenth century's mind-body discourse is framed by the Three Hypotheses, or the doctrines of physical influx, occasionalism and pre-established harmony. In both philosophical and medical arenas, physical influx dominates the science of mind and body and, at one point, Kant himself develops his own version of it. However, in the 1760s he refutes not only the notion of physical influx but also the coherency of the problem it is designed to address. In studying which notions he rejects and why, one recognizes that Kant does not cast off the poles of mind and body, nor does he refute the brute fact that they relate. Rather, he rejects the problem of their causal relationship as poorly formed and unsolvable. That is, he rejects the problem of the interaction of mind and body as fruitless for both physicians and philosophers alike.

In this section, I will explain how Kant provides crucial insights into the mind-body union and its relation to the race concept. This accomplishment stands despite the fact that Kant rejects the basic terms of the mind-body problem while also producing three texts on race that do not address the problem in any way recognizable to his contemporaries. This point itself calls for a brief summary of just what Kant does discuss in *Of the Different Races of Human Beings* (1775), which was expanded in 1777; *Determination of the Concept of a Human Race* (1785); and *On the Use of Teleological Principles in Philosophy* (1788), his three essays dedicated to race. On the basis of this summary, I will examine certain elements that support Voegelin's claims that Kant is both a major player in the development of the race concept and that the concept is best understood on the basis of the mind-body union, although this investigation requires that I again depart significantly from Voegelin's writings. Despite Kant's attention to physical characteristics, his notion of race applies to more than just bodies. His attention to both physical and mental race traits raise the question of how these characteristics relate to form racial unities of minds and bodies. The answer lies in Kant's designation of racial characteristics, both mental and physical, as those aspects of the person that regenerate unfailingly. In his theory of regeneration one discovers that the necessity and irreversibility of certain characteristics create a union of mind and body based on the permanent agreement between certain body types and certain psychic traits. In Kant's writings on race, the problem of the mind-body union is no longer to be conceived as one of interaction and unity in space, as physical influence had presumed, but rather one of repetition in time, across generations. That is to say, Voegelin's integration of race into the mind-body discourse is tenable if one recognizes the radical reorganization of the problem along the axis of time in Kant's writings on race. If in reading Descartes one encounters a problem of *why* mind and body unite at birth, and following Bonnet one discovers a question of *where*, in Kant's work one will see the question transformed for a third time, now into one of *when* mind and body unite. When the problem of the mind-body union is configured along the axis of regeneration or repetition in time, then 'race,' as Kant conceives it, becomes a legitimate solution. This solution to the problem of unity is however but the first step in the recovery of another mind-body problem, a problem that is effectively generated by this union of mind and body as it is formulated by Kant.

Along with the problem of developing a science of sexual reproduction, the relationship between mind and body is a topic of intense dispute throughout Europe in the eighteenth century. Although these two discourses should not be separated, suffice it to say much of the latter debate pivots around the camps, or Three Hypotheses, of physical influx, occasionalism, and preestablished harmony. These solutions to the problem of the mind-body union were roughly associated with Descartes, Malebranche, and Leibniz, respectively.[6] Readers may wonder about the omission of materialism, but, as the *Encyclopédie* indicates, at this time it is still seen as a form of Spinozism, and as Ann Thompson has detailed, material theories of the mind "remained on the level of an intuition" in the eighteenth century.[7] Familiar to many, allow me to just briefly review the basic tenets of the Three Hypotheses. First, preestablished harmony denies intersubstantial causation but argues in favor of intrasubstantial causation on the basis of monads. As I mentioned in chapter 2, in terms of minds and bodies, this amounts to Leibniz's doctrine of concomitance wherein, "everything that happens through itself in the one corresponds perfectly to everything that happens in the other, just as if something passed from one to the other."[8] Second, occasionalism denies any causal powers whatsoever, be they within a substance or between substances. In this case, God is the cause of any interaction between substances, including minds and bodies.[9] Finally, physical influx asserts a real causal influence of substances. Regarding mind-body causation, this latter position can be traced at least to Descartes's pineal gland, which could both affect and be affected by the soul.

Eric Watkins has studied the rise of physical influx and Kant's early interest in the project. While occasionalism gained very little traction in eighteenth-century Germany, much of the debate took place over the relative merits of Leibniz's preestablished harmony and physical influx.[10] In a philosophical context, it seems as though physical influx overtook preestablished harmony as the dominant account of the mind-body union when Martin Knutzen, Kant's teacher, published his 1735 *Systema causarum efficientum*, in which he details why one must recognize that change that appear to be caused by other finite substances are verily caused by these other substances.[11] Among doctors and physicians, physical influx was buttressed by new studies in the nervous system and brain disorders, and by midcentury there was a virtual explosion of writings attempting to specify the mode of mind-body interaction through the application of methods from natural history, natural philosophy, and medicine to the soul. John Yolton reports that this physical science of the mind generally addresses the problem of how the body, and specifically the brain, interacts with the soul, since it was assumed that the soul could affect the body, an entity lower on the chain of being.[12] The problem of the body's effect on the mind brought an intense focus on causal theories of sensation in a variety of physiological and medical works.

Of course, speculation on the loci of interaction between soul and body are not unique to the eighteenth century if one notes that Western philosophy has long debated the roles of the brain, heart, blood, and other organs in relation to the soul.[13] Yet, never had this question spurred empirical research to the extent one finds here. In chapter 2 I discussed at length how Bonnet was developing a complex science of the nervous system and 'seat of the soul' not only in his 1754 *Essai de psychologie* and 1760 *Essai analytique sur les facultés de l'âme* but throughout his published works and correspondence. He was far from alone in this project. For instance, in France, La Peyronie studied brain-damaged patients in his attempt to locate precisely where the soul exercises its functions in the brain.[14] Guillaume-Lambert Godart, in his 1755 *La physique de l'âme humaine*, follows La Peyronie in locating this point in the corpus callosum.[15] Also working in France, Jean-Paul Marat argues that the soul must be located in the meninges, since it is here that the nervous system unites to "form one simple uniform substance."[16] At Oxford, Thomas Willis locates the 'lucid' or intellectual soul in the whole head, although conscious perception is rooted in the corpus striatum specifically.[17] In Germany, Haller, following Boerhaave, locates the seat of the soul in the crura, corpora striata, thalami, pons, medulla oblongata, and cerebellum, simultaneously. Gary Hatfield points out how J. F. Abel and K. C. E. Schmid, also in Germany, had developed popular textbooks developing general laws for studying the mind and its spatial location in the body.[18] There truly are too many authors to list, but the general project of mid-eighteenth-century neurophysiology is perhaps best summarized by La Peyronie who, in 1741, articulated the research program that followed from his espousal of physical influx:

> The soul is united to the body; through the laws of this union the soul acts on the body and the body acts on the soul. At what point in the body is this reciprocal commerce immediately executed? It is this point, this site, this seat, this instrument that I search for in this memoir.[19]

In eclipsing preestablished harmony and occasionalism, physical influx answers the question of *if* mind and body truly interact, only to bring about the question of *where* that interaction occurs. While Bonnet's work represents an important iteration of this problem of location, a neuro-anatomical study of the soul and its relation to the body dominates much of the second half of the century.

Kant himself felt the effects of this trend, claiming in a letter to Mendelssohn in 1766 that the body's effect on the mind is philosophy's key problem:

> In my opinion, everything depends on our seeking out the data of the problem, how the soul is present in the world, both in material and non-material things. In other words, we need to discover the nature of that power of external agency, and the nature of that receptivity or capacity for being affected, of which the union of soul and body is only a specific case.[20]

However, by the 1760s Kant's enthusiasm for solving this problem had waned. Over the next three decades he cites several authors investigating the causal relationship of mind and body, arguing not that their individual solutions were wrong, but that the problem itself is mistaken. This can be seen in Phillippi's 1772 lecture notes, where Kant specifically targets Bonnet's *siège de l'âme*, which Kant seems to understand as a dense cluster of nerve fibers with an immediate, though mysterious, relation to the mind. Of this doctrine, Kant states,

> The transition of bodily motion into spiritual motion cannot be further elucidated, hence Bonnet and several others err severely when they seek to infer from the brain to the soul with any certainty.[21]

Shortly thereafter, in the winter of 1773, Kant takes aim at Ernst Platner's *Erfahrungsseelenkunde* in a letter to Herz. Platner's *Anthropologie für Aertze und Weltweise* had attempted an account of the interaction between soul and body on the basis of Haller's writings on the nervous system. Like Bonnet, his project focuses on the nerves in an attempt to locate the soul in the brain, specifically the brain marrow, and thereby determine their modes of interaction. Kant's rejection of this project is significantly more forceful and categorical than that from the previous year. Outlining his Anthropology lectures to Herz, Kant states,

> I shall seek to discuss phenomena and their laws rather than the possibility of modifying universal human nature. Hence the subtle and, to my view, eternally futile inquiries as to the manner in which bodily organs are connected to thought I omit entirely.[22]

In a third instance, Kant writes to Samuel Thomas von Sömmering in 1795 commenting on his *Über das Organ der Seele*. Here again he makes his disapproval of the task clear by bluntly stating that the project of establishing a seat of the soul "is not only unsolvable for [metaphysics] but also in itself contradictory."[23]

This final instance is worth further consideration. To philosophers, Sömmering is hardly a household name, but he is nevertheless a prominent scientist of the late 1700s, having just published his six-volume *Vom Baue des menschlichen Körpers* at the time Kant writes him.[24] Sömmering's book on the seat of the soul begins with a description of the anatomy of the brain and a detailed overview of the nervous system. His hypothesis, which owes no small debt to Bonnet (who is frequently cited), states that the nerves unite in the brain's ventricles through a liquid found within the brain's cavities. It merits mention that this project is the background of his attempt to develop a comparative anatomy in *Über die Korperliche Verscheidenheit des Negers von Europaer*, which argues that the African's lack of intellect is owed to a diminutive brain and crude nervous system. Kant's critique highlights Sömmering's attempt to locate the soul in a particular organ or realm of the brain. He argues that while the physiological problem of where the body's various nerve endings unite can be solved through empirical research, the further problem of how and where that terminus interacts with the soul is a metaphysical question.

This problem cannot be resolved, least of all empirically, since if one is to locate the soul in space, it must be studied as a body. However, there are no grounds for studying the soul this way, since the soul can only perceive itself as a series of representations in time. Thus, Kant argues that in order to give the soul a location, one would have to treat it as a body, thereby spatially perceiving that which can only be experienced in time—a clear contradiction.[25] Sömmering might have anticipated this criticism had he reviewed the *Critique of Pure Reason*, wherein Kant had stated that the problem of locating the soul is "an imaginary science," performed only by those confused enough to "treat their own representations as objects."[26]

Moreover, Kant's appraisal should not be understood as merely a disdain for one of the Three Hypotheses. Kant does not take his rejection of physical influx as an opportunity to argue in favor of any forms of occasionalism or preestablished harmony, both of which by that time had widely fallen out of favor. Instead, when Kant designates the interaction between body and mind as an "eternally vain investigation" or "contradictory," one must recognize him rejecting the very terms of the problem. As I detailed at length in the previous chapter, what Bonnet, Platner, and Sömmering have in common is a methodological approach to the union that begins by asking *Where?* This question, which has spurred so much neuro-anatomical experimentation, is derivative of the deeper assumption of interaction or causation that defines not only physical influx but also the project of a racial comparative anatomy as it is taken up by Bonnet, Charles White, Sömmering, and others. This approach presumes the union is an interaction in space between two objects, which then forces one to locate the soul in space in order to discover the causal interaction that would reveal the union. Kant himself recognizes that the problem of mind-body interaction entails the further problem of location early on in his *True Estimation of Living Forces*.[27] Well before writing any of his essays on race, Kant clearly decides that the problem of how the unity of the person arises out of interaction or causation is a poorly formed question upon which philosophy has no bearing. By rejecting the terms of the problem these thinkers and many others hoped to solve, Kant effectively removes himself not just from the debate over how and where minds and bodies interact, but from the landscape of the Three Hypotheses altogether.

On these grounds, after a certain point early on in his career, Kant simply does not engage the mind-body discourse of his contemporaries, labeling it a frivolous and interminable endeavor. This makes it difficult to recognize Voegelin's assertion that one must grapple with the unity of mind and body if one hopes to comprehend the race idea. In rejecting the very prospect of a philosophical determination of mind-body inter-action, Kant certainly does not heed Voegelin's precept if what is meant by 'mind-body unity' is some sort of causal relationship between enti-ties in space, as is orthodox in eighteenth-century Europe. Additionally, beyond the issue of Kant's repeated rejection of the problem of mind-body interaction, one must also reckon with the fact that Kant's three essays on race make no attempt to intersect with his contemporaries' mind-body discourse. If, in his writings on race, Kant does want to provide a theory of human difference from a point of common descent on the basis of physical influx, several precedents are available, not the least of which is Bonnet's *Palingénésie* from 1769. Instead, Kant's most significant engagements with the concept of race do not proceed along the contours of any of the Three Hypotheses. In these essays, the prob-lems Kant seems most concerned with are the refutation of polygenesis, the distinction between 'race' and 'variety,' the purposiveness of racial characteristics, and the proper jurisdiction of natural history in con-trast to natural description. The mind-body union, framed in terms of physical influx, is simply not a theme. If Voegelin or anyone else wants to position Kant as a preeminent figure in the history of the concept of race, and that concept is truly a subset of the mind-body union, then this triumvirate is anything but obvious in Kant's own work.

Angelica Nuzzo has provided some explanation as to why this might be the case. She argues that Kant's disenchantment with physical influx begins with his belief that proponents of mind-body interaction, and

Christian Wolff in particular, misrepresent space. In his justification of physical influx, Wolff claims that although the soul is immaterial, it nevertheless interacts with the body in space. 'Space,' on Wolff's account, is in fact nothing other than the field within which substances interact. Knutzen agrees with Wolff, and one sees their influence on Kant when he adopts their ideas on space and mind-body interaction in his 1747 *Thoughts on the True Estimation of Living Forces*. As Nuzzo explains, Kant will reject both this approach to space and mind-body interaction in his 1766 *Dreams of a Spirit-Seer* and break ground on a new transcendental concept of space in the 1768 *On the Ultimate Ground of the Differentiation of Regions in Space*. Nuzzo claims that from this point on in Kant's work space no longer refers to the realm in which a metaphysically independent soul interacts with the body. Rather, space relates to how a necessarily embodied consciousness is present to the world. She details how Kant proves this in "The Refutation of Idealism" in the second edition of the *Critique of Pure Reason*. In these pages, Kant argues that consciousness, which is always empirically determined in time and never given as an empty abstraction, is perpetually changing. Yet, change presupposes something permanent in relation to which the changes can be determined. This permanence can only be found "through the existence of actual things which I perceive outside me."[28] The perception of things outside me requires a body. Thus, there can be no consciousness in isolation of the body, or, as Nuzzo quotes Maurice Merleau-Ponty, "a perceiving mind is an incarnated mind."[29] This leads Nuzzo to write that "Kant completely revolutionized"[30] the mind-body problem by first reconceiving space such that it is no longer the medium within which an immaterial mind interacts with a material body, and second, by prioritizing space over time such that the temporality of consciousness depends on the body's spatiality as the transcendental condition of what makes possible the representation of objects outside it.

Nuzzo undoubtedly provides an excellent study of Kant's place in the history of the mind-body problem. However, her claim that Kant revolutionizes Descartes's mind-body problem depends as much on her reading of Descartes as it does Kant. It may very well be the case that Kant solves, or better, dissolves the problem of how mind and body interact, a problem that is, roughly speaking, 'Cartesian.' But Descartes's writing is not 'Cartesian,' and I have demonstrated a different mind-body problem in Descartes's work that does not refer to the question of how mind and body interact in the space of the brain. Descartes never gets to that question because he fails to explain how the mind enters the body at birth when the body's supposedly unique accommodation is no different than other mundane phenomena. Since the body is not sexually generated for the sake of the soul, Descartes lacks an explanation as to how it can ever be in the brain to interact with the body in the first place. Thus, while I agree with Nuzzo that Kant does indeed revolutionize the mind-body problem, I disagree with her both about the dimensions of the problem he revolutionizes and the way in which he revolutionizes it. In my estimation, Descartes's mind-body problem is a problem of sex. In the wake of Descartes's work there is undoubtedly a discussion of how minds and bodies interact and where they make contact. I provided some of that context earlier. However, the debates around physical influx are also profoundly engaged with the doctrine of preformation and the mysteries of sexual reproduction. I detailed one instance of this overlap in chapter 2. One cannot simply divorce the mind-body discourse from the study of sex in Modern Europe. With a properly contextualized understanding of the mind-body problem, one sees that one of the ways Kant revolutionizes the mind-body problem is through his reinvention of how minds and bodies relate at birth and across generations. Kant accomplishes this with a radically new theory of sex that he calls 'race.' As I will explain, Kant's concept of race does require that the mind is necessarily incarnated, just as Nuzzo demonstrates in her reading of the *First Critique*, but Kant's essays on race accomplish this along different axes and in light of a somewhat different problem. As I have emphasized throughout the previous two chapters, that problem is undoubtedly one of how mind and body relate, but that issue is inextricably related to questions of sexual reproduction and human difference.

To grasp Kant's innovations on these fronts, one must consider how, in inventing a concept of race, Kant transfigures the terms of the problem such that the relationship between mind and body becomes not one of spatial interaction, but rather one of a persistent, invariable repetition in time across generations.

In constructing a scientific idea of race Kant does not reject the poles of mind and body that constitute each of the Three Hypotheses. Although physical characteristics occupy center stage, most notably in Kant's essay from 1785, mental and moral characteristics are hardly excluded from classification. In his 1777 essay on race, Kant does not overlook what he believes to be the industrial and cultural disinclinations of the Negro race:

> [H]umid warmth is generally preferential to the robust growth of animals. In short, there arises from these conditions the Negro, who is well-fitted to his climate—that is, strong, fleshy, nimble, but, under ample care of his motherland, lazy, soft and dallying.[31]

Here one finds the somatic type, 'strong, fleshy, nimble' paired with the mental type, 'lazy, soft and dallying.' Similarly, in 1788, Kant writes of Americans that they are not only copper colored but also "too weak for hard labor, too indifferent for industry and incapable of any culture."[32] Of course, his extensive considerations of skin color, particularly that of the Negro race, should not distract from the fact that race was very much an idea about bodies for Kant. In 1785, Kant was so concerned with establishing the purposiveness of racial characteristics that he made skin color a principle of racial classification. This led him so far as to define race as a concept that applies to the body, without mention of the mind:

> Physical characters by means of which human beings (irrespective of gender) *distinguish* themselves from one another—but, to be sure, only those that are heritable—come into question in order to establish the division of the species into classes.[33]

Nevertheless, Kant's interest in incorporeal hereditary differences cannot be dismissed. In *Observations on the Feeling of the Beautiful and the Sublime* from 1764 Kant had already defined the scope of the race concept in writing, "So essential is the difference between these two kinds [Black and White], and it seems to be just as great with regard to the capacities of the mind as it is with respect to color."[34] Regarding his later works, his extensive commentary on the racial designation of certain talents, cultural and intellectual traits, propensity for industry, and other psychic qualities play a crucial role not only in his concept of race but, as several authors have noted, history as well.[35] For example, consider an important passage from the early 1780s to which I will later return:

(1) The American people acquire no culture. It has no incentives; because affect and passion are absent in it. They are not in love, thus they are also not fertile. They hardly speak at all, do not caress one another, also do not care for anything, and are lazy, they paint their faces in an ugly manner.

(2) The Negroes race, one could say, is exactly the opposite of the American; they are full of affect and passion, very lively, talkative and vain. They acquire culture, but only a culture of slaves; that is, they allow themselves to be trained. They have many incentives, are also sensitive, afraid of beatings, and also do many things out of honor . . . ; they are full of affect and passion, very lively, chatty and vain. It can be educated, but only to the education of servants, i.e. they can be trained. They have many motives, are sensitive, fear blows and do much out of concern for honor.

(3) It is true that the Hindis have incentives, but they have a strong degree of composure, and they all look like philosophers. Despite this, they are nevertheless very much inclined toward anger and love. As a result, they acquire culture in the

highest degree, but only in the arts and not the sciences. They never raise it up to abstract concepts; a great Hindustani man is the one who has gone very far in deceit and who has a lot of money. The Hindus always remain as they are, they never bring culture further, although they can begin to cultivate themselves much earlier.

(4) The race of the whites contains all incentives and talents in itself; and so one must observe it more carefully. To the white race belong all of Europe, the Turks and the Kalmucks. If ever a revolution occurred, it was always brought about by the whites, and the Hindus, Americans, Negroes never had any part of it.[36]

Of course, Kant is not entirely innovative in classifying peoples according to their mental characteristics. Others before him, including Abbé Jean-Baptiste Dubos, Montesquieu, and, of course, those figures discussed in chapter 2 had included both moral and physical traits in their accounts of how climate creates human differences. In any case, these passages indicate that, despite his criticisms, Kant does not depart from the Three Hypotheses by excluding mind or body from his notion of race. For example, he does not argue, with Hobbes, that the soul does not exist, nor does he argue that the soul transcends racial classification—a strategy encountered in Buffon's work. Mind and body are certainly both elements of Kant's race concept.

Although Kant does not articulate these mental traits in the rubric of a comparative anatomy in terms of causes or effects of relative body types, his essays on race do nevertheless construct a kind of unity between psychic and somatic traits. Consider for instance how the term 'white' applies not just to "tender, white skin, reddish hair and pale blue eyes,"[37] but also "all tendency to cultivation and civilization" and the constant "progress in perfection."[38] Or, consider that the Hindu race unfailingly reproduces an "olive-yellow skin color"[39] but also intellectually, "they will never achieve abstract concepts." There is a pairing of body and mind here, but not a union achieved in terms of physical influence. The problem Kant is addressing in these and a host of other similar passages is not that of the interaction between soul and body. His concern is the establishment of certain racial types, which is to say, the classification of certain necessarily hereditary traits. The way in which mind and body are united in these essays lies in the problem of the way in which these specific mental and physical characteristics are 'racial.' That is to say, one must understand how Kant's concept of race unites the Negro's strength to his or her laziness, white skin to cultivation, or copper-red skin to perpetual apathy, and so on.

In developing a concept of race Kant struggles to develop a coherent vocabulary highlighting certain traits that are heritable in a way that becomes irrevocable to the lineage.[40] Among the terms Kant employs in this context are a number of variations on the noun *Art*, including *abartung, anartung, ausartung, einartung,* and perhaps most significantly, *nachartung.* Kant draws from this language when he first attempts to define his concept of race in 1775. In *Of the Different Races of Human Beings*, he begins his definition with a distinction between regeneration and degeneration:

> If the marks of the phyletic origin agree with their point of origination, then they are called regenerations (*Nachartungen*); however, if the subspecies could no longer provide the original formation of the phylum, then it would be called a degeneration (*Ausartung*).[41]

In 1775, Kant believes races are *Ausartungen* insofar as "[o]ne cannot hope to find the original human shape unchanged anywhere in the world now."[42] In relation to this distant historical point, races are degenerations on account of the various adaptations that the local climate has stimulated. However, one learns that races are more accurately described as regenerations, as Kant defines *Nachartungen* in terms of those hereditary traits that "persistently preserve the distinctive character of their variation in all transplantings."[43] Regeneration becomes synonymous with Kant's race concept through the constant preservation of certain traits, a notion often expressed as the *unausbleiblich nachartung*, or 'unfailing regeneration,' as well as the *unausblieblich erblich, unausbleiblich Anartung*, or the 'unfailingly hereditary.'

Contrary to Kant's contemporaries, particularly Buffon and Blumenbach, who defined race as a degeneration, it is regeneration that defines Kant's race concept. Again, races certainly are degenerations to the extent that none of the four races can reproduce the original type, but when Kant addresses race, he consistently does so from the point of view of the origin of the race, in which case progeny unfailingly regenerate their ancestors. For example, Kant's definition of 'race' in his 1775 essay highlights the necessary and permanent nature of certain differences:

> Among the subspecies, i.e., the hereditary differences of the animals which belong to a single phylum, those which *persistently* preserve themselves in *all* transplanting (transpositions to other regions) over prolonged generations among themselves and which also *always* beget half-breed young in the mixing with other variations of the same phylum are called *races*.[44]

This unfailing repetition of certain differentials, even in mixed-race progeny, is what constitutes the lawfulness of Kant's race idea, distinguishing it from other mental and physical traits that do not repeat themselves with any constancy. Kant makes this triumph of regeneration and the limits of degeneration quite clear when he writes:

> Once a race like the current [American] one had established itself through the long residence of its original people in northeast Asia or in the neighboring America, this race could not be transformed into another one through any further influences of the climate. For only the phyletic formation can degenerate into a race; however, once a race has taken root and has

suffocated the other germs, it resists all transformations just because the character of the race has then become prevailing in the generative power.[45]

That is to say, 'race' is not simply the opening up of certain permanent differences within the species. It is at the same time a profound and equally permanent closing off or suffocation of other racial possibilities. Each of Kant's four races can be accounted for in positive terms such as 'fleshy,' 'uneducable,' or 'cultivated,' but each race can also be expressed in negative terms like 'those who, no matter the environment, could never be other than fleshy,' or 'those who could never be other than uneducable,' and so on.[46] This stands in contrast to Kant's contemporaries such as Buffon, Blumenbach, or even Meiners and Kames, who all held out the possibility of ongoing degenerations or improvements of each race, depending on the climate.[47]

The importance of Kant's inclusion of both physiological and psychological traits as well as his formulation of 'race' in terms of necessary, permanent regenerations is revealed in certain comments Kant directs against Georg Forster in his final essay on race from 1788. In his critique of monogenesis, Forster had objected to Kant's claim that nature had implanted certain predispositions in the original human seed that would be suited for the complete spectrum of Earth's climates. How could these predispositions develop at the expense of other possibilities? What would happen if a population migrated to a new climate? Does this inability to further adapt not ascribe a certain myopia to God that contradicts His very nature? In this line of questioning, Kant believes that Forster has fallen into abstraction. In addition to the fact that Kant simply cannot cite any migrating populations ("And where have Indians and Negroes attempted to expand in northern regions?"[48]), Kant explains that this is not an accidental phenomenon, but rather a necessary effect of race. The sedentary nature of these people is a race trait, and as such, it is inherited unfailingly and universally. Thus, even if one brought them to the harsher European climate, they would never adapt the proactivity and will necessary to survive there, since racial characteristics lie beyond the influence of the climate once the process of regeneration is set. That is to say, by making certain adaptations necessary for survival in certain climates yet fatal liabilities in others, nature has prevented Forster's concerns from ever actually arising. Kant makes the possibility of migration, and all consequent adaptations, null on the basis of an embryology that stipulates a rigid, permanent repetition of race traits.

Kant expounds on this point in a long footnote detailing how, regardless of social conditions, there is a direct connection between natural predispositions and one's drive to activity. Because race traits lie potentially in the original stock and are only aroused through climatic stimulation, each race develops only the psychological capacities, in this case the will to work, necessary to survive in a given climate. Accordingly, the hospitable environment of the Indian and Negro races has stimulated only as much of this drive as is necessary, leaving it relatively weak. Moreover, under the law of unfailing inheritance, this "inner predisposition extinguishes just as little as the externally visible one."[49] That is to say, the psychological makeup of a race has developed in the same way as their skin colors, and accordingly it is equally immutable.

Kant's engagement with Forster highlights how the unfailingly hereditary nature of both mind and body traits develop and continue in unison. As the generative power responsible for these differential traits hardens and settles into a series of permanent regenerations, the differences defining each race's mind and body become permanently united in the lawfulness of their inheritance. In other words, although the original stock supports a contingent variety of psychological capacities and body types, the stimulus of the climate has actualized one particular arrangement that precludes any other. Kant insists that the interaction between seed and climate that produces black skin, fleshiness, and strength is the same process that will produce the Negro's laziness, limited interest in work, and a psychology best suited to servitude. For Kant, it is a fact of sexual generation that these traits will repeat in unison perpetually. Bound by the law of unfailing, necessary inheritance, mind and body

Table 1. Kant's Four Unities of Mind and Body

	Moral and Psychological Character	Corporeal Character
Hunnish (American)	No impulses or talents; weak compulsion to reproduce; incapable of culture; no historical role whatsoever	Copper skin tone; black hair; beardless chin; flat face; slit eyes; reddish skin; thin lips; weak
Negro	Intense yet fleeting impulses; lazy; can be educated to the point of servitude; incapable of historical revolution	Thick, turned-up nose; thick lips; oily, black skin; high concentration of iron in the blood; strong; fleshy; supple
Hindu (East Indian)	Capacity for pragmatic, technical thought; no abstract thought; limited capacity for culture; incapable of historical revolution	Olive-yellow skin color; cold blood and hands
White	Possess all talents of the species; compulsion to cultural progress and civilization; exclusive role in history and historical revolutions	White skin

can be unified and classified under the headings of four racial types in table 1.[50] These characteristics will be repeated indefinitely across generations, creating a bond in time between body and mind. This theory of sex accounting for the mind-body union can be further clarified through the following three points.

First, while physical influx and comparative anatomy investigate the union by taking the individual at the present moment as its object, race, as Kant understands it, unites mind and body only by studying a series of individuals. Because the unfailingly hereditary nature of mental and physical race characteristics can only be discerned over the course of several generations, the unity of these traits must be discovered historically. No anatomical analysis of the individual will reveal that which is inherited unfailingly from his or her ancestors. This is why Kant writes at the end of his 1777 essay, "[T]he description of nature (the condition of nature at the present time) does not suffice to explain the manifold diversity of human deviations. We must, therefore, venture to offer a history of nature."[51] On the basis of this temporal approach, the mental and physical type united under the heading 'Hindu,' for example, is the unification of a series of minds and bodies in time, rather than a singular mind and body in space. Of course, this is not to say that the results of the generational analysis cannot be retroactively applied to the individual. Though the union is only manifested by a serial repetition, that series is constituted by individuals that consistently display certain mind-body traits. For this reason, once Kant has discerned racial traits on the basis of a serial analysis, he knows that certain corporeal characteristics will be united with certain mental types. This provides a scientific basis for what Kant could only stipulate in 1764 regarding the inference from a Black individual to that individual's stupidity.[52]

Second, as table 1 illustrates, the unity of mind and body is not one, but rather fourfold. This is just to say that because 'race' is a union of mind and body, and there are four races, there must also be four unions. Thus, 'Hindu' is one sort of union insofar as this term signifies the necessary and permanent bond between a pragmatic mind and olive-yellow skin. Again, the union is one insofar as race unites the spheres of mind and body, in this case, olive-yellow skin to a pragmatic mind in each and every Hindu individual. Nevertheless, this is just one of four possible unions, and each individual stands as a particular bond of mind and body that falls within one of four racial categories. For this reason, 'race' is composed of four permanently distinct mind-body unions.

Finally, each race is a union of mind and body revealed over the course of a series of unfailing regenerations. However, this is not to say that the mind-body union constitutes the whole of Kant's race concept.

In fact, the concept of race is itself a composite of two other concepts: monogenesis and regeneration. On the one hand, the concept of regeneration provides the reliable, scientifically lawful basis for classification. On the other, the concept of monogenesis guarantees that this classification is of differences within the species, not between species. It is the first concept that permits the designation of certain mind-body traits as permanently united across an infinite series of regenerations. The second concept allows Kant to argue that these four unions are unions of *human* minds and bodies, but monogenesis is not essential to the union as such.

To summarize, despite Kant's rejections of the mind-body problem popular with his contemporaries, one does find a mind-body union in his three essays on race. This union is the generational union of certain mental and physical characters, united under the four headings White, Negro, Hunnish and Hindu. Each of these races articulates a unique relation between body and mind that cannot be located in space, but instead must be studied over time. It does not relate consciousness to nerve fibers or brain states, but rather it unites skin color to mental dispositions and capacities. These unions cannot be discovered through a dissection of individual bodies, since their permanent, hereditarily necessary element is only revealed over a series of generations. In this way, the racial unions of mind and body are not anatomical but rather serial, to be discovered only through the medium of time. This is to say, in short, Kant's concept of race is a theory of sex that provides an account of how generations relate to each other as well as how mind and body, and in thinking sex and the union simultaneously, 'race' accomplishes what Descartes, Bonnet, and others could not.

It has recently been said that Kant invented the concept of race.[53] Yet, as I mentioned in chapter 1, one must recognize that concepts are not invented *ex nihilo*. As Gilles Deleuze and Félix Guattari explain, "All concepts are connected to problems without which they have no meaning and which can themselves only be isolated or understood as their solution emerges."[54] If Kant does invent the concept of race, this invention can only be made intelligible along the contours of a newly invented problem. Here, as in the previous chapter, readers have seen how not only Bonnet but numerous philosophical, medical, and scientific authors articulated the mind-body problem as a question of *Where*? As Sömmering or Bonnet demonstrates, once these authors decide there is a real causal relation between soul and body, the project requires them to then locate the site of this interaction. Bonnet, who did attempt a history of the mind-body union, only endeavors that history on the presumption that he could locate the union in relation to a preexistent egg embodying all future life. As I noted, his history fails insofar as it is illegitimately predicated on a certain spatial arrangement. Arguing that the soul, which exists in time, cannot be anatomically located in the body, Kant rejects the basic terms of this problem. Accordingly, Kant's essays on race do not address mind and body according to the question of where they interact or even if they interact. Kant's reterritorialization of the mind-body union occurs when the problem of *Where*? is displaced in favor of *When*? Rather than attempting to first locate the soul in space, natural history positions both body and mind in time.[55] Studied in the medium of time and without reference to spatial anatomy, the problem of their unity becomes something more than a fruitless endeavor, as it finds its solution in the process of repetition or regeneration. Of course, one cannot deny that the body occupies space, and that the skin, for example, exists in space. However, racially speaking, skin color and other race traits are not discovered in space. In a move that owes no small debt to Buffon's redefinition of the species discussed in chapter 1, according to Kant, the raced body, like the mind, can only be discovered in time. Only once mind and body are positioned hereditarily, in time, can one determine their unity as a necessary bond of mind and body types across generations.

Recall the governing hypothesis of Voegelin's two texts on race: "The race concept is a part of the body-soul problem; the former requires for its adequate understanding complete clarity about the latter and therefore about the nature of man."[56] I have been pursuing this hypothesis through the works of several authors, arriving at mostly negative conclusions. Hitherto, every author examined prior to Kant has failed to coherently respond to the mind-body problem while simultaneously lacking any coherent doctrine of a human race. Now, looking at Kant's

work, in what way might race be 'part of' the larger problem of the relationship between body and mind? For this thesis to be as historically
accurate as it is innovative, readers must admit various reformulations
of the mind-body problem throughout the long development of the
race idea. In the history of the formulation of the problem I have been
developing, Kant stands as the most radical advancement, and philosophers should recognize the notion of a mind-body union inherent in
his concept of race. One can highlight this aspect of Kant's work while
acknowledging that Kant's race writings do not engage with any of the
popular eighteenth-century solutions to the mind-body problem. In other
words, if the problem is stated in terms of interaction, then reasonable
solutions do include doctrines wherein the mind and body are denied
any interaction, or God is the mediator of any perceived interaction, or
the interaction is an actual causal relationship occurring somewhere in
the body. Yet, if philosophers will allow that these are not the only solutions, but also that interaction or causality is not the only problem, then
the term 'body-soul problem' is open to a broad range of interpretations.
If the philosopher approaches this problem as a race question, then, as
Voegelin's work demonstrates, the anatomy of the brain, the details of
the nervous system, and the seat of the soul are superseded by questions
surrounding embryology, heredity, and sexual reproduction. Tracing
these themes, one is able to recognize a mind-body problem developing in Europe that ultimately terminates in Kant's science of the races.

For a long time now, not all, but many philosophers have been
fairly certain that the mind-body problem is a problem of relations, be
it between minds and bodies or brain states and consciousness.[57] This,
however, is not a problem for Kant's theory of race. I understand that for
some it may seem strange to think the mind-body problem in terms of
sex, regeneration, and heredity. It may seem even more foreign to consider 'race' as the solution to the problem. Yet, I doubt it seems strange
to authors such as Linda Alcoff, who understands race as the veritable passageway from a person's physical exterior to an interior realm
of consciousness. In her own words, she describes race as the product

of "habits of visual discrimination"[58] that organize a field of perceived physical racial differences so as to "provide purported access to a subjectivity through observable, 'natural' attributes, to provide a window on the interiority of the self."[59] Likewise, mind-body relations should not be a problem for the carpenter to whom Kant refers in the *Observations on the Beautiful and the Sublime* whose physical darkness is said to so obviously envelope his mental stupidity. In one of history's subtle repetitions, the mind-body union is not a problem for Malcolm X in eighth grade when his dark body supposedly carries a mental stupidity that makes him suitable only for carpentry.[60] In each case, race is the vehicle from the exterior to the interior. Philosophy's orthodox problem of the mind-body union is not a universal problem. Its solution is lived every day and known intimately through these "habits of vision" for which Kant institutes a 'science.'

Accordingly, one can further Voegelin's aim of integrating the development of race with Modern philosophy in claiming that Kant's race concept is not merely 'a part of' the mind-body problem, but it is actually a feasible solution. Nonetheless, the resolution of this problem is not its end, nor has the aim of this book ever been to 'solve' the mind-body problem. This would potentially terminate the discourse in a way that would perhaps be fatal to my ultimate goal, which is to reopen the mind-body discourse in a way that recognizes the organic knowledge of those most familiar with a racial non-being. The true value of Kant's concept of race as a solution to the mind-body problem only lies in its potential to open onto a truly other mind-body problem, to which my attention should now turn.

THE OVERTURNING OF THE MIND-BODY PROBLEM

The principle of reason reads, *nihil est sine ratio*, or 'Nothing is without reason.' I have already taken note of two other moments in the history of this principle's maturation and its relation to the mind-body discourse.

In chapter 1, readers saw how Descartes establishes the reason for the mind's existence, writing, "God is the cause of me, and I am an effect of him."[61] A demonstration of the cause of the soul is necessary because Descartes believes that if anything exists, then it must have an efficient cause. His axiom of the cause effectively determines the essence of every being as an effect, and every being, including the *res cogitans*, is insofar as it is caused. Although this axiom is not identical to the principle of reason found in Leibniz's work, a number of commentators agree it holds an important place in the development of Leibniz's *principium magnum, grande et nobilissimum*.[62] In chapter 2, readers saw that Bonnet, working in Leibniz's wake, is able to deploy the principle of reason quite explicitly. Inquiring into the being of the Hurons and others, I found that their existence was secured by a reason that Bonnet formulated as the unity of nature. Since nature permits no gaps, there must be a perfectly smooth gradation of beings populating the Great Chain, and thus, the Huron, Iroquois, Hottentot, and every other being for that matter are necessary for the sake of nature's harmony. Even though Bonnet departs from the Cartesian scheme and gives an account of the Huron as an essentially inferior being, this inferiority is protected from a fall into non-being precisely because there is a reason, a necessity even, accounting for this denigrated status. Although the metaphysical ideas of Descartes, Leibniz, Buffon, and Bonnet differ in so many ways, there is a general consensus that every being is grounded in a 'reason,' be it an efficient or final cause, and a being *is* only when grounded in this way. Kant claims to provide "the only possible proof of the principle of sufficient reason" in his Second Analogy of Experience, although he had written on it at length in several precritical texts and lectures.[63] I have addressed Kant's scientific notion of 'race' and discovered that each race is a unity of mind and body. On what ground does this unity stand?

Today, this question persists under various guises. Perhaps race is grounded in a psychological disposition humans inherited through natural selection? Or is its reason found in the social constructions of power? Could the reason for the races even lie in certain economic necessities?

This approach, guided by the demand to provide a reason, is nearly as old as the principle of reason itself. For instance, the need to render reasons for human difference was expressed by Jean-Baptiste Dubos when in his 1719 *Réflexions critiques sur la poésie et sur la peinture* he asked, "*Why are all the nations so different in courage, stature, inclinations, and mind, if they all came from the same father?*"[64] The ubiquity of this interest in the reason for human difference is reflected in the fact that travel literature was second only to the novel in eighteenth-century European print culture,[65] and Kant addresses its importance in writing, "The information the new travels offer about the diversity of the human race has so far tended more to stimulate the mind to further research on this point than to satisfy it."[66] This 'further research' should be understood in light of the guiding metaphysical principle of Modern science and its demand that there be an answer to *why* one finds these differences within the species.

In this section, I will be inquiring into Kant's writing on race through the lens of the requirement that every being render a reason for its existence. Guided by this demand, one will at last discover another mind-body problem, one that concerns the being of Kant's racial mind-body unions detailed earlier. Although Kant famously addresses the principle of reason in the Second Analogy in the *Critique of Pure Reason*, I seek the application of this principle to his specific notion of 'race.' For that reason, and because race falls under the jurisdiction of natural history for Kant, I investigate the role of the principle vis-à-vis the repetition of racial characteristics, or more generally, the regeneration of the species. This is to say, one must grasp how sexual regeneration not only provides a foundation for a certain mind-body union, but how it is also necessary to the realization of certain endowments essential to the species. Accordingly, this will turn my attention away from the Second Analogy and toward Kant's work on history and culture to comprehend how, without a long history of regeneration, the innate capacity to reason would itself be without reason.

Before digging into this analysis I must stress again that, according to Kant, there are two historical phases of the species. The first period is one of degeneration whereby an original human stock adapts to a certain geographic environment. This period accounts for the emergence of difference within the species, while the second phase of the process, regeneration, accounts for the permanence of these differences across four races. When one inquires into the reason grounding the existence of human races, one must be careful to continuously distinguish between Kant's concepts of degeneration and racial regeneration, since these phenomena do not share the same reasons, taken either as final or efficient causes. Properly speaking, there is no truly racial degeneration in Kant's work, since he consistently defines 'race' in opposition to degeneration:

> I would translate [race] by means of *deviate form* [Abartung] (progenies *classifica*) in order to distinguish it from a *degeneration* [Ausartung] (degeneratio s. progenies *specifica*), something which we cannot allow, since it runs counter to the laws of nature (in the preservation of the species in unchangeable form).[67]

Although degeneration is not racial, and thus not the site of Kant's mind-body unions, it nevertheless has a role to play in explaining the reason for the origins of human difference and Kant is not unique in attempting to render a reason for this process. Allow me to briefly review Kant's thoughts on degeneration in order to identify them, set them aside, and prevent them from confusing or obscuring an understanding of the reason for the properly racial regenerations, which, again, comprise the very fabric of the mind-body union.

Prior to Kant, reasons for degeneration could be located in the influence of the mother's imagination on the fetus,[68] the myth of Ham,[69] climatic influence,[70] or, most worrisome for Kant, the theory of polygenesis.[71] Kant's own attempt to explain the origins of the differences reported in the travelogues is well documented in recent literature on Kant's theory of race.[72] The most pertinent lines appear in his 1775 and 1777 versions of *Of the Different Human Races* in a section titled "Of the immediate causes of the origin of the different races." Here, Kant claims that the original development of the races is due to two causes, one 'productive,' the other 'occasional.' The productive causes of each race are found in the original germs (*Kieme*) and predispositions (*Anlagen*) of the species, which were furnished by the prudence of Nature "to equip her creature through hidden, inner provisions for a variety of future circumstances to the end that the creature might preserve itself and be suited for the difference of climate and land."[73] Of course, these inner predispositions develop differently according to the occasional causes responsible for arousing one or the other preexisting form. The occasional cause is the environment, which never genuinely creates anything but only brings about certain modifications provided by Nature laying latently in the seed. The traits of each of the four races are present from the start, and the appropriate characteristics are only actualized in accordance with environmental circumstances. This teleological account applies not only for humans but equally governs the development of animals and plants, allowing Kant to explain differences found in birds and even grain.[74]

The phenomenon of degeneration has for its reason the conservation of the species, as Nature placed various endowments in the germs of the original stock "because it was required for the preservation of the kind."[75] The 'because' here appeals to the distinct reason that grounds this specific process: degeneration is for the sake of bare survival. Yet, in this context, 'survival' does not just refer to the individual. Rather, degeneration is for 'the preservation of the kind,' and by 'kind' Kant means the progeny of this type or species. Strictly speaking then, degeneration is for the sake of regeneration, or regeneration is the reason for degeneration. Thus, if there is any remaining possibility of the reader confusing degeneration with that which is properly racial, bear in mind that even though regeneration comes after degeneration in time, given the logic of teleological thinking, regeneration is ontologically first, standing as the ground or reason for any adaptation.

I am interested in the reason that would account for Kant's four racial mind-body unions. Insofar as this unity is found in a serial repetition, it will not be accounted for by the reason Kant furnishes for degeneration.

What is the ground of those mind-body unities that constitute the four races, understood as regenerations? Again, this is a different question from 'where did the races come from and how did they emerge?' Insofar as I seek the reason for the races, Kant must explain why these four types persist, since it is that very persistence of differences within the species that is properly racial. What is the reason underlying the 'survival' or repetition of those physical and mental traits charted in table 1? To answer this question, Kant draws on a tradition familiar from chapter 2: a theory of the species' historical progress, which is something more than simply reproducing.

In discovering Kant's racial mind-body unions, I emphasized that races are strictly studied in time. However, the chronological succession of generations is not itself 'history' in Kant's sense of the word. In Kant's philosophy, to properly speak of the history of the species, one must account for a coherence or unity underlying seemingly chaotic facts and events, and for that, one must study the history of the species in terms of its beginning and end. Yet, merely observing, one finds no goal or narrative directing the will of all members of the species and it seems, "everything in the large is woven together out of folly, childish vanity, often also out of childish malice and the rage to destruction."[76] History cannot simply be grounded in empirical observation, since it does not aim to understand just one or the other distinct event. Rather, history is a theoretical endeavor that involves the study of the species as a whole, including all its past and future generations.[77] If any narrative might tie these disparate and even contradictory behaviors together to unite them, then one needs some a priori guideline.

Specifying this parameter is, in part, the project of Kant's first and most extensive work in the philosophy of history, the *Idea for a Universal History with a Cosmopolitan Aim* from 1784. Kant provides this interpretive rule in the First Proposition: "All natural predispositions of a creature are determined to develop themselves completely and purposively."[78] In the next sentence, Kant restates this precept in negative terms: There is no organ without a purpose, and no arrangement that does not realize its end. Kant emphasizes the necessity of this a priori principle in warning that if one strays from it, "then we no longer have a lawful nature but a purposelessly playing nature; and desolate chance takes the place of the guideline of reason."[79] In his 1788 essay on race Kant calls this the 'principle of purposes,'[80] but it is already present in the *Idea*, such as when he claims, "[N]ature does nothing superfluous and is not wasteful in the use of means to its end."[81]

This 'guideline' of reason or principle of purposes must be heard according to its vital wellspring, the principle of reason. Again, this principle can be summarized in two formulae: either, 'Every being has a reason,' or 'Nothing is without reason.' In the First Proposition of the *Idea* one finds both iterations formulated according to a specific application: 'Every natural predisposition, even those yet to be developed, has a reason or purpose,' and, 'No predisposition is without reason or purpose.' In the tradition of Leibniz's and Bonnet's writings, 'reason' refers to the final cause. This makes history, in Kant's specific sense of the word, a rational, metaphysical endeavor grounded in the principle 'everything in nature has a reason,' or 'nothing is wasteful,' or even just 'nothing is without reason.'

Concerning the human species, one latent predisposition stands out: the capacity for rational thought. For Kant, this capacity is not given at birth, as one finds in Descartes's Third Meditation. Here, reason is given but only potentially, not actually, and 'history,' in Kant's philosophy, is essentially the narrowing of this gap between potential and actual reason. When one asks what causes this gap to close, one is inquiring into the efficient cause of rational thought itself. Throughout this study, readers have repeatedly seen philosophers and scientists alike study the capacity to reason as an effect defined by its cause. For instance, for the likes of Descartes or Buffon, reason is an effect of God. In Bonnet's work one discovers a historical account of reason grounded in a cause, which he identifies as the development of the body's sense receptors and nervous system. Kant is also studying reason as an effect, but not in terms of an immediate relationship to God, nor through an anatomical and causal relationship to the body. In Kant's philosophy reason is, in a way, an effect of nature, but not at all in the sense Bonnet intended. In Kant's philosophy, nature, in the form of certain predispositions, does actualize the innate capacity to reason, but only indirectly through culture, and that is in large part brought about by 1) a natural inclination to reproduce and 2) a natural inclination to antagonism.

How is sexual reproduction, which, I repeat, comprises Kant's racial mind-body unions, necessary to the development of the capacity to reason? In the *Idea* Kant provides a clue as to how it is *not* necessary when he writes,

> Reason itself does not operate instinctively, but rather needs attempts, practice and instruction in order to gradually progress from one stage of insight to another. Hence every human being would have to live exceedingly long in order to learn how he is to make use of all his natural predispositions.[82]

While he was not the first (or last) thinker to promote the doctrine of palingenesis, readers know that Bonnet, following Leibniz, does in fact think life is not only 'exceedingly long' but actually infinite. In chapter 2, readers saw that Bonnet's theory offers a history of the maturation of reason based on the perpetual rebirth of the individual. It is not clear whether Kant is referring to palingenesis here, but he is at least aware of the doctrine, since he publishes an article this same year explicitly denying it.[83] In any case, because reason is not given, like instinct, it must be developed over time, but because Kant rejects palingenesis, and each individual lives only a short time, then the species will require "an immense series of generations"[84] to develop its predisposition to reason. Four years later in the *Critique of Practical Reason* Kant solves this problem by referring to the immortality of the soul.[85] However, in Section 83 of the *Critique of Judgment* he returns to his belief that historical progress requires the regeneration of the species.[86]

This then is the reason for regeneration as Kant states it in the first two propositions of the *Idea*: 1) Humans have a natural predisposition to reason; 2) that capacity is neither given in its fully developed state, nor is an individual's life long enough for it to develop; 3) therefore, an individual must reproduce *in order to* "[transmit] its enlightenment to the next [generation]." And furthermore, this occurs "in order to finally propel its germs in our species to that stage of development which is completely suited to its aim."[87] Although it may seem odd, regeneration is a natural predisposition, and in *Religion within the Limits of Reason Alone*, Kant classifies it as a primary "predisposition to animality." Insofar as nature does nothing superfluous in its allotment of predispositions, the predisposition to propagate the species must have a reason: it is necessary to the 'transmission of enlightenment.'

However, reason does not simply mature as the species merely reproduces itself, and the 'transmission of enlightenment' is not the same as the capacity to reason in its mature form. Regeneration is a necessary but insufficient condition for the complete development of reason. When Kant says regeneration is necessary to transmit enlightenment to the next generation, he is also alluding to his notion of 'unsocial sociability.' This too is a predisposition that "obviously lies in human nature."[88] It is twofold, consisting of the contradictory inclinations to both socialize and individualize, resulting in the species' "propensity to enter into society [. . .] combined with a thoroughgoing resistance that constantly threatens to break society up."[89] This propensity accounts for so much of the vanity, jealousy, and even warfare that characterize what appears to be the chaos of human affairs. But the inclination to evil is not without reason. As Kant states in *Religion*, "[N]ature, indeed, wanted to use the idea of such rivalry only as a spur to culture."[90] That is to say, on the basis of this discord, the species is compelled to transcend its *Rohigkeit*, or barbarism, and progressively develop a culture or civil society.

Culture is the reason for unsocial sociability, but, once again, the latter is not a sufficient condition for the former. The transition from a natural condition of instinctual bondage to a rational, ethical community cannot be accomplished in a single generation. As Kant emphasizes in the following passage, regeneration is necessary if the evils of unsocial sociability are to bear fruit:

Now it is this resistance that awakens all the powers of the human being, brings him to overcome his propensity to indolence, and, driven by ambition, tyranny and greed, to obtain for himself a rank among his fellows, whom he cannot stand, but also cannot leave alone. Thus happen the first true steps from crudity toward culture, which really consists in the social worth of the human being; thus all talents come bit by bit to be developed, taste is formed, and even, through progress in enlightenment, a beginning is made toward the foundation of a mode of thought which can *with time* transform the rude natural predisposition to make moral distinctions into determinate practical principles and hence transform a pathologically compelled agreement to form a society finally into a moral whole.[91]

This 'moral whole' is none other than Kant's final end of creation, or *Endzweck*, which he variously refers to as the 'kingdom of ends,' the 'invisible church,' the 'ethical community,' or the 'kingdom of God on Earth.'[92] Accordingly, culture is not an end in itself, but it is a prerequisite for that end. Insofar as I seek a reason for regeneration and not a summation of Kant's critical philosophy, it suffices to underscore that the species transcends its barbarity and achieves reason with the aid of two elements: 1) a propensity for culture, understood as "the fruits of unsociability,"[93] and 2) 'time' as Kant states in the preceding quote. And by 'time' Kant means sex, insofar as the necessary time for the development of culture is only provided by a long series of regenerations.

Accordingly, regeneration, on the basis of which I discovered a solution to the problem of how minds and bodies unite, finds its reason and necessity in this schematic. Most importantly, I must stress that regeneration is necessary to the continuous progress of culture, and it finds its reason in culture. As a natural predisposition, and an essential component of human nature, it must be heard as part of Kant's claim in the *Critique of Judgment* that "only culture can be the ultimate purpose that we have cause to attribute to nature with respect to the human species."[94] Thus, it is anything but 'desolate chance' that the species regenerates. It is necessary because reason cannot mature in a single generation, and without it there could be no accumulation and 'transmission of enlightenment' that defines the progress of culture. As the reason for the regeneration of the species, culture is also its ground. Consequently, in *Anthropology from a Pragmatic Point of View*, when Kant defines the character of the species, understood as a chain or succession of individuals, he defines that succession according to its reason, or *why* that succession occurs: "to bring about the perfection of the human being through progressive culture, although with some sacrifice of his pleasures of life."[95] Without this progress, the predisposition to reason would lay dormant, and would then "have to be regarded for the most part as vain and purposeless,"[96] a proposition that contradicts the basic principle of Kant's philosophy of both nature and history: nothing is without reason.

The idea of the progress of culture across generations undergoes several revisions in the *Critique of Judgment*, most notably Kant's reinterpretation of history on the basis of reflective judgment as well as his introduction of the cultures of skill and discipline.[97] Yirmiyahu Yovel has argued that in the *Idea* Kant dogmatically ascribes a purpose to nature itself. Yovel's interpretation is not without critics, but even if one does recognize precritical and critical phases in Kant's philosophical history, the principle of purpose or reason remains a constant theme.[98] In developing the *telos* of history as a reflective end, Kant is able to integrate the main themes of the *Idea* with his critical project. Without going into the details of reflective judgment here, a theme that has received ample attention in the secondary literature,[99] suffice it to say the practice of ascribing ends to the species and nature as a whole gains legitimacy once one acknowledges that although nature operates mechanistically, one cannot grasp anything like nature as a whole or its history without assuming a purpose or end to its activities. Since this purpose is not given empirically, Kant makes the notion of teleologically organized history an a priori condition for the possibility of comprehending the species and its regeneration, while simultaneously denying that this end determines the actual being of objects, as noumena. According to the Copernican principle that governs this reinterpretation of the *Idea*, one must recognize that the reason for the regeneration of the individual is not found in nature. It is now a reason supplied by cognition. But this transition does not make the reason any less of a ground, nor does it signal a surrender on Kant's part to ground the regeneration of the species in a reason. In fact, the situation is quite the opposite insofar as the principle of reason remains a governing precept of beings. The transcendental method, when applied to the specific case of history, dictates that the historian must supply the purpose or reason for events in order to get beyond the chaos of random occurrences and think them in terms of a historical narrative. Far from rejecting the principle of reason, this reformulation only reemphasizes Kant's commitment to rendering reasons. Not only does every predisposition have a reason or purpose, but the reason for assuming that principle now must be expressed as one grounded in the condition for the possibility of history. This is why Heidegger would claim the transcendental method features a profound allegiance to the principle of reason:

> [Kant's] thinking is, as a Rational cognition, the rendering of sufficient reasons for what can and cannot appear to humans as a being—it is the rendering of sufficient conditions for the manner in which what appears can appear, as well as how it cannot appear.[100]

In incorporating the themes of the *Idea* into his critical project, Kant effectively doubles down on the principle of reason: while the claim that regeneration occurs for the sake of the progress of culture still stands, this teleological interpretation of sex is further grounded in the cognitive demands of the historian, since without that teleology events could not appear historically. In other words, while teleology provides reasons for events, the transcendental method provides the reason for teleology insofar as it "represents the unique way in which we must proceed in reflection on objects of nature with the aim of a thoroughly interconnected experience."[101] I emphasize this to point out that although Kant rarely spoke of the principle of reason in his works on history and race, the seeking of reasons pervades this work, and the introduction of reflective judgment in the third *Critique* should, among other things, be understood as Kant's solution to the problem of rendering a transcendental reason for the regeneration of the species. This attention should not be surprising considering what is at stake, which is nothing less than the determination of what has a reason and what does not, or, more fundamentally, what attains the status of being and what does not. And so, when one asks with Kant, 'Why does the species regenerate?' one is essentially making a determination on the being of regeneration and, in turn, the species. I have demonstrated why this phenomenon occurs: for the sake of culture or the 'transmission of enlightenment.'

That Kant recognizes the immediate racial implications of this grounding of regeneration in the progress of culture must not be underemphasized, and the point is best observed in the context of his clash with J. G. Herder. Zammito writes that the disagreement between Kant and Herder over historical progress and the species' cultural development should be seen as "one of the most important events in the literary life of Germany in the last years of the eighteenth century."[102] The relevant text from Herder is his *Ideas for a Philosophy of the History of Mankind*, of which Kant wrote a scathing review in November of 1785. Herder had written one section in particular to draw the ire of Kant, entitled, "The happiness of human beings is everywhere an individual good; consequently, it is everywhere climatic and organic, a child of practice, tradition, and custom."[103] Here, Herder takes aim at a number of themes from Kant's *Idea*, none more significant than the idea that the reason for a species' self-regeneration lies at the end of history understood as a federation of European states. For Herder, the reason for each individual's existence is self-justifying: "Its existence is to it an end and its end is existence,"[104] and to claim that the human race, considered as a whole, must receive a certain cultural education is "incomprehensible."[105] Accordingly, the reason for each individual does not lie in sexual regeneration, but rather in the happiness each person finds in life, no matter what form that life may take. Kant underscores this theme in his thinking, quoting Herder's claim that, "each human individual has the measure of his happiness within him."[106] Clearly, this stands in direct opposition to Kant's *Idea*, which, Herder believes, insists on an arrangement of states based on a European model in order for the species to develop its predisposition for reason, live peacefully, and only then, at the end of a long historical process, find happiness.

Herder's identification of what Kant calls "this shadowy image of happiness which each individual creates for himself"[107] as the reason for the existence of the human species stands in direct contradiction to Kant's doctrine of cultural progress and the fulfillment of the political and moral destiny of the species. For Kant, the question becomes, if the development of culture (on the basis of a propensity for selfishness and unsocial sociability) is the reason for the regeneration of the species, then *why* do peoples exist lacking this propensity? To highlight the lack of a reason for an 'indolent,' 'uncultured' human species, Kant draws on a concrete example: the Tahitians. In this most striking passage Kant inquires into the existence of a human individual who "does not yield in the enjoyment of his happiness to any of those who come after him":

> [A]s far as the value of [the Tahitians'] existence itself is concerned—i.e. the *reason why* they are there in the first place, as distinct from the conditions in which they exist—it is in this alone that a wise intention of the whole is revealed. Does the author really mean that if the happy inhabitants of Tahiti, never visited by more cultured nations, had been destined to live for thousands of centuries in their tranquil indolence, one could give a satisfying answer to the question of *why they exist at all*, and whether it would not have been just as good to have this

island populated with happy sheep and cattle as with human
beings who are happy merely enjoying themselves?[108]

In studying this quote, first note that his invocation of the Tahitians here
is far from idiosyncratic. As I stated earlier, travel writings are tremendously popular in eighteenth-century Europe, and Kant sees them as a
significant resource for the development of anthropology.[109] Travelogues
had long been of interest to German academics where Haller, for example,
ran a reading group entirely devoted to their study.[110] In the second
half of the century, Georg Forster's *Reise um die Welt* (*A Voyage Round
the World*) from 1777 is particularly notable. This work meticulously
details the life of the South Pacific Islanders, creating a compilation of
data appropriated by a range of subsequent academic debates on politics, anthropology, history, and human nature. Excerpts are published
on multiple occasions in *Der Teutsche Merkur*, the work inspires several
novels, and, due to Forster's friendships with German intellectuals, it is
disseminated among the likes of Goethe, Schiller, Herder, Sömmering,
and, of course, Kant.[111] The text is instrumental in shaping the German
imagination of life in the South Pacific, and, judging from his 1788 essay
on race in which he engages Forster at length, Kant must have read this
work with intent. For Forster, Tahiti is simultaneously uncivilized and
utopian. He describes it as a life of "uninterrupted tranquility and continual sameness, suited only to a people whose notions are simple and
confined."[112] It is "an easy life free from cares, in the happiest climate
in the world,"[113] an attitude reflected by Kant in the *Groundwork* (also
from 1785) where he goes out of his way to make an example of the
Tahitians' purported lack of development and "idleness."

For my study of the mind-body problem, this passage is of particular
importance because when Kant addresses the Tahitians, he invokes the
principle of reason twice. First, he claims the Tahitians as such, without
contact with Europe, have no reason to exist, and so one cannot answer
"why they exist at all." Kant then continues, asking if there is any reason
for the island not to have been populated with sheep. This formulation

must be seen as asking into the *ratio existentia* of these people: why are the Tahitians here and not something else? In either case, for Kant, a people defined by 'uninterrupted tranquility and continual sameness' has no reason. The *Why*? finds no *Because*... Whereas in the *Idea* Kant opposes cultural progress to indolence and laziness, one now sees this is not an exercise in abstraction for him. He may then have had the Tahitians in mind, although he will later cite peoples without reason in the form of the New Hollanders, the Fuegians, the Greenlanders, Lapps, Samoyeds, and the Yakuts.[114]

A people without reason? If 'nothing is without reason,' if "Nature does nothing superfluous,"[115] then, as an uttering of being, the principle of reason renders 'the happy inhabitants of Tahiti,' who undoubtedly regenerate and yet do so for no reason, a kind of nothingness. To what exactly is this nothingness directed? As I have explained, the particularity of the Tahitian is a result of degeneration, where they developed the dispositions necessary for this climate. As I discussed, this process has a reason, which is survival or regeneration. Kant has no need to ask into the why of their degeneration, since by 1785 he has already published extensively on that question. Kant however does provide a hint as to what is without reason. He writes: "the happy inhabitants of Tahiti," living "for thousands of centuries in their tranquil indolence." What is this 'tranquil indolence,' this stagnant enjoyment, without change, for thousands of centuries? Clearly, it could not be an individual Tahitian, nor a degenerative adaptation. Those phenomena clearly do not endure long enough. Rather, it is nothing other than a regeneration, or more precisely the unfailing regeneration I have identified as Kant's definition of 'race.' When Kant asks, "[W]hy are they really there?" the 'they' is racial.[116] Yet, as I detailed earlier, 'race' is a series of unfailing regenerations, and this repetition is none other than a mind-body union. If this particular kind of regeneration, or 'race,' is without reason, then one not only encounters a race that stands without being, but one must also recognize the eruption here in this passage of *a unity from which being withdraws*. While it is true that sex produces the series of individuals that make up the race, the reason for this ongoing sexual regeneration goes missing. It goes missing precisely because it is the sexual regeneration of a mind-body union that will never be other than indolent in mind and brown in body. And so, for Kant, *the Tahitian race is a oneness that reproduces its own nothingness.* As a race without reason, this non-being can be replaced or exterminated altogether, and precisely *nothing* is lost:

> Man has such a propensity to perfect himself that he deems superfluous a people who achieved their development and are simply happy, and he believes the world would lose *nothing* if Tahiti was engulfed [*die Welt würde nichts verlieren, wenn auch otaheite unterginge*].[117]

Could Kant not have said, with Herder, that every individual has his or her own reason for existence? Or even following Bonnet, could he not have consistently maintained that inferior types are necessary to the unity and perfection of nature? Could he not have said that through the process of adapting to the climate, the Tahitian nevertheless retains the prospect of enlightenment and cultural progress?[118] Kant accepts none of these options, and instead one finds the problem of races without reason infecting not just the Tahitians, but all non-White people.

I have explained that the reason for the regeneration of the species after its initial phase of degeneration is defined as a full development of reason on the basis of culture. And yet, when Kant formulates and defines the moral or psychological characteristics that regenerate unfailingly and are thus specific to each race, he does this precisely according to each races' participation in cultural progress. Nowhere is this clearer than in the previously cited *Menschenkunde* lectures from the early 1780s (see above p. 118–119). Here, each race is evaluated according to its fitness to participate in the species' progress toward its ultimate and final end. From the Americans, who have 'no prospect,' to the Negroes, who respond only to heteronomous coercion, to the Hindus, who lack the capacity for abstract rational thought, each of the races represents a merely stagnant regeneration.[119] As Kant puts it in his own words, "We find people who do not appear to progress in the perfection of human nature, rather they have come to a standstill, while others, as in Europe, always progress."[120] Insofar as the reason for regeneration is to serve as a vehicle for the 'transmission of enlightenment,' a race that has 'come to a standstill' survives without reason. Each individual is born without reason. As such, they are a groundless unity, subject to the same status as the Tahitian.

Everyone is familiar with the mind-body problem, if by that phrase one is designating the problem of how *a* being can nevertheless not be *one*. A being is necessarily *one*, and it is contradictory to say otherwise. This is of course the precept that Descartes violated, and he is widely credited (accurately or not) with inaugurating this particular mind-body problem.[121] Whether philosophers are asking into the relationship between Cartesian substances, or, with the decline of substance dualism and the rise of physicalism, they are concerned with the association of physical processes and consciousness, one orthodox formulation of the problem is one of unity.[122] There is no question of there being evidence of Descartes's participation in solving this problem insofar as he tried to explain the interaction and causal influence of minds and bodies. There is also no question as to the attention and resources that have been dedicated to this problem both by historians of philosophy and the contemporary philosophy of mind. Moreover, it is the problem I have been occupied with in the previous chapters, although my concern was with the sexual generation of the unity, thus leading to the problems of sex in both Descartes's and Bonnet's work, respectively. In these previous formulations of the mind-body problem, readers witnessed how theories of generation and regeneration played significant roles not just in the construction of the person, but more significantly, the raced human being. If the mind-body problem is understood in this way, a problem of *a being without unity*, then readers have equally seen that Kant's innovative definition of 'race' solves this problem insofar as it scientifically establishes a unity of mind and body *in time*. Yet, this solution to the problem of when mind and body unite cannot respond to the governing ontological question: *Why* do they unite? To be sure, regarding the White race, this problem does not arise. On the other hand, for Kant's Negroes, Hindus, and Americans, when a reason for regeneration goes missing, then each race stands as mind-body unities without being. That is to say, rather than a being without unity, one finds with these races *a unity without being*. This problem is not the mind-body problem philosophers are familiar with today and it cannot be reduced to that industry. Nevertheless, it warrants being called *another mind-body problem*, since it is precisely Kant's characterization of the unity that generates this nothingness. This problem must be recognized as the problem of a racial non-being, a problem that philosophy should credit Kant with having instituted. In this way, Kant's philosophy completes the *Umwälzung*, or overturning, of the mind-body problem. Two further points are crucial to an understanding of this very specific brand of non-being.

First, one must be clear what it means for this nothingness to be 'racial.' As I have made clear, that which lacks being is precisely the unity of mind and body. In earlier chapters, I discussed the difficulties of accounting for the place of the mind in the process of generation. Readers saw, for instance, how a thinker like Buffon, drawing from a Cartesian construction of the human being, could not account for a racialized human being, understood as a mind-body unity, because he located the generation of the mind in a transcendent source. Bonnet, though he is not a canonical figure in the history of European racism and he does not use the term 'race,' came closer to formulating a viable theory of human difference when he located the mind in the process of palingenesis and then tied its development to the development of the body. This allowed him to not only discount God's involvement in every human 'birth'; it also allowed him to hierarchize minds according to body types.

Kant, in inventing a racial non-being, goes beyond any of the previous constructions insofar as he not only unites minds and bodies across generations in time, thereby making minds and bodies hereditary; he also makes the nothingness itself hereditary. This is of course not to say that 'non-being' could somehow be discovered in the genes of non-White people. As concepts of metaphysics, being and unity are not available for such an analysis. Nor is this nothingness in space, as one is accustomed to thinking when they say, 'I opened the cupboard and nothing was there,' or 'They drilled for oil and found nothing.' Again, a racialized nothingness, precisely because it is racial in Kant's sense, operates in time. It is a lawful, necessary, unfailing repetition without reason, and thus one must say that the nothingness is hereditary.

Because this non-being is hereditary, it cannot be confused with other studies of non-being throughout philosophy such as Heidegger's 'nothingness' grounding Western science or even the non-being Marilyn Frye discovers in the concept of 'lesbian.'[123] Simply put, these manifestations of non-being are not hereditary and thus not 'racial' as Kant understands the word. However, just because this nothingness is hereditary, and thus in time, that is not to say it is 'historical' in the strict Kantian sense of the term. The distinction between a racial regeneration without reason and a history without reason can be further clarified if one contrasts Kant's racial non-being with yet another encounter with a nothingness from Western philosophy: Nietzsche's nihilism.

Nietzsche famously interprets the history of Western metaphysics as an endeavor without reason or purpose: "What does nihilism mean? That the highest values devaluate themselves. The aim is lacking; 'why?' finds no answer."[124] It could be argued that all I am uncovering here is an early precedent to nihilism, wherein everyone, even the European, has no reason. However, when Nietzsche discusses the nothingness that characterizes nihilism, he is referring to a certain history of the West, understood as an auto-degeneration or devaluation, which then opens onto a transvaluation. That is, Western metaphysics' lost faith in progress, reason, unity, being, truth, and the like is a necessary "pathological transitional stage"[125] in Western history, one that culminates in the *Übermensch*. The nothingness I am analyzing in Kant's work cannot be seen as a precedent to European nihilism. I have shown that the racialized nothingness is in time, but is not historical in the strict Kantian sense because non-White races play no role in the narrative of progress.

Again, as a racial mind-body union, the medium of non-white people is strictly time, a status they share with White Europeans, but, according to Kant, non-Whites are in time the way, for instance, Turgot thought plants are in time: each generation is merely a repetition of the same and "time does no more than restore continuously."[126] Non-Whites are held outside linear time.[127] Nietzschean nihilism on the other hand is profoundly historical not in the sense that nihilism has a history; rather, nihilism is the very lawfulness of the historical narrative Nietzsche presents. Even though Nietzsche interprets Western history as a decline and a confrontation with its own groundlessness, for that very reason he never strips Europe of its essentially historical nature. The 'nothingness' of nihilism is not then a lack of history. Instead, it is the logic of history in its decline and eventual rise, historical revolutions that would be irrelevant to the Negroes, Hindus, and Americans, given Kant's characterization.

This important difference between being merely in time and being historical perhaps explains why the cultivation of history has been a key strategy for certain antiracist movements seeking to combat annihilation. Readers already saw this at work in Malcolm X's thinking at the beginning of this book. He underscores the bond between a racial non-being and the total privation of history in declaring, "When you have no knowledge of your history, you're just another animal; in fact, you're a Negro; something that's nothing."[128] Three years later Kwame Ture will argue that the cultivation of Black history is "absolutely essential" and a "vital first step" in establishing Black power.[129] These are not the only thinkers decades ahead in grasping the logic of this problem as well as the possible contours of its solution, and I will return to this field of experts shortly. For now, I only intend to emphasize that Kant's racialized nothingness is distinctly in time (on account of it being racial) but nevertheless stripped of any historical reason (making it nothing).

Malcolm X's distinction between animality and non-being is equally significant to a second point of clarification: the racism expressed in Kant's mind-body problem is not a racism of inferiority. There is without doubt an ongoing and robust debate in the recent secondary literature on whether and how Kant hierarchizes the races. Often without hesitation, many authors accept the problem of a racial hierarchy in Kant's corpus as most pressing. Emmanuel Eze demonstrates this tendency when he interprets Kant's racial classification as a hierarchy of skin colors, wherein "the ideal skin color is the 'white' (the white brunette) and the others are superior or inferior as they approximate whiteness."[130] Similarly, Pauline Kleingeld locates the problem of Kant's so-called 'early racism' in the way he "connects his understanding of race with a hierarchical account according to which the races *also* vary greatly in their capacities for agency and their powers of intellect."[131] Todd Hedrick has defined Kant's racism as a racism of "inequality,"[132] and Peter K. J. Park asserts, "Kant's description of the races [...] entails a hierarchy of worth."[133] To emphasize this racism of inferiority, Charles Mills has even invoked the anachronistic term *Untermenschen* or 'subpersons' to highlight an "inferior metaphysical standing."[134]

There is no question that Kant does perpetuate this sort of hierarchal thinking at times in his writing. For instance, one finds evidence for a racial hierarchy in passages such as this:

> [H]umanity is in its highest degree of perfection in the white race. The yellow Indians have somewhat lesser talent. The Negroes are much lower, and lowest of all is a part of the American races.[135]

This is not unlike Bonnet's schematic, where according to the chain of being, one finds a necessary hierarchy of minds and bodies, wherein each link in the chain finds its reason in the whole.[136]

Nevertheless, Bonnet's inferior beings, though less than, nevertheless *are*. As I noted in chapter 2, a rationale of inferiority also has its roots in the principle of reason, although the principle is applied to the Tahitians and others according to a radically different logic. When Kant says there is no reason for the Tahitians to exist, asking "whether it would not have been just as good to have this island populated with happy sheep and cattle as with human beings who are happy merely enjoying themselves?" one cannot interpret this as a racism of inferiority, but rather a racism of non-being. Serequeberhan, for example, conflates these two forms of racism when he interprets this passage writing, "[Kant] himself thinks that the Tahitians are 'nothing,' i.e., mere sheep."[137] But still, in Western metaphysics, a sheep is not nothing. A sheep is a being. A sheep has a why, a reason, a ground. The Tahitians are radically other than sheep, since they could be Tahitians or they could be sheep, but they have reason to be neither sheep nor Tahitian. They occupy an alterity not just to sheep but to any being whatsoever, just as non-being designates a radical alterity to being. It is then precisely not the case that the Tahitians are inferior, like animals, but rather they are without reason, or without any ground whatsoever. In recent literature, Larrimore comes closest to noting this distinction when he highlights the presence of a racial 'waste' in Kant's work. In his reading of Kant's 1755 essay, *Universal Natural History and Theory of the Heavens*, Larrimore notes that Kant's early views on the creation of the universe represent a kind of theodicy that allows for God's generation of certain pockets of waste, which rather than calling into question the divine creation, only edify His omnipotence. As Larrimore explains, "A teleology that extended down to the minutest detail of creation would not tell of a God of infinite majesty, but of a penny-pincher,"[138] and in this text, written two decades before his first publication on race, the example of those without reason is not a Tahitian but the inhabitants of Venus.[139]

It may seem that I am really splitting hairs here. After all, is nothing not inferior to something, thereby creating a hierarchy? However, this conflation would be a grave mistake. The difference between an inferior race and a racial non-being is as radical as it is disastrous. Recall from the last chapter that one doctrine of racial inferiority segregates in time and creates a 'not-yet human.' Bonnet, among many others, represents non-Europeans as progressing, but always in Europe's wake. This creates a kind of subhuman that stands to be exploited as an object, but since the object has a reason or a purpose, it must not be eliminated. Césaire testifies

to this through his own experience of 'thingification.' Long makes it a
basic principle of the sugar plantation. By contrast, a race without reason
cannot lack being and simultaneously be designated an inferior rung on
a chain of beings. If these races without reason are truly a nothingness,
regenerating without reason, then they cannot be exploited, since they
stand without political or economic use. Insofar as non-Whites represent
a pure negativity and cannot be folded into a hierarchy of beings, their
status demands a new treatment. As Pierre-André Taguieff has written,
the sort of racism that renders non-Whites non-beings that cannot be
instrumentalized but may nevertheless threaten or infiltrate a superior
race is the racism not of colonial exploitation, but genocide:

> The Other who cannot be made inferior, that is, acceptable
> within the strict measure of his allocation to an inferior place
> on a common scale, may be defined only as exterminable. The
> genocidal logic imposes itself on the basis of the Other's inca-
> pacity to be ranked on a hierarchal scale.[140]

Accordingly, Kant's claim that "[a]ll races will be extinguished . . . only
not that of the Whites"[141] should be understood in the context of this
racism of non-being I am elucidating here.[142]

I readily concede that one often finds 'thingification' and non-being
side by side in both ideology and practice. The proximity of these racisms
is manifest, for example, in Said's observation of the colonial machinations in Palestine and elsewhere:

> Imperialism was the theory, colonialism the practice of chang-
> ing the uselessly unoccupied territories of the world into useful
> new versions of the European metropolitan society. Everything
> in those territories that suggested waste, disorder, uncounted
> resources, was to be converted into productivity, order, taxable,
> potentially developed wealth. You get rid of most of the offend-
> ing human and animal blight—whether because it simply

sprawls untidily all over the place or because it roams around unproductively and uncounted—and you confine the rest to reservations, compounds, native homelands, where you can count, tax, use them profitably, and you build a new society in the vacated space.[143]

What is important here is just that Kant's racism is not necessarily monolithic, and it is certainly not merely expressed in the sort of hierarchy detailed in the previous chapter. While, at times, one does find Kant edifying a tradition that characterizes non-White people as 'less than,' it is crucial to recognize in his work the inauguration of a racism that characterizes non-Whites as nonexistent and thereby disposable.[144]

Kant's defenders will argue that his openly racist remarks are unfortunate but nevertheless remain peripheral to his critical project. In this spirit, one might claim that Kant's philosophy of history and racial development is conjectural and should be classified among other minor works. After all, at one point he even states that his philosophy of history is 'just a thought.' However, two points are relevant in rebuttal. First, there is significant evidence pointing to the fact that Kant does not see racial difference as marginal to his critical enterprise. If one looks in particular at the opening paragraphs of his 1788 essay on race, Kant clearly sees the mystery of racial difference as one of the key problems teleological principles would resolve. In these pages Kant argues race is a metaphysical concept grounded in certain a priori principles, not the least of which is the 'principle of purposes.' Of course, Kant's need to legitimate teleological principles is a main concern for both his writing on race and the *Critique of Judgment*, which of course completes his critical project. This is to say I agree with Jon M. Mikkelsen who, in his introductory remarks to *On the Use of Teleological Principles in Philosophy*, writes that one simply cannot divide Kant's racism from his critical project given the fact that his racism is expressed through teleological and transcendental principles.[145]

More importantly however, it seems to me the conversation around whether Kant's thoughts on race are merely personal and hence irrelevant biases or if they infiltrate his critical project is motivated by the question of whether Kant and his philosophy are 'truly racist.' As I wrote in the introduction, I do not think philosophers should be framing the question in this way. Not only does that approach claim to have racism all figured out so as to reduce it to a homogeneous and static definition, which can then be applied to a particular offensive statement; it also focuses all of its attention on the perpetrator of racist statements at the expense of the victims. By contrast, my concern from the outset has been with the phenomenon of a racial non-being as it manifests itself in the experiences and writings of the targets of racism, Malcolm X being but one of many examples. Investigating when and how racial non-being was instituted, I have been led back to Kant. In that regard, even though it is clear that Kant's race thinking is anything but peripheral to his philosophy, a genealogy of present-day racism makes that of secondary importance. All the texts are in play, so long as one can demonstrate their novelty and their lasting impact. This is to say that for those interested in better understanding racism, its many manifestations, and its developments, in order to better combat it, the question need not be 'Was Kant racist?' or 'Did Kant's racism intersect with his critical works?' Judged up or down, I fail to see what difference that could make to the lives of those in the crosshairs of racist violence today. I do admit that it is quite easy to see how a positive or negative verdict on that question could impact professional Kant scholars, although it is a mystery as to how the well-being of that demographic came to occupy center stage in the critical philosophy of race. That said, it is worth noting that in *Toward Perpetual Peace* from 1795 Kant does distance himself from his belief that "native inhabitants were counted as nothing."[146] This is has been cited as evidence of the fact that Kant had a change of heart, although there is good reason to think that is not the case.[147] Furthermore, given the extent of Kant's thinking on race, his efforts to integrate those ideas into his critical program, the fact that he continues to reauthorize the publication of his essays on race into 1799,[148] and the importance of his debate with Herder to eighteenth-century popular discourse, it is doubtful that a single passage from *Perpetual Peace* manages to put the genie back in bottle regarding racial non-being.

The overriding goal of this study has been to better understand the mind-body problem and its history. With that end in mind, I have been led to ask what, if any, experience of racism is inaugurated by Kant's philosophy? Or, what, if any, genealogy of racism would include Kant? What antiracist opportunities are found within that genealogy? The projects overlap because I have been using Voegelin's hypothesis as a guiding thread. In response to these questions I have discovered that Kant institutes a racial doctrine of minds and bodies regenerating without reason. To recapitulate this finding, notice again how there are two ways to formulate the principle of reason. Stated negatively, it reads, 'Nothing is without reason.' If one eliminates the double negation, it reads, 'Every being has a reason.' When Kant states that non-White people regenerate without reason, he deploys the principle so as to say non-White = non-being. That is, being withdraws from non-White races. One can eliminate the double negative and the formula becomes: White = being, or the White race *is*. Understood in this way, it is redundant to speak of non-White non-being. Kant makes those terms synonymous according to a basic philosophical principle: "Nature does nothing superfluous and is not wasteful."[149] Kant's White race, understood as a mind-body unity that has reason for its regeneration, is the sole race to which this precept applies. This means that when critical race theorists speak of the 'property of whiteness' or 'whiteness as property,'[150] one must be especially careful to include this fundamental principle of Western metaphysics among those things belonging strictly to the White race. When I claim that Kant invents a racialized nothingness, I mean to say, conversely, that Kant makes the principle of reason White property.

With that, I can conclude this study of another mind-body problem. Superficially, this study has been about the past insofar as I have developed a history of racism and the mind-body union in Modern Europe. Yet philosophically, a genuine historical return is the prerequisite for any authentic futurity. In that spirit, I close with a consideration of this racism's future in philosophy.

SOLUTIONS AND EXPERTS

The goal of this book has never been to solve the mind-body problem. From the outset I assigned myself the task of uncovering another problem concealed and harbored by orthodox histories of the problem in the Modern European period. The recovery of another problem is necessary not because it allows a final verdict on the meaning of the problem, nor is it necessary because it comes to any final conclusions on Kant's racism, or Leibniz's involvement in the rise of White supremacy, or Buffon's role in constructing a science of race. Insights into these questions are peripheral to my main concern: the relationship between a regime of racism and the mind-body problem, the latter understood not only as a discourse but, more importantly, a job industry. In addressing this relationship I took Eric Voegelin's work as a rough guide, testing his hypothesis that 'the race concept is a part of the body-soul problem; the former requires for its adequate understanding complete clarity about the latter and therefore about the nature of man.' This quote has been the guiding thread of an investigation through which I uncovered the problem of a unity without being. This discovery allows me to further update Voegelin's hypothesis. That is, while Voegelin is interested in the relationship between 'race' and the mind-body problem, I have found a problem that expresses something much less innocent than 'race.' Insofar as Kant's thinking on race makes the principle of reason White property, this other mind-body problem found in his work has to be seen as a kind of genocidal racism, as I have detailed. As I explained in the introduction, because in this instance the mind-body problem is a problem of White supremacy, and yet White supremacy is not exhausted by this particular logic or history, Voegelin's hypothesis should be amended so as to read: 'The body-soul problem is a part of white supremacy; the former requires for its understanding complete clarity about the latter and therefore about the nature of man.' Given this claim, a prerequisite to understanding the mind-body problem is a study of racism, namely, that genocidal racism that estranges non-Whites from being. In practice, students interested in the mind-body problem would require a very different training from what they receive now. Yet, that training is only a prelude to the important task of finding a solution. Once the problem has been set out, the questions only multiply: What kind of solutions does this call for? Are solutions even possible in this epoch of genocide? Who is qualified to articulate them? What precedents are there in the study of a racial non-being? Where do the field's current mind-body specialists stand in relation to these experts?

The solutions appropriate to the mind-body problem in its orthodox formulation include concepts such as identity theory, functionalism, eliminativism, and monism. These solutions apply to a problem of relations, associations, or causation. With Kant as a guide, I have argued that 'race' should be included above all among these proposed solutions, since it succeeds in providing a coherent account of the mind-body relation. Also thanks to Kant, readers have seen that the White race is the only mind-body union with a ground, purpose, or reason, and, accordingly, the problem of a racial non-being does not apply to White people. As I emphasized in the introduction, insofar as the mind-body problem confronting non-White people over the past two centuries is *another* mind-body problem, it calls for *another* assemblage of solutions along with *another* field of experts. Philosophy should not look to neuroscientists or psychologists or CAT scans for these answers. Encounters with and intimate studies of a racialized nothingness are unlikely at the top tiers of academia. Yet, despite the fact that Kant's doctrines of heredity, progress, and teleology are by now laughably outdated, the phenomenon those doctrines conspire to produce is as entrenched as ever. To better grasp its current manifestations and glimpse these other authorities I have been alluding to for too long now, allow me to survey a few rare moments when a racial non-being does find its way into print.

I already noted Malcolm X's statement on the nothingness that is non-Whites stripped of history. Kant could not have said it better himself, although, clearly, Kant intends this as a permanent condemnation, while X's speech to the Organization of Afro-American Unity lays out a program of resistance. Similar eruptions and encounters with non-being can be found across a breadth of sources and with varying degrees of theorization. Consider, for instance, Michelle Alexander who, in reporting on the redundancy in the term 'Black criminal,' cites two youths from Washington, DC, emphasizing their ontological status as a kind of non-being. These individuals tell of their interactions with police, " 'We can be perfect, perfect, doing everything right and they still treat us like dogs.' 'No, worse than dogs,' another student adds, 'they treat us like we are nothing.' "[151] This exchange is reminiscent of Wynter's analysis of 'N.H.I.,' or 'No Humans Involved,' a phrase used "to refer to any case involving a breach of rights of young Black males who belong to the jobless category of inner city ghettoes,"[152] directed at those whose status is defined as a lack. In this case, the 'lack' is specified as a lack of being itself, and, again, the racism of non-being is not an experience of inferiority. That is, the people are not dogs; they are nothing in the eyes of the police. As a Blackness without being, the logic of their treatment cannot be exploitation, but rather elimination. Elsewhere, these eyes that interpret non-Whites as non-being, and thus eliminable, find their literary expression most famously through Ralph Ellison's invisible man who states, "[Y]ou often doubt if you really exist. [. . .] You ache with the need to convince yourself that you do exist in the real world."[153] Charles Mills cites this very invocation of non-being as the starting point for African-American Philosophy.[154] In another engagement with a racialized nothingness Huey P. Newton describes his ontological status in America as that of a 'non-entity' when he writes,

> In a society where a man is valued according to occupation
> and material possessions, he is without possessions. He is
> unskilled and more often than not, either marginally employed

or unemployed. Often his wife (who is able to secure a job as a maid, cleaning for White people) is the breadwinner. He is, therefore, viewed as quite worthless by his wife and children. He is ineffectual both in and out of the home. He cannot provide for, or protect his family. He is invisible, a nonentity. Society will not acknowledge him as a man.[155]

One again discovers an extended treatment of a racialized non-being in James Cone's analysis of the permissibility of genocide in America and the need for a survivalist theology of liberation. Cone claims, "By white definitions, whiteness is 'being' and blackness is 'non-being.' Blacks live under the sentence of death."[156] The phenomenon is again apparent in bell hooks's critique of White feminism when she argues that the condition for White women's appropriation of Black history is the simultaneous denial of their existence.[157]

Beyond the United States, one discovers a similar non-being in Arab and African contexts. Frantz Fanon, for example, describes how non-Whites fall into non-being when they are denied historicity and thereby pressed into a pathological self-doubt:

Because [the colonial situation] is a systematized negation of the other person and a furious determination to deny the other person all the attributes of humanity, colonialism forces the people it dominates to ask themselves the question constantly: "In reality, who am I?"[158]

In sharp contrast to the logic of hierarchal domination, Fanon claims this racism is encountered as a problem of non-being: "A feeling of inferiority? No, a feeling of not existing."[159] In addition to Said's comment on Palestine and the Middle East as a quasi-wasteland cited earlier, he writes of his own personal experience, "The life of an Arab Palestinian in the West, particularly in America, is disheartening. [. . .] [H]e does not exist, and when it is allowed that he does, it is either as a nuisance or as an Oriental."[160] In the introduction, I cited Nasrallah's condemnation of the 'war on terror,' since that agenda aims only at denying Arab peoples' right to historical self-determination. The Lebanese author Samir Kassir affirms that historical denial in terms of a relegation to non-being when he writes,

> The Arab people are haunted by a sense of powerlessness; permanently inflamed, it is the badge of their malaise. Powerless to be what you think you should be. Powerless to act to affirm your existence, even merely theoretically, in the face of the Other who denies your right to exist, despises you and has once again reasserted his domination over you.[161]

Non-being is further aligned with a lack of history in the work of Algerian author Albert Memmi. He describes his ontological condition as precisely that of an Arab non-being, without history:

> He has been torn away from his past and cut off from his future, his traditions are dying and he loses hope of acquiring a new culture. He has neither language, nor flag, nor technical knowledge, nor national or international existence, nor rights, nor duties. He possesses nothing, *is no longer anything*, and no longer hopes for anything.[162]

Achille Mbembe elaborates on this theme. Just as Kant stripped the regeneration of non-White people of a purpose when he excluded them from the historical narrative, one again finds a lack of history affiliated with an alienation from being:

> The removal of the native from the historically existing occurs when the colonizer chooses—and has the means to—not to look at, see, or hear him/her—not, that is, to acknowledge any human attribute in him/her. From this instant, the native is only so far as he/she is a thing denied, is only as something

deniable. In short, from the standpoint of a 'self' of one's own, he/she is nothing. In the colonial principle of rationality, the native is thus that thing that is, but only insofar as it is nothing. And it is at the point where the thingness and its nothingness meet that the native's identity lies.[163]

If this brief array of quotes could be summarized faithfully, it would be worth noting how, on the one hand, because non-being is articulated racially these authors highlight themes of temporality and historicity. On the other hand, because non-White people are displaced into a zone radically alienated from being, one should not be surprised to find the vocabulary of elimination, violence, and death. These two details would suggest that the fundamental experience of a racial nothingness takes hold at the junction where history departs and genocidal violence supervenes.[164]

Certainly the limited sampling of quotes does not do justice to the depth of thinking these authors (and others I am sure to have unknowingly overlooked) have accomplished on this theme. My point is simply to document the proliferation of the problem after Kant, and preempt philosophers' tendency to dismiss this sort of problem by simply pointing out that Kant was 'wrong' about the races or 'mistaken' in his philosophy of history. It cannot be simply 'wrong' or dismissed as one individual's jaundiced prejudice when this phenomenon stands as the fundamental experience of so many lives around the world, nor would it be a sufficient reparation for philosophy to now just explain away a past mistake. Kant's thinking on these themes is still very much alive. Alternately, other critics may be quick to point out that the aforementioned thinkers need neither Kant nor the moniker 'mind-body problem' to accomplish their research. True, yet, once again, my aim was never to legitimate extant discourses by assimilating them to a European tradition. The goal of the analysis is to provincialize a discourse and reappropriate jobs and resources, the necessity of which is witnessed by the fact that nearly all of those authors cited are not or were not employed as philosophers. Yet, it is beyond doubt that these thinkers have gone the farthest in detailing an important philosophical problem regarding the allegiance between non-Whiteness, non-being, ahistoricity, and death. This cluster of terms should trace its genealogy back to Kant, and regarding the mind-body problem, this is the Kantian tradition.

Philosophy has a long-established practice of hiring and funding those experts best suited to addressing those problems that define its 'core areas.' On this account, philosophy's mind-body discourse is no different, as each year it absorbs millions of dollars in salary, benefits, and research funds at departments and research centers around the world. My study, while it offers no solution, raises the necessity of broadening who philosophy recognizes as a mind-body expert in a way that invites the industry to pay those individuals with a most intimate knowledge of the problem, understood as a racial nonexistence. In fact, the field will need to fund these experts, just as it does now with its current understanding of what the problem is and who the experts are. From the passages previously cited, readers know who these other mind-body experts are. Furthermore, if one simply follows Kant's dictate, one knows that this problem of a unity without being defines the life of all non-White people, which Kant defines as a majority (three-quarters) of the species. Proportionately, it is reasonable for professional philosophy and its mind-body industry to allocate a majority of its assets, including salaries, benefits, offices, research centers, travel grants, conferences, journals, and other resources currently deemed essential to the solution of one of philosophy's longstanding and most pressing problems. To some extent these resources are already shared among extant interpretations of the problem. Today the words 'mind-body problem' can refer to a problem of how cognition relates to brain states, to questions of personal identity, to the evolution of consciousness, or the problem of interaction. With Kant's contribution, philosophers can recognize the univocity of this term 'mind-body problem' and the problem of racism. It is worth noting that for those philosophers dismayed by the virulent racism of a man widely recognized as the most important figure of Modern philosophy, it is his racism, which is truly another mind-body problem, that opens onto the possibility of a significant reallocation of resources in a core area of a major academic field. Furthermore, for those concerned about philosophy's historical allegiance to White supremacy, when Kant's writings are understood as a crucial toehold for employment, this may finally allow the field to recognize his work on race as something other than unadulterated evil.

Again, to be clear, this is not a call for the study of and resistance to racism to wholly assimilate itself to the philosophy of mind in its current state. As a critical history, this is a historical circumscription of the current discourse. Rather than assimilation, this study calls for a professional displacement. This suggestion may seem unrealistic given the current economic situation of philosophy in general at the time of this writing. Philosophers today may very well dismiss the notion of surrendering the bulk of a subfield to a global majority 'without reason.' Still, it is not entirely obvious what is most unrealistic in all this, and exactly to whom it seems unreasonable. Is it more fanciful to think philosophy can carry on with an imperial hubris that calls European philosophy 'Philosophy,' and European thought from 1600–1800 'The Modern Period,' and a mind-body problem canonized almost exclusively by White thinkers 'The Mind-Body Problem'? Might there be alternative histories and problems entrenched in the fundamental experiences of people outside Europe that nevertheless can share in the discussions of mind and body, modernity, and philosophy?[165] Or maybe it is a greater fantasy to believe everything is settled once academics demonstrate the historical contingencies and 'social constructs' that erroneously rendered certain peoples essentially irrelevant? It is by now quickly becoming a piety for philosophers to confess that the Enlightenment was, to some extent or another, a racist enterprise. Is it unthinkable to ask what material reparations the field owes to those impacted by this tradition? Likely though, it is most unrealistic to think philosophy today might allow genuine experts on one of the field's most enduring problems to remain relegated to redundancy and poverty. Not only philosophy but academia as a whole likes to credential its 'diamonds in the rough.' But what about the rough? Can the rough think? Might they not have a unique expertise on one of the field's most prominent and enduring discourses?

Like many academics, here in Alabama and in my former positions I have written numerous references for young people. Recently, I provided a recommendation letter for an Arab asylee to work in a telephone call center. Another student, a Black woman, asked if I could refer her for a maid position at the Holiday Inn. A former student with a felony record for illegal possession needed someone to refer him as a line cook. A Somali student, degree in hand, once asked for a recommendation to a Walmart warehouse. I fill these requests just like my colleagues and everyone else. I do not expect much benevolence for these individuals, and yet, I do wonder if history might not find it scandalous how casual and everyday it is that I recommend these young people to become cheap surplus labor with such routine and regularity. To this day I have not had anyone ever ask into my methodology, my research, my qualifications, or my credentials when I submit my recommendation letters in those situations. Nor do I often wonder myself. Now that I have written them and other 'redundants' this rather long recommendation letter (and, if the reader has been following along from the beginning, that is all I have been doing) for high-paying academic jobs in the philosophy of mind, will the response be so casual and everyday? Or will we be suspicious of the possibility that these 'non-beings' might now come and be paid good money to express themselves at our hotel conferences? Whatever the case may be, I suspect that if we are going to, as Wynter says, "marry our thought so that we can pose the questions whose answers can resolve the plight of the [nonexistent categories],"[166] then we will at some point need to further open the field to those whose very existence is itself the solution to a mind-body condemnation.

INTRODUCTION

1. X (1990), 27.
2. Ibid.
3. In discussing her relationship with God, she recalls asking Him for help in recovering her son, effectively requesting that He make her heard among those that ignore her. See Truth (1998), 47–48.
4. Garvey (1926), 18.
5. Ibid.
6. Ibid.
7. X (1990), 64.
8. X (1992), 83.
9. Ibid. p. 63.
10. Gutiérrez (1988), 56
11. Nasrallah (2011), 120.
12. Fanon (2004), 236; (2011), 674.
13. Fanon (1967), 35; (2011), 719.
14. Arendt (1966), 158.
15. See Voegelin (1940), 283–317.
16. Voegelin (1997), 2.
17. Voegelin (1998), 8.
18. Ibid., 78–79.
19. Ibid., 89–90.
20. On the racism and violence peculiar to orientalism, see Harfouch (2017).
21. See Brantlinger (2013).
22. There are truly just so many, but I can cite a few examples of this framing here. Westphal writes, "How did my neurons *contact me* or my

mind or consciousness, and *stamp* there the image of the cup of coffee for me? How did the sensation of a cup of coffee *arise from* the mass of neurons? It's a mystery" (Westphal [2016], 5, my emphasis). Searle writes, "What is the relation of our minds to the rest of the universe? This, I am sure you will recognise, is the traditional mind-body or mind-brain problem. In its contemporary version it usually takes the form: how does the mind relate to the brain?" (Searle 1984, 14). In his introduction to the problem Robert Kirk writes, "[T]he following double question will serve as a brisk statement of the problem: (a) What is it to have thoughts and feelings? and (b) *how are thoughts and feelings related to the physical world*?" (Kirk 2003, 6), my emphasis.

23. See Levine (1983), 354–361.

24. Moody (2014), 178. My emphasis.

25. Chalmers (2010), 105. My emphasis.

26. When Colin McGinn describes an 'unsolvable problem,' the terms of the impasse are expressed precisely in terms of a relationship between two that somehow interact:

> How is it possible for conscious states to *depend on* brain states? How can technicolor phenomenology *arise from* soggy grey matter? [...] We know that brains are the de facto *causal basis* of consciousness, but we have, it seems, no understanding of how this can be so. It strikes as miraculous, eerie, even faintly comic. Somehow, we feel, the water of the physical brain is *turned into* the wine of consciousness, but we draw a total blank on the nature of this *conversion*. [...] The mind-body problem is the problem of understanding how the miracle is wrought, thus removing the deep sense of mystery. We want to take the magic out of *the link between* consciousness and brain." (McGinn 1989, 349, my emphasis)

27. To take just one of many examples, Jaegwon Kim situates the current debate in relation to Descartes in writing,

Giving an account of mental causation—in particular, explaining how it is possible for the mental to exercise causal influences in the physical world—has been one of the main preoccupations of the philosophy of mind over the last two decades. The problem of course is not new: as we learn early in our philosophy classes, Descartes was confronted forcefully by his contemporaries on this issue, to explain how there could be causal transactions between minds and bodies. (Kim 1998, 30)

Also consider Jonathon Westphal's description of the problem when he writes,

The hard problem is to understand how our experience of whiteness, and with it our consciousness of whiteness, could arise from the purely physical systems operating in the visual cortex. The idea is that we can understand experience by the physical processes that go on when we perceive, but that there are properties of the experiences that cannot be understood in this way. These are *qualia*, and for Chalmers they are not physical. Fair enough, but this new twentieth-century 'hard problem' is simply a souped-up version of an old problem which [. . .] appeared with Descartes and his critics in 1641. [. . .] Chalmers's hard problem of consciousness is just the mind-body problem with a new name, complete with a very sharp distinction between the more easily understood physical processes, and consciousness or qualia, or mind. (Westphal 2016, xi)

28. Such an endeavor would be similar to what Michel Foucault does in books like *The Birth of the Clinic* or *The Order of Things* when he excavates a historical a priori determining the conditions for the possibility of any statement. If I were undertaking such a project, I would not be focused on the truth or falsity of individual solutions to the mind-body problem, but rather I would be interrogating "a limited space of communication,"

wherein interlocutors find themselves deployed in the same conceptual landscape. It is not by accident that Foucault's archaeological method-ology ultimately mutated into a technique of 'problematization,' since it is precisely the terms of the problem that structure the conditions of the discourse. At times Foucault, echoing Husserl and Heidegger, would call this a kind soil, within which various concepts and solutions take root. On this theme see Han (2002), 171. Deleuze and Guattari understand this well when they write about problems as a kind desert that con-cepts populate without dividing it up. See Deleuze and Guattari (1994), 36–37.

29. See, for example, MacDonald (2003).

30. Furet (1984), 56.

31. Bergson (1972), 1528.

32. Bauman (2004), 12.

33. Deleuze (1994), 158.

34. Smith (2015), 196.

35. Kleingeld (2007), 590.

36. Fanon (2008), 72.

37. Ture and Hamilton (1992), 4.

38. Mills (1994).

39. Crenshaw (1988).

40. This latter approach to racism in philosophy's canon is illustrated, for instance, by the historian Peter K. J. Park's recent book (2013). Also, Said explicitly calls for a genealogical approach to colonialism in (1990).

41. Authors such as Charles Mills, Kristie Dotson, and Leonard Harris have already been answering this question. Mills (1998) remains one of the most widely read works on racism in philosophy classes in part because he is able to speak through the language of social contract theory. Dotson (2013) and Harris (2002) adopt a similar approach in forcing the languages of epistemology and ethics to speak to their concerns.

42. Headley (2006), 339.

43. 'Critique' is, of course, most commonly associated with a German tradition that includes Marx, Hegel, and Kant. For an overview of the critical method in their work, see McCarthy (1985); Antonio (1981).

44. Horkheimer (2002), 229. My emphasis.

45. Unger (1983), 580.

46. In these sentences, I am only parroting Derrida, who discusses this meaning of the word *contre* or 'counter' in (2004), 17–18.

47. See, for example, Rhode (1990); Dalton (1987). For a brief history of the relationship between critical theory and the race question, as well as the shortcomings of the former, see Outlaw (1990), 69–82.

48. In her article "Looking to the Bottom: Critical Legal Studies and Reparations," Mari Matsuda argues that certain calls for reparations constitute a "critical legalism" insofar as they use the constitution and legal system to reinterpret concepts of justice and liberty in the service of those at the margins. She situates her argument in a long line of scholars who have found impetus for social change within conservative legal documents, including Frederick Douglass's appropriation of the Constitution. This is just to say that one does not need Hegel or Marx to find precedent for an approach that seeks to "draw transformative power out of the dry wells of ordinary discourse," as Matsuda writes. The movement out of/within has its own history that is not entirely German. See Matsuda (1995), 63–79.

49. Crenshaw et al. (1995), xiii.

50. See, for example, Said (1979), 71–72. His effort to use the history of orientalism to expose the caricaturing of Arabs and Islam constitutes the basis of Said's humanism.

51. Lewis Gordon attributes this approach to Fanon, who understands 'critique' in the sense of a sociodiagnostic of how knowledge is produced and races are constructed 'rationally.' I am emphasizing this aspect of the critical project, but as Gordon points out, this is not the only meaning of the word 'critical' in the history of the race discourse. See Gordon (1999).

52. Concerning the impotence of a distinct race discourse in the academy, Wynter warned against this in quoting Bradley. See Wynter (1994), 57. Additionally, in a related context, Alcoff cites Colin McGinn, who boasts, "[F]eminism now has a place in many philosophy departments, for good or ill, but it has not made any impact on the core areas of the subject" (cited in Alcoff 2013, 16–43).

53. X (1964), 23.

CHAPTER 1. Descartes's Fundamental Mind-Body Problem

1. Searle (1984), 14–15.

2. See Descartes, *Oeuvres*, III, 661 (hereafter cited as AT).

3. See Spinoza, *Ethics*, Part III, Prop. 2; Leibniz, *The Monadology*, Para. 17.

4. Fontenelle (1989–2001), 529–530. Cited from Schmaltz (2008), 9.

5. Authors that depict Descartes's mind-body problem as a problem of interaction include Wilson (1978), 218; Williams (1978); Cottingham (1986), 119.

6. For example, see, Rodis-Lewis (1950); Hoffman, (1986); Skirry (2001); Broughton and Mattern (1978); Alanen (1996); Richardson (1982); Baker and Morris (1996).

7. AT VII 228.

8. AT III 491.

9. See AT III 493; AT III 508; AT IV 166; AT VII 219; AT VII 228; AT IV 346.

10. Baker and Morris (1996), 170.

11. When Aristotle defines nature in book 2 of the *Physics* (192a21–23), he defines it in terms of movement and change. In interpreting these passages, Aquinas writes, "For those things are said to be born which are generated after having been joined to a generator, as is clear in plants and animals, thus the principle of generation or motion is called nature" (Aquinas 1999, 76).

12. Gilson (1951), 155–156.

13. Stone Haring (1956).

14. AT XI 407.

15. AT X 521.

16. AT VIII 27.

17. AT IX 28.

18. AT VII 108; see also 164: "Concerning every existing thing it is possible to ask what is the cause of its existence."

19. "But I think it is clear to everyone that a consideration of efficient causes is the primary and principal way, that we have of proving the

existence of God. We cannot develop this proof with precision unless we grant our minds the freedom to inquire into the efficient causes of all things, even God himself. For what right do we have to make God an exception, if we have not yet proved that he exists" (AT VII 238). For further analysis of Descartes's axiom of the cause and its place in the history of the principle of reason, see Carraud (2002), chapter 2.

20. Jean-Luc Marion develops this reading in (1999), 105. He goes on to explain how even the existence of the 'I' is governed by causation. See ibid., 112–113. Parts of this section follow the general contours of what Marion elsewhere has called Descartes's "onto-theology of the cause." See Marion (2007), 145.

21. AT V 156; also see Marion (1999), 113.

22. AT VII 48.

23. An analysis of this axiom, with special attention paid to Descartes's views on cause and effect, is found in Schmaltz (2008), 49–86.

24. AT VII 49.

25. AT VIII 12.

26. AT VIII 344. Descartes considers the possibility of the parents producing a rational soul in his *Sixth Reply*, but he does not pursue it (AT VIII 425).

27. AT VIII 51–52.

28. AT VIII 50–51.

29. AT III 491.

30. AT VIII 24.

31. Suarez (2000), 55. My emphasis.

32. AT XI 407.

33. Fernel (2005), 15–16.

34. Gilson (1951), 52.

35. AT I 533

36. See, for example, Sennert, "Practica Medicinae VI," in (1650), 740. Sennert formulates the soul's bond with the body's innate heat as the standard Aristotelean view. However, it should also be noted that when Sennert refutes the soul's divine origin and the physiology of its

subsequent bond with the innate heat, it is specifically Fernel to whom he directs his attack. See Sennert (1637), book 4, chapter 2, 134–141; Michael (1997).

37. A partial bibliography of Fernel includes Figard (1903); Sherrington (1946); Roger (1960); Zanier (1987); Hirai (2005).

38. Fernel (2005), 318 Latin, 319 English.

39. Fernel does not believe that the sun sends down a form that had been generated and completed extra-terrestrially. However, the sun does instill the power of a form into a freshly generated being by illuminating it. Fernel explains, "[Heavenly bodies] instill into the freshly generated thing the power and nature of the substances from which they emanated, and insert a form in such a way that the illumination radiating from the Sun's light into a visible and prepared body, and bathing in it, introduces into that body not just illumination, but also in the end some of its own light too" (ibid., 320 Latin, 321 English). This hinges on a complex relationship between *lux* and *lumen*, which is well beyond the scope of this study. See Forrester (2003), 258 Latin, 259 English; also ibid., 76–83.

40. Ibid., 552 Latin, 553 English.

41. Ibid., 548 Latin, 549 English.

42. There is a long and notable history of heat's role in conception. For example, Solmsen (1957); Kleywegt (1984); Matthen (1989); Plochmann (1953); Preus (1977); Boylan (1986).

43. Fernel (2005), 198 Latin, 199 English.

44. AT VII 441–442.

45. Fernel (2005), 204 Latin, 205 English.

46. Ibid., 212 Latin, 213 English.

47. Ibid.

48. Ibid.

49. Ibid., 214 Latin, 215 English.

50. Fernel (2005), 258 Latin, 259 English.

51. Ibid., 262 Latin, 263 English.

52. On Harvey's relationship with Descartes, see Fuchs (2001); French (1994). On Harvey's relationship to Fernel, see Bono (1990). A general

bibliography of William Harvey includes Pagel (1967); Pagel (1976); Webster (1967); White (1986).

53. Harveo (1666), 490; Harvey (1847), 502.

54. Harveo (1666) 491; Harvey (1847), 504. See also Harvey (1995), 157.

55. Gyeke (1998), 63.

56. Gilson (1951), 73.

57. Harvey (1949), 71.

58. French (1994), 179.

59. AT VI 46–50; AT I 263; AT II 501.

60. AT XI 202.

61. For a thorough account of Descartes's rejection of Aristotelean physics in favor of mechanical explanations of nature, see Hattab (2009).

62. AT VI 46.

63. AT XI 228.

64. AT VI 46.

65. See Des Chene (2001), chapter 2.

66. AT XI 407.

67. Details on the meaning of 'life' in Descartes can be found in Bitbol-Hesperies (1990).

68. Vincent Aucante's excellent commentary in these texts can be found in (2000).

69. See AT XI 507; AT XI 506; AT XI 509.

70. AT XI 253.

71. AT XI 254.

72. On fetal development as a sort of nutrition, see Gaukroger (2000), 393.

73. Descartes famously struggled to account for the generation of bodies. For insights into this, see Aucante (2006), 65–79.

74. Fernel (2005), 572 Latin, 573 English.

75. Ibid., 578 Latin, 579 English.

76. AT XI 281.

77. Fernel (2005), 16 Latin, 17 English. For context on the teleological nature of dispositions beyond Fernel's writings, see Des Chene (1996), 179–181.

78. It is important to note here that love is not the only passion at the start of life. In subsequent paragraphs of the *Passions* Descartes explains the origins of hate, joy, sadness, and desire. These passions arise as a result of the suitability of the 'aliment' in the heart. That is to say, the suitability of the body's accommodation incites various passions in the soul. For example, the soul may 'hate' the body at the beginning of life if a foreign fluid enters the heart and cannot properly maintain the vital heat. Thus, several passions aside from love may be endured at the beginning of life. Yet, Descartes prioritizes love insofar as this is the passion felt when the accommodation is most suitable, thus causing the soul to bond with the body, instituting the union. Other passions originate at the commencement of life as a result of various occurrences in the heart, but this is only possible once the bond has been created. Love is, in a way, the condition for the possibility of the processes described in Articles 108–111. A possible precedent for this prioritization of love in regard to the soul-body union at the beginning of life could perhaps be found in Ficino (1985), 112–114.

79. Kim (1998), 30.

80. Westphal (2016), xi.

81. Voegelin (1998), 90.

82. Hannaford (1996), 183.

83. Smith (2015), 67. See also 17–18.

84. AT VIII 124.

85. AT VIII 124.

86. AT VIII 51.

87. 'Huron' is a name imposed by the French that comes from the Old French word *hure*, meaning 'rough' or 'boorish.' Likely, these philosophers are referring to the Wyandot.

88. AT VII 139. He elaborates on this passage in his interview with Burman where he says, " 'Idol' is in fact the equivalent of our 'idea.' In forming the idol, therefore, they are in a way forming a real idea, but it is a materially false idea" (AT V 156).

89. AT VI 16.

90. See Reiss (2005).

91. AT VI 2.

92. See Garber (2001).

93. AT VI 2, my emphasis. He elaborates in writing,

> As for myself, I have never presumed that my mind was in any way more perfect than those of common people; I have even often wished to have as quick a wit, or as clear and distinct an imagination, or a memory as ample and ready as other people. And I know of no other qualities that contribute to the perfection of the mind, because as far as reason or sense is concerned, it is the only thing that makes us men and distinguishes us from animals, and I wish to believe that it is whole in each of us. I follow in this the common opinion of the philosophers, who say that there are differences in degree only among the *accidents*, and not for the *forms* or *natures of individuals* within the same species. (AT VI 2)

94. See Jordan (1968), 179 and 194.

95. Poullain de la Barre (2002), 82. Two helpful introductions with analyses and critiques of his general project can be found in Amorós and McAlister (1994); La Vopa (2010).

96. Buffon (2007), 183.

97. A host of authors have recently detailed how Buffon's innovations around the notions of species and varieties or races must be understood in their historical context. See Sloan (1979); Doron (2012); Farber (1972); Sloan (1987).

98. Cited in Roger (1997a), 314.

99. Buffon (2007), 1019.

100. Doron (2012), 103.

101. Sloan (1979), 118.

102. Ibid., 117–118. This argument is also developed in Doron (2012).

103. Buffon (2007), 186.

104. Ibid., 190.

105. Ibid., 184. "It is impossible to recognize the mind under any other form than that of thinking, which is extremely general, simple, and uniform. This form is not divisible, extended, impenetrable, nor possesses any other quality of matter. The mind, therefore, which is the subject of this form, must be indivisible and immaterial. Our bodies, on the contrary, as well as all external objects, have many forms, each of which is compounded, divisible, and destructible." The details of Buffon's embryological ideas can be found in Ibrahim (1987); Bowler (1973); and a very clear discussion of how the reality of the species is rooted in Buffon's ideas of sexual reproduction is found in Farber (1972).

106. Buffon (2007), 499.

107. Ibid., 501 (my emphasis). See also ibid.: "L'empire de l'homme sur les animaux est un empire légitime qu'aucune révolution ne peut détruire, c'est l'empire de l'esprit sur la matière, c'est non seulement un droit de Nature, un pouvoir fondé sur des loix inaltérables, mais c'est encore un don de Dieu, par lequel l'homme peut reconnoître à tout instant l'excellence de son être." And Ibid., 829: "[C]ette lumière pure, de ce rayon divin, qui n'a été départi qu'à l'homme seul."

108. AT VIII 50–51.

109. See Hoquet (2005), 706–708.

110. Buffon (2007), 560. Also see Curran (2011), 111. A discussion of this important quote in the context of the meaning of 'degeneration' can be found there.

111. Cited from Doron (2012), 95.

112. Cited from ibid., 96.

113. Buffon (2007), 385–386: "[T]ous ces Sauvages ont l'air rêveur, quoiqu'ils ne pensent à rien, ils ont aussi le visage triste et ils paroissent êtres mélancoliques."

114. Wattles (1989), 297–303.

115. Curran (2009). He does provide a plate of an albino woman, which Hoquet does not mention.

116. Hoquet (2007), 153. Cf. also Hoquet (2014), 24.

117. Buffon will attempt to develop this science in his 1764 *Des époques de la nature*. See Phillip R. Sloan's article detailing the developments of this shift in (1973).

118. Galton (1865), 322.

119. A comprehensive overview of Gobineau's ideas can be found in Biddiss (1970). See also Kale (2010); Boissel (1993); Taguieff (1998), 38–43. An important rebuttal comes from the nineteenth-century philosopher Anténor Firmin in (2002), 60. See also Bernasconi (2008); Fluehr-Lobban (2005); Russell (2014).

120. Gobineau (1983), 352.

121. Ibid., chapter 6, book 1, entitled "Dans le progrès ou la stagnation, les peoples sont indépendants des lieux qu'ils habitant."

122. Ibid., 1149. Elsewhere he writes the mind is the "result of a supreme force that the individuals receive from a domain higher than themselves" (ibid., 1148).

123. He writes, "These active forces, these life-giving principles, or if we want to consider them under a concrete idea, this soul, remained hitherto unnoticed and anonymous. It must be ranked among the cosmic agents of the first degree" (ibid., 1149).

124. Ibid., 1148.

125. Gobineau illustrates the importance of this 'supreme force' when he addresses the common origins of Greek and Roman thought. Consult ibid., 170; Gobineau (1999), 33.

126. Although it is beyond the scope of this study, suffice it to say that the decline of civilization is owed to the corruption of the Aryan intellect through miscegenation or 'blood mixing.' On the relation between the blood and the intellect in Gobineau's work see Gaulmier (1981). Also see Nale (2014) (this article is used by permission of The Pennsylvania State University Press).

127. Gobineau (1983), 229; Gobineau (1999), 95.

128. Falguni Sheth has written on a similar maneuver in the human rights discourse of the twentieth century. See Sheth (2009), 80.

CHAPTER 2. A Thing Not-Yet Human

1. "The most straightforward causal connection between segregation and inequality is spatial. When important goods are asymmetrically distributed across space and groups are sorted into separate spaces containing more or less of these goods, group inequality results. Race-based spatial effects are pronounced for numerous goods, including jobs, consumer goods, professional services, and environmental quality" (Anderson 2010, 27).

2. See "On Violence," Fanon (2004).

3. Fanon (2008), 101; (2011), 161.

4. Bhabha (1994), 342.

5. Bunge (1980), 25–26.

6. Rostow (1990), 5.

7. See Johnson (2010), 28.

8. Mill (1998), 453.

9. Cited from Chakrabarty (2000), 30.

10. Bhabha (1994), 342.

11. Claude Perrault articulates the implausibility of Descartes's views on generation when he writes in 1690, "For, I believe, in the end, that it is hardly more conceivable that the world was able to shape itself out of matter from chaos than that an ant could create its kind from the homogenous substance of the seed of which people believe it is begotten." Those opposed to the idea include biologists dubious of mechanistic physics, skeptics who refuse to believe that physics alone could account for animal generation, as well as Augustinians who reject the idea that spermatic fluids could be empowered in a way contrary to the omnipotence of God. See Roger (1997b), 272.

12. Malebranche, an early adopter of this view, cites Swammerdam when he formulates the basic hypothesis of preformation in his 1674 *Récherche de la verité*, which he summarizes in writing, "[A]ll the bodies of men and animals to be born until the fulfillment of time were perhaps produced at the creation of the world; what I mean is that the females of the first

animals were perhaps created containing all those of the same species that the animals have since engendered, and that are to be engendered in the continuation of time" (cited from ibid., 269).

13. Bowler (1971), 221–224.

14. Zammito (2002), 305.

15. Bernasconi (2001), 24.

16. Zammito (2002), 305.

17. Chakrabarty (2000), 8.

18. Cited from Said (1992), 80–81.

19. Conder (1879), 9.

20. Césaire (2000), 42.

21. See the work of scholars such as Daniel Garber, Pauline Phemister, Charlotte Witt, François Duchesneau, Richard R. T. Arthur, and Justin E. H. Smith.

22. Briefly, some orientalists, unable to racialize Arabs phenotypically, do so on the basis of language. This science of linguistic races is something the orientalist anti-Semitic author Ernest Renan explicitly credits Leibniz with inventing. See Harfouch (forthcoming).

23. This theme is emphasized throughout *Orientalism*. See for instance where Said addresses the "primitive simplicity" imperialists attributed to Arabs, making it "as if the Arab had not been subject to the ordinary processes of history" (Said 1979, 230).

24. Smith (2002), 167.

25. Leibniz (1998), 278. See also Arthur (2007), 170–171.

26. Leibniz (1998), 33. Also see Smith (2002), 164. Smith writes, "In Leibniz's view, the doctrine of concomitance hangs together with the doctrine of preformation of animal bodies: Given a concomitance between souls and bodies, it must be the case that all organic bodies originated concomitantly with souls." Also see Arthur (2007), 149.

27. Leibniz (1976), 337.

28. Ibid., 608.

29. Leibniz (2007b), 176.

30. Ibid.

31. Leibniz (2007a), 139.

32. Cited from Fouke (1991), 40.

33. Cited from ibid.

34. Bonnet (1769), 287.

35. Leibniz (2007), 167.

36. Roger (1997), 501.

37. For a complete overview of the development of Bonnet's thinking on preformation, see Mazzolini and Roe (1986), 23–32.

38. Marx (1976), 80–81.

39. See Duchesneau (2006).

40. Bonnet (1769), 268.

41. On Bonnet's relationship to Leibniz, see Whitman (1895); Rieppel (1988); Duchesneau (2006).

42. Leibniz (1996), 58.

43. Ibid.

44. Bonnet (1765).

45. As the Cambridge historian J. B. Bury reports in his ground-breaking study on the idea of progress from 1920, this interpretation of history is one that had just begun to emerge in the centuries preceding Bonnet. On Bury's account, it seems that even though the Greeks and Romans were aware of cultural or intellectual advances, they lacked a formal doctrine of progress. This was due to several factors, including the Greeks' relatively short recorded history, the Stoic idea that nature followed a pattern of recurring cycles, and a general acceptance of faith (*moira*). Through a series of events beyond the scope of my discussion, he details those events and thinkers responsible for formulating an idea of progress. See Bury (2014), 4. Without question, Bury's account has received considerable updates, criticisms, and challenges over the past century, including those from John Baillie, Robert Nisbet, Karl Lowith, George Iggers, and David Hopper. See Baillie (1951); Nisbet (1980); Lowith (1949); Iggers (1982); Hopper (1991). Despite whatever quibbles there may be over the details, it is sufficient here to note that 'progress' is a quintessentially Modern idea, one that had not existed long but was

nevertheless a legitimate interpretation of history by the time Bonnet was writing in the mid-eighteenth century.

46. See Blaise Pascal's quote from 1647 in Taguieff (2004), 160. Pascal is not alone in this sort of thinking as he was joined by the likes of Bernard le Bovier de Fontenelle, who expresses a nearly identical sentiment, writing in his *Digression sur les anciens et les modernes* from 1688. See ibid., 163.

47. Taguieff writes, "If man is perfectible, then progress is inscribed in his nature: human nature is no longer a principle of limitation, rather it becomes the condition for the possibility of movement toward the good" (ibid., 176).

48. Turgot (1973), 41.

49. Ibid.

50. Ibid., 44.

51. For this context, see Harrison (2001).

52. Bonnet and Haller (1983), 1145, 1218.

53. See Taguieff (2004), 176.

54. Bonnet (1769), 272.

55. Marx (1976), 107.

56. Ibid.

57. This recalls some of the most famous passages of the *Essay*, particularly of book 2.7. Locke is an important figure in the history of the race debate both for his definition of property and his involvement in the slave trade. The best contextualization of Locke's theory of property in the race context comes from Harris (1993), 1721–1724. See also Tully (1983); Bernasconi and Maaza Mann (2005). However, his epistemological innovations should not be overlooked in the history of the development of racism. On the historical allegiances between empiricism and racism, see Bracken (1973).

58. Bonnet (1782), 36–7.

59. Buffon (2007), 471.

60. Bonnet (1769), 62.

61. Without having studied Bonnet, and working in a different historical context, Voegelin addresses this important, though not comprehensive,

aspect of race thinking when he writes, "[R]ace speculations of the sort we are familiar with today [. . .] require a basic reciprocal spiritualization of the body and embodiment of the spirit into the union of earthly-human existence as their foundation" (1998, 90). Also see Grober (1995), 36.

62. Anderson (1982), chapter 4.

63. Also, for Bonnet, the memory of our lives in this world throughout all its manifestations and the identity of the individual secured by this memory is essential to our moral accountability at Judgment Day. Here Bonnet is again closely in conversation with Locke. See Grober (1993), 239.

64. At Bonnet (1769), 286, he writes, "I employed nearly my entire *Essai Analytique* to demonstrate how a being, at first sensitive or sentient, can raise itself by natural means to the quality of a rational or thinking being."

65. Bonnet (1760), 456.

66. Ibid., 458.

67. Bonnet (1755), 350.

68. Bonnet (1769), 288.

69. See Anderson (1982), 107.

70. Johannes Fabian has argued persuasively that this conversion of space into time was essential to the emergence of anthropology and the way in which that field has defined its object of investigation. See Fabian (1983), 143–144. See also Quijano (2007).

71. Bonnet (1769), 179, 171.

72. Bonnet (1760), 473.

73. Bonnet (1783), 149–150.

74. Claude Perrault (1628–1703) was a French author of fairy tales. Sébastien Le Prestre de Vauban (1633–1707) was a famed military strategist.

75. There are many synonyms for 'historicism' throughout the literature including 'developmentalism,' 'the problem of the ambivalent temporality of modernity,' or 'the denial of coevalness.' Roger Nisbet has called it the 'Comparative Method.' See Nisbet (1975), 218. See also Jacques (1997).

76. See Shell (2006), 69. By comparison, Susan Shell attempts to characterize Kant's understanding of history and 'primitive peoples'' writing:

"The non-European peoples (especially those of Africa and of America) contribute to the achievement of man's moral destiny on Earth, less directly than in the manner of an inner wasteland, providing an historically emergent humanity with a means of gauging the distance it has traveled from its (otherwise unknowable) inner point of origin—that is, a means of measuring its progress." However, without a footnote, it is difficult to see this in Kant's thought. In fact, as I will detail in the next chapter, it is even difficult to see how these peoples even might serve this limited purpose in Kant's work.

77. Mill (1998), 453.

78. This is reminiscent of how former prime minister of Jamaica Michael Manley expresses the confusion of working-class Jamaicans who fail to realize "that the escalator which they imagined was marked 'up' is in fact the inner, smaller part of a larger escalator which is unmarked but actually going down. This larger escalator is the economic system which imperialism put in place" (1983, xiii).

79. Bonnet (1760), 120.

80. Bonnet (1769), 36.

81. Bonnet (1755), 351.

82. Bonnet (1769), 38.

83. On the evolution of final causes in the Modern period, see Osler (1996).

84. For discussion of this aspect of Leibniz's work, see McDonough (2008). For an evaluation in the context of the history of the principle of reason, see Carraud (2002), chapter 5, especially 391–399.

85. Leibniz (1976), 478–479.

86. Ibid., 478: "But when one pushes forward his inquiry after reasons, it is found that the laws of motion cannot be explained through purely geometric principles or by imagination alone."

87. Leibniz (1996), 475.

88. Leibniz (2007b), 151.

89. The paradigmatic interpretation is found in Couturat (1901). Also see Look (2011); Carraud (2002), chapter 5; Sleigh (1982).

90. Bonnet (1769), 243.

91. See Lovejoy (2011), chapter 4.

92. Following Leibniz's 'principle of plenitude,' which postulates at least one individual mediating any two distinct kinds, between each step in the hierarchy there is virtually an infinite number of intermediate degrees. Leibniz himself makes several mentions of the chain of being, as cited in ibid., 144–145. Bonnet's source for the idea of the chain of being however could not have been Leibniz, since he already elaborated the idea in his 1743 *Insectologie*, published four years before he discovers Leibniz. Lorin Anderson notes that he probably learned the idea from Alexander Pope's 1734 *Essay on Man*, although he was no doubt later encouraged by Leibniz's views. See Anderson (1982), 6–9. Bonnet summarizes his own understanding of the chain of being neatly and succinctly, and with a nod to the principle of reason, when he writes, "There are no breaks in nature; all is graduated, nuance. If between any two beings there were an empty space, what reason would there be for passing from one to the other?" Bonnet (1782), 52.

93. For a thorough and philosophically interesting summary of this context, see Moran (2002).

94. In this work, comparative anatomy falls under the heading 'ethnology': "Ethnology demands to know what was the primitive organic structure of each race?—what such race's moral and physical character?—how far a race may have been, or may become modified by the combined action of time and moral and physical causes?—and what position in the social scale Providence has assigned to each type of man?" Nott and Gliddon (1854), 49.

95. White (1795), 64.

96. Bonnet (1782), 21.

97. Taguieff (2001), 130. Jordan (1968), 496.

98. Long (1774), 356.

99. Ibid., 352.

100. Ibid.

101. Ibid., 383.

102. Ibid.

103. Ibid.

104. Ibid., 374–375.

105. Jordan (1968), 492.

106. Buffon (2007), 560.

107. Long (1774), 372.

108. Ibid., 771.

109. See Williams (2014). It is true that Williams is technically an apprentice, but his testimony was used as evidence that apprenticeship was no different from slavery and abolition had not taken hold. Williams does mention better conditions under slavery, although it does not prove the benevolence for which Long takes credit. Consider where Williams writes, "When I was a slave I never flogged [*sic*],—I sometimes was switched, but not badly, but since the new law begin, I have been flogged seven times, and put in the house of correction four times" (1).

110. Long (1774), 391–392.

111. Bonnet (1770), 131.

112. Long (1774), 375.

113. Bonnet (1769), 179.

114. Ibid., 283.

115. Bonnet (1770), 91.

116. Bonnet (1769), 10; see also 129, 133; and Anderson (1982), 112–113.

117. Cited from Savioz (1948), 138.

118. Bonnet (1770), 172.

119. Ibid., 123.

120. Bowler (1973), 278.

121. Grober (1993), 234.

122. Bonnet (1770), 29.

CHAPTER 3. "All races will be extinguished . . . only not that of the Whites"

1. Voegelin (1998), 8

2. Ibid., 78–79.

3. Ibid., 78; also see 136–137 and 144.

4. Voegelin (1997), 10.

5. Nuzzo (2008) is a notable exception, which I discuss later.

6. There is a case made for Descartes as an occasionalist. See Baker and Morris (1996), 138–167.

7. See Thompson (2001).

8. Leibniz (1989), 33.

9. See Ablondi (2008).

10. Watkins (1998).

11. Watkins (1995).

12. Yolton (1991), 87.

13. Crivellato and Ribatti (2007).

14. Yolton (1991), 103.

15. Godart (1755), 74–123.

16. Marat (1773), 49.

17. Meyer and Hierons (1965).

18. Hatfield (1995).

19. La Peyronie (1741), 199. Also see Kaitaro (1996), 564. Of course, this approach has not gone away. The twentieth century mind-body discourse still can be found debating the location of mind-body interaction. See, for example, Eccles (1973), 214–219.

20. Kant (1967), 56. See also Zammito (2002), 43; Sytnik-Czetwertyński (2013).

21. Cited from Zammito (2002), 297.

22. Kant (1967), 79.

23. Kant (1990–), 12: 35 (cited hereafter as AA); (2007a), 225.

24. For context and commentary, see Marino (1994), 127–142.

25. AA 12: 32; Kant (2007a), 223.

26. Kant (2007b), A 395. Also see Harrington (2013).

27. AA 1: 19; Kant (2007a), 19. Also see Watkins (2005), 106–108.

28. Kant (2007b), B 276.

29. Nuzzo (2008), 338, fn. 79.

30. Ibid., 45.

31. AA 2: 438; Kant (2013), 67.

32. AA 8: 176; Kant (2013), 186.

33. AA 8: 99; Kant (2013), 136. See also Kleingeld (2007). She argues that Kant's racial hierarchy is predicated on moral characteristics, which, as early as 1779, he saw as detachable from "the physical theory of race itself" (579). She argues that although he 'attached' and 're-attached' his mental stereotypes throughout his career, he ultimately excluded predispositions of the soul from his concept of race. See my brief discussion of the problems with this approach to racism in the history of philosophy in the introduction. In addition to those comments I would note that, curiously, Kleingeld does not support this argument with any evidence from Kant's essays explicitly addressing race, instead relying on 1) A letter to Johann Jacob Engel where Kant employs the phrase "attached principles of a moral characterisation," which Kleingeld stipulates to mean 'detachable moral characteristics' (579); 2) A sentence in *Perpetual Peace* that equates American Indians' military courage to that of mediaeval European knights (589); 3) Kant's endorsement of Girtanner's *Über das Kantische Prinzip für Naturgeschicte* (1796), which, according to Kleingeld, does not mention the moral characteristics of races *aside from a few comments about the laziness of 'North American savages'* (590). In a later text, she develops these themes in order to buttress the notion of a Kantian 'cultural diversity.' See (2012), chapter 4. Also see Muthu (2003), chapters 4 and 5. Kleingeld is right to investigate the questions of separation and unity of minds and bodies in the race context. However, 'separability' never simply means that one can discuss the mind without the body or vice versa. One would start with what Voegelin calls the 'isolating construction,' exhibited by Buffon, for example, to understand what sorts of mind-body 'separability' were available to Kant. One could then recognize how far Kant is from adopting these rigorous ontological and genealogical separations of mind and body. In a separate article, Kleingeld argues that Kant never explains how minds and bodies relate in the race context (2014, 49). However, as I explain, that is in part what Kant's concept is about and why it is unique in Modern Europe.

Despite philosophy's best hopes for Kant, to my knowledge, Kant never retreats from his view that minds are shaped by the same processes that race bodies. As I explain later, this is the basis of 'race' as the solution to the mind-body problem. Further discussion of Kleingeld's 2007 argument can be found in Bernasconi (2011). Concerning the importance of Kant's racial hierarchy to his political thought and cosmopolitanism, see Hedrick (2008).

34. AA 2: 253; Kant (2007a), 59.
35. See Larrimore (1999); Bernasconi (2003); Shell (2006); Cohen (2009).
36. AA 25: 1187; Kant (2012b), 320–321.
37. AA 2: 441; Kant (2013), 69.
38. AA 15: 377–378.
39. AA 2: 433; Kant (2013), 63.
40. See McLaughlin (2007).
41. AA 2: 430; Kant 2007a), 85.
42. AA 2: 441; Kant (2007a) 95.
43. AA: 2: 430; Kant (2007a), 85
44. AA 2: 430 (my emphasis); also see AA 8: 101; Kant (2007a), 85
45. AA 2:442; Kant (2007a), 96.
46. Notice the legacy of this idea in, for example, Schelling's work: "Now that which is *developed* (but not, on that account, *brought forth*) through external influence is called *germ* or *natural predisposition*. Those determinations of the formative drive within the sphere of the general concept of the species, therefore, are able to be presented as *original natural predispositions* or *germs*, which were all united in the primal individual—but such that the prior development of the one makes the development of the other impossible." Cited in Bernasconi (2014), 248.
47. For example, Meiners (2013). Regarding the potential improvement of the Negro, see 204. Also see Kames (1776), 38.
48. AA 8: 174; Kant (2007a), 209.
49. Ibid.
50. This chart is roughly inspired by one found in Lagier (2004), 185.
51. AA 2: 443; Kant (2013), 71.

52. AA 2: 255; Kant (2007a), 61.

53. Bernasconi (2001), 1.

54. Deleuze and Guattari (1994), 16.

55. Although I emphasized the differences between Buffon and Kant on the ancestry of mind and body, Kant's debt to Buffon on this point must be acknowledged. Though Buffon lacks a rigorous science of human races, his redefinition of 'species' as a constant succession of individuals rather than a collection of similar traits certainly sets an important precedent for Kant's innovations on race. On Buffon's rethinking of the species concept, see Roger (1997a), 314.

56. Voegelin (1998), 8.

57. It seems to me that David Chalmers, for example, might dispute this formulation of philosophy's contemporary mind-body problem. Although some argue that there is nothing new in his 'hard problem' of consciousness (see note 27 in the introduction), Chalmers makes clear that he is not interested in the mechanism of interaction between mind and body. Chalmers wants to know, "how could a physical system give rise to conscious experience?" (1996, 25). I do not believe Kant's race concept responds to this question, although his concept of degeneration can explain why a certain raced body arises with a particular raced conscious experience. Moreover, I doubt that Chalmers's 'hard problem' can stand as the hardest problem of minds and bodies once one reckons with Kant's overturning of the mind-body problem.

58. Alcoff (2006), 196.

59. Ibid., 192.

60. X (2001), 118.

61. AT V 156.

62. For example, Marion (1999), 108.

63. On the development of Kant's understanding of the principle of reason, see Longuenesse (2001), particularly 76. For an analysis of this proof, see her article (1994). Alternately, see Allison (2004), 246–256.

64. Dubos (1719), 238; cited in Curran (2011), 79. My emphasis.

65. Noted in Zhang (2013), 264.

66. AA 8: 91.

67. AA 8: 163–164; Kant (2013), 177.

68. This view can be traced as far back as Empedocles and can be found in works dating to as late as 1788. See Huet (1993), 5. For a discussion of the maternal imagination in a racial context, see Kidd (2006), 68–69. Kant himself mentions this possibility, but by the second half of the eighteenth century this view was arcane. Christoph Girtanner, in his summary of Kant's natural history in 1796, dismisses this doctrine as "precisely as old as it is wrong." See Girtanner, (2013), 223.

69. The actual biblical account of a 'curse' put on the offspring of Ham, found in Genesis 9:18–27, includes no account of physical attributes, asserting only that Ham's descendants would endure eternal slavery. Nevertheless, in large part as a justification for slavery, a number of texts stated that this punishment was somehow accompanied by a darkening of the skin. See Davis (2006), 64–73.

70. Curran's recent archival work has uncovered an essay contest held by the Académie royale des sciences de Bordeaux in 1739 dedicated to theories of the causes of blackness and African hair. The essay competition resulted in sixteen submissions, which as a whole, hypothesized how the influences of climate, over a long period of time, resulted in degeneration, with whiteness standing as the original state of mankind. See Curran (2011), 81–87.

71. Among others, including David Hume, Henry Home Lord Kames describes this hypothesis in 1774: God "created many pairs of the human race, differing from each other both externally and internally" (1776, 45). At genesis, God created several pairs of human beings and, in his benevolent perfection, He fitted them appropriately for each climate so that each pair could preserve itself eternally. Thus, on Kames account what Kant would call racial difference is in fact a difference of species, and this phenomenon is grounded in the providence of God, who willed that each kind should preserve itself eternally.

72. For example, see Lagier (2004), 23–29; Cohen (2006).

73. AA 2: 434; Kant (2007a), 89.

74. AA 2: 434; Kant (2007a), 89. Kant's preferred illustration is the skin color of the Negro. See also AA 8: 102–104; Kant (2013), 138–140

75. AA 8: 98; Kant (2007a), 135.

76. AA 8: 18; Kant (2009), 10–11.

77. On the methodology of the essay at hand, see Allison (2009), 24–45. On the meaning of 'history' in the *Idea*, see Yovel (1980), 142.

78. AA 8: 18; Kant (2009), 11.

79. Ibid.

80. AA 8: 169; Kant (2013), 181.

81. AA 8: 19; Kant (2009), 12.

82. AA 8: 19; Kant (2009), 11.

83. See Kant (1991b), 208. The significance of the short life span to the development of culture is also noted in his 1786 *Conjectural Beginning of Human History* (AA 8: 117).

84. AA 8: 19; Kant (2009), 11.

85. AA 5: 122.

86. On this theme, see Ypi (2010).

87. AA 8: 19; Kant (2009), 12.

88. AA 8: 20; Kant (2009), 13.

89. Ibid.

90. Kant (1960), 22.

91. AA 8: 21; Kant (2009); 13–14 (my emphasis).

92. On the relationship between Kant's moral theory and his philosophy of history, see, for example, Yovel (1980).

93. AA 8: 22; Kant (2009), 15.

94. AA 5: 431.

95. AA 7: 332; Kant (2007a), 417.

96. AA 8:19; Kant (2009), 12.

97. For a more comprehensive discussion of culture in Kant's work, see, for example, Rotenstreich (1989); Deligiorgi (2005), chapter 3 in particular; Castillo (1990).

98. Yovel (1980), chapter 4; A discussion of this debate is also found in Deligiorgi (2005), 105.

99. A very small sampling includes Allison (2009); Zammito (1992), chapter 7; Huneman (2007).

100. Heidegger (1996), 76.

101. AA 5: 184.

102. Zammito (1992), 330.

103. Sikka (2007).

104. Ibid, 516.

105. Kant (1991), 220.

106. Kant (1991b), 219

107. Ibid

108. Ibid., 219–220.

109. "Travel belongs to the means of broadening the range of anthropology, even if it is only the reading of travel books" (Kant 2006, 4).

110. Gascoigne (2007), 144.

111. Zhang (2013), 265; also see Carhart (2007), chapter 8.

112. Forster (2000), 381.

113. Ibid., 379. On the 'happiness' of the climate, see also 151.

114. See AA 5: 378 and AA 5: 369. Shell nearly concedes this point on 168 of (1996).

115. AA 8: 19; Kant (2007a), 12.

116. AA 8: 177. Kant seems to think the South Sea Islanders are possibly of his Negro race.

117. AA 15: Reflexion 1500 1775–1777. My emphasis.

118. Lagier (2004), 174. Lagier raises precisely this possibility in noting, "The maximal population could effectively be considered as a biological optimum for the species, the racial differentiation permitting man to colonize the entire world in full possession of his faculties under every horizon."

119. On the cultural abilities of Kant's races, see Cohen (2009), 39. See also Wilson (2009), 205. On Kant's 'tag-team' with Christoph Meiners in the formulation of ahistorical peoples, see Park (2013), chapter 4.

120. From his Pillau lectures as cited in Louden (2014), 223.

121. I discussed this in chapter 1 and the introduction, but for good measure, see, for instance, Nagel (1994), 65: "The mind-body problem

is a natural outgrowth or by-product of the overwhelmingly successful methods of physical science which have driven the scientific revolution of our era since the seventeenth century. That is why the problem received its essential modern formulation from Descartes, who participated in the beginnings of that revolution."

122. On the decline of substance dualism in the nineteenth century, see Heidelberger (2003).

123. Frye (1983), 152–173.

124. Nietzsche (1968), 9.

125. Ibid., 14.

126. Turgot (1973), 41.

127. Sharpe brings this up throughout her study of the ontological negation of Black people. On the long durée of the 'hold,' see 128, for example, but the entire book addresses the theme of repetition and the 'ditto ditto' along the lines of a genocidal construction of time. See Sharpe (2016).

128. X (1992), 83. On his broad definition of 'Black,' see 62.

129. Ture and Hamilton (1992), 37, 38.

130. Eze (1995), 217.

131. Kleingeld (2007), 574; see also 576.

132. Hedrick (2008), 246.

133. Park (2013), 94.

134. Mills (2005), 171.

135. Cited in Louden (2011), 132.

136. See AA 8: 180; Kant (2013), 190. It is however important to note that in 1788 Kant describes the idea of "a descending natural chain of organic being" as a "game with which many a person has certainly amused themselves, but then given up because nothing is to be gained by it."

137. Serequeberhan (1996), 343.

138. Larrimore (1999), 119.

139. On the destruction of peoples as a sign of the richness of nature, see Kant (2008), 100.

140. Taguieff (2001), 125. Taguieff dismantles the notion of a monolithic racism in these pages, generating what he calls an 'other-racialization,' exemplified by colonialism, and 'self-racialization,' most conspicuous in

National Socialism. Although Kant does not fit easily in either of these categories, it is a helpful rubric. See Taguieff's section entitled "Inequality and Difference: Two Logics of Racialization," 120–133.

141. AA 15: Reflexion 1520.

142. For a discussion of this quote and Kant's place in the history of genocidal ideology, see Bernasconi (2005).

143. Said (1992), 78.

144. It is worth mentioning the disparity here between the logic of bio-power and that of this non-being. If, as Foucault writes of biopower, "Such a power has to qualify, measure, appraise, and hierarchize," and, since the eighteenth century it has "acted as factors of segregation and social hierarchization, exerting their influence on the respective forces of both these movements, guaranteeing relations of domination and effects of hegemony," then we are not discussing that here. Biopower is governed by a calculation of the "more or less." (Quoted from [1984], 266, 263, and 279, respectively.) This includes Agamben's understanding of the Holocaust as an incessant elimination of the inferior types, without boundaries. See Agamben 1988, 146–147. For this reason, it seems that there can be no biopolitics of the sort of nothingness found in Kant's work.

145. Mikkelsen (2013), 170–171.

146. Kant (2011), 106.

147. See Ypi (2014). However, this cannot be taken as clear evidence that Kant believes non-White peoples are equal to Europeans or that their existence is historically meaningful. Inés Valdez (2017) convincingly demonstrates how Kant's anticolonialism in *Towards Perpetual Peace* coexists with both his racial hierarchy and his belief in the purpose-lessness of non-White peoples. Emphasizing his political and economic context, she argues that Britain's colonial dominance is crucial to under-standing Kant's essay. Kant is concerned with specifying the kind of antagonism that facilitates historical progress. As he makes clear in the First Supplement, he still believes unsocial sociability and war are Nature's means of achieving peace, but he now believes this is only the case if the two warring parties are relatively equal in strength. British

naval dominance in the colonies and aggression against non-Europeans is antagonistic, but it does not compel progress because the adversaries are so mismatched. This results in a refined understanding of antagonism, but not a rejection of his racism. As Valdez argues, Kant's anticolonial- ism in 1795 implies a racial hierarchy, since a unified system of Right is needed to protect an inherently weak people from wanton violence in contrast to the 'productive' warfare among equal parties. Accordingly, non-White races are an obstacle to progress insofar as they populate a territory but do not spur competition with European peoples. Their status as an obstacle to progress notwithstanding, non-Whites are still historically worthless.

148. Larrimore (2008).

149. AA 8: 19; Kant (2009), 12.

150. I am alluding to Harris (1993).

151. Alexander (2012), 200. See also, Sharpe: "As another young Black man reports, 'When you're young and you're black, no matter how you look you fit the description.' You 'fit the description' of the nonbeing, the being out of place, and the noncitizen always available to and for death" (2016, 86).

152. Wynter (1994), 42.

153. Ellison (1980), 4.

154. Mills (1998), 9. Also implied in Bell's first rule of racial standing. See Bell (1992), 111.

155. Newton (2002), 133.

156. Cone (2010), 12.

157. hooks (2015), 140–142.

158. Fanon (2004), 182; (2011),625.

159. Fanon (2008), 113; (2011), 175. On Fanon's 'zone of non-being,' see Kawash (1999); Gordon (2007).

160. Said (1979), 27. Also see Said (1990), 213.

161. Kassir (2013), 4.

162. Memmi (1969), 127–128, my emphasis. I would additionally point out that despite the fact that a number of prominent Arab authors testify

to the experience of nonexistence, professional philosophy usually only manages to edify that status. See, for just one instance, the flyer for PIKSI 2017, http://www.piksi.org/wp-content/uploads/2016/12/piksi_poster_2017_V2.pdf (accessed May 29, 2017).

163. Mbembe (2001), 187.

164. Given this formulation, if it is accurate, it might be tempting seek a solution to this other mind-body problem in recognizing that non-European philosophies do exist, they do have a history, and they are of value. Perhaps then medieval Islamic thought has some insight into the problem of mental causation? Or perhaps Akan thinkers can help philosophy with the problem of other minds? However, such an integration is not a sufficient counteragent to the kinds of racism discussed here. If the solution to Kant's mind-body problem is a mere rendering of reasons, then one is drawn into the further questions of just what renders reasons to whom? Governed by the logic of the principle of reason, is it not the subject to whom reasons are rendered? Is that which does the rendering not then an object, or a tool, the very inferior being encountered in chapter 2 while looking at the role of the principle of reason in the logic of the plantation colony? While it may paper over Kant's mind-body problem, this strategy would seem to do little to alleviate the predicament of a racialized non-being, for when a tool is no longer useful, it becomes waste. This creates a situation where one either renders reasons for their being, and that reason is affirmed by a subject, or one has no reason at all, creating an oscillation between thinghood and nothingness. To accept these terms and render a reason to philosophy seems then to be only a half-measure. Given a situation where one is either a tool in the realization of a *telos* or one is irrelevant to any *telos*, it would seem that a way out of this dilemma would call for a rethinking of these historical narratives. For readers have seen that this brand of racism aspires less to a command and control over geographic areas than to the exclusive ownership of the meaning of time and the idea of history. Without a decolonization of time, one in which reasons are not rendered, nor is one rendered without reason, non-White people appear to be trapped between thinghood and nothingness.

(On this theme see Mbembe 2001, "Out of the World." On the pitfalls of alternative histories as a decolonial tactic, see Nandy 1995.) While only one position is properly 'another mind-body problem,' neither situation is acceptable. Of course, all this is only to conjecture in the direction of a possible solution. What remains certain is the current constitution of academic philosophy, and the philosophy of mind in particular, remains so utterly overmatched in the face of this problem on account of the fact that those most intimate with the nuances of a racialized nothingness remain largely invisible.

165. A question posed in Dabashi (2013).

166. Wynter (1994), 65.

REFERENCES

Ablondi, Fred. 2008. "François Lamy, Occasionalism, and the Mind-Body Problem." *Journal of the History of Philosophy* 46: 619–629.

Agamben, Giorgio. 1998. *Homo Sacer: Sovereign Power and Bare Life.* Translated by Daniel Heller-Roazen. Stanford: Stanford University Press.

Alanen, Lilli. 1996. "Reconsidering Descartes' Notion of the Mind-Body Union." *Synthese* 106, no. 1: 3–20.

Alcoff, Linda Martín. 2006. *Visible Identities: Race, Gender, and the Self.* Oxford: Oxford University Press.

———. 2013. "Philosophy's Civil Wars." *Proceedings and Addresses of the American Philosophical Association* 87: 16–43.

Alexander, Michelle. 2012. *The New Jim Crow: Mass Incarceration in the Age of Color Blindness.* New York: The New Press.

Allison, Henry E. 2004. *Kant's Transcendental Idealism.* New Haven: Yale University Press.

———. 2009. "Teleology and History in Kant: The Critical Foundations of Kant's Philosophy of History." In *Kant's Idea for a Universal History with a Cosmopolitan Aim: A Critical Guide,* edited by Amélie Oksenberg Rorty and James Schmidt, 24–45. Cambridge: Cambridge University Press.

Amorós, Celia Ana Uriarte, and Linda López McAlister. 1994. "Cartesianism and Feminism: What Reason Has Forgotten; Reasons for Forgetting." *Hypatia* 9, no. 1: 147–163.

Anderson, Elizabeth. 2010. *The Imperative of Integration.* Princeton: Princeton University Press.

Anderson, Lorin. 1982. *Charles Bonnet and the Order of the Known.* Dordrecht: D. Reidel.

Antonio, Robert J. 1981. "Immanent Critique as the Core of Critical Theory: Its Origins and Developments in Hegel, Marx and Contemporary Thought." *The British Journal of Sociology* 32, no. 3: 330–345.

Aquinas Thomas. 1999. *Commentary on Aristotle's Physics*. Translated by Richard J. Blackwell, Richard J. Spath, W. Edmund Thurlkel. Notre Dame: Dumb Ox Books.

Arendt, Hannah. 1966. *The Origins of Totalitarianism*. New York: Harcourt, Brace and World.

Arthur, Richard T. W. 2007. "Animal Generation and Substance in Sennert and Leibniz." In *The Problem of Animal Generation in Early Modern Philosophy*, edited by Justin E. H. Smith, 147–174. New York: Cambridge University Press.

Aucante, Vincent. 2000. *Descartes: Écrits physiologiques et medicaux*. Paris: PUF.

———. 2006. "Descartes' Experimental Method and the Generation of Animals." In *The Problem of Animal Generation in Early Modern Philosophy*, edited by Justin E. H. Smith, 65–79. New York: Cambridge University Press.

Baillie, John. 1951. *The Belief in Progress*. New York: Charles Scribner's Sons.

Baker, Gordon, and Katherine J. Morris. 1996. *Descartes' Dualism*. London: Routledge.

Bauman, Zygmunt. 2004. *Wasted Lives: Modernity and Its Outcasts*. Cambridge: Polity.

Bell, Derrick. 1992. *Faces at the Bottom of the Well: The Permanence of Racism*. New York: Basic Books.

Bergson, Henri. 1972. *Mélanges*. Paris: PUF.

Bernasconi, Robert. 2001. "Who Invented the Concept of Race? Kant's Role in the Enlightenment Construction of Race." In *Race*, edited by Robert Bernasconi, 11–36. Oxford: Blackwell.

———. 2003. "Will the Real Kant Please Stand Up? The Challenge of Enlightenment Racism to the Study of the History of Philosophy." *Radical Philosophy* 117: 13–22.

———. 2005. "Why Do the Happy Inhabitants of Tahiti Bother to Exist at All?" In *Genocide and Human Rights: A Philosophical Guide*, edited by John K. Roth, 139–148. New York: Palgrave.

———. 2008. "A Haitian in Paris: Anténor Firmin as a Philosopher against Racism." *Patterns of Prejudice* 42, no. 4–5: 365–383.

———. 2011. "Kant's Third Thoughts on Race." In *Reading Kant's Geography*, edited by Stuart Elden and Eduardo Mendieta, 291–318. Albany: State University of New York Press.

———. 2014. "Heredity and Hybridity in the Natural History of Kant: Girtanner and Schelling in the 1790s." In *Reproduction, Race, and Gender in Philosophy and the Early Life Sciences*, edited by Susan Lettow, 237–258. Albany: State University of New York Press.

Bernasconi, Robert, and Anika Maaza Mann. 2005. "The Contradictions of Racism: Locke, Slavery and the Two Treatises." In *Race and Racism in Modern Philosophy*, edited by Andrew Valls, 89–107. Ithaca: Cornell University Press.

Bhabha, Homi. 1994. *The Location of Culture*. New York: Routledge.

Biddiss, Michael. 1970. *Father of Racist Ideology: The Social and Political Thought of Count Gobineau*. London: Weidenfeld and Nicolson.

Bitbol-Hesperies, Annie. 1990. *Le Principe de vie chez Descartes*. Paris: Vrin.

Boissel, Jean. 1993. *Gobineau biographie: mythes et réalité*. Paris: Berg International.

Bonnet, Charles, and Albrecht von Haller. 1983. *The Correspondence Between Albrecht von Haller and Charles Bonnet*. Edited by Otto Sontag. Bern: Hans Huber.

Bonnet, Charles. 1755. *Essai de psychologie*. London.

———. 1760. *Essai Analytique sur les facultés de l'âme*. Copenhagen: Frères C. L. & Ant. Philibert.

———. 1765. *Traité d'insectologie*. Paris: Durand.

———. 1769. *La palingénésie philosophique*. Vol. 1. Geneva: Claude Philibert and Barthelemi Chirol.

———. 1770 *Contemplation de la nature*. Amsterdam: Marc-Michel Rey.

———. 1782. *Contemplation de la nature.* Vol. 1. Hamburg: J. G. Virchaux.

———. 1783. *Oeuvres d'histoire naturelle et de philosophie de Charles Bonnet.* Vol. 7. Neuchatel: Samuel Fauche.

Bono, James J. 1990. "Reform and the Languages of Renaissance Theoretical Medicine: Harvey versus Fernel." *Journal of the History of Biology* 23, no. 3: 341–387.

Bowler, Peter J. 1971. "Pre-formation and Pre-existence in the Seventeenth Century: A Brief Analysis." *Journal of the History of Biology* 4, no. 2: 221–244.

———. 1973. "Bonnet and Buffon: Theories of Generation and the Problem of Species." *Journal of the History of Biology* 6, no. 2: 259–281.

Boylan, Michael. 1986. "Galen's Conception Theory." *Journal of the History of Biology* 19, no. 1: 47–77.

Bracken, H. M. 1973. "Essence, Accident, and Race." *Hermathena*, no. 116: 81–96.

Brantlinger, Patrick. 2013. *Dark Vanishings: Discourse on the Extinction of Primitive Races, 1800–1930.* Ithaca: Cornell University Press.

Broughton, Janet, and Ruth Mattern. 1978. "Reinterpreting Descartes on the Notion of the Union of Mind and Body." *Journal of the History of Philosophy* 16: 23–32.

Buffon, Comte de. 2007. *Oeuvres.* Edited by Stéphane Schmitt. Paris: Gallimard.

Bunge, Mario. 1980. *The Mind-Body Problem: A Psychobiological Approach.* Oxford: Pergamon Press.

Bury, J. B. 2014. *The Idea of Progress: An Inquiry into Its Origin and Growth.* New York: Dover.

Carhart, Michael C. 2007. *The Science of Culture in Enlightenment Germany.* Cambridge: Harvard University Press.

Carraud, Vincent. 2002 *Causa sive ratio: La raison de la cause de Suarez à Leibniz.* Paris: PUF.

Castillo, Monique. 1990. *Kant et l'avenir de la culture.* Paris: PUF.

Césaire, Aimé. 2000. *Discourse on Colonialism.* Translated by Joan Pinkham. New York: Monthly Review Press.

Chakrabarty, Dipesh. 2000. *Provincializing Europe: Postcolonial Thought and Historical Difference.* Princeton: Princeton University Press.

Chalmers, David. 2010. *The Character of Consciousness.* New York: Oxford University Press.

Cohen, Alix. 2006. "Kant on Epigenesis, Monogenesis, and Human Nature: The Biological Premises of Anthropology." *Studies in History and Philosophy of Biological and Biomedical Sciences* 37: 675–693.

———. 2009. *Kant and the Human Sciences: Biology, Anthropology and History.* London: Palgrave Macmillan.

Conder, C. R. 1879. "The Present Condition of Palestine." *Palestine Exploration Quarterly* 11: 6–15.

Cone, James. 2010. *A Black Theology of Liberation.* Maryknoll: Orbis Books.

Cottingham, John. 1986. *Descartes.* Oxford: Basil Blackwell.

Couturat, L. 1901. *La logique de Leibniz d'après des documents inédits.* Paris.

Crenshaw, Kimberlé Williams. 1988. "Race, Reform, and Retrenchment: Transformation and Legitimation in Antidiscrimination Law." *Harvard Law Review* 101, no. 7: 1331–1387.

Crenshaw, Kimberlé, Neil T. Gotanda, Gary Peller, and Kendall Thomas. 1995. *Critical Race Theory: The Key Writings that Formed the Movement.* New York: New Press.

Crivellato, Enrico, and Domenico Ribatti. 2007. "Soul, Mind, Brain: Greek Philosophy and the Birth of Neuroscience." *Brain Research Bulletin* 71: 327–336.

Curran, Andrew. 2009. "Rethinking Race History: The Role of the Albino in the French Enlightenment Sciences." *History and Theory* 48: 151–179.

———. 2011 *The Anatomy of Blackness: Science and Slavery in the Age of Enlightenment.* Baltimore: Johns Hopkins University Press.

Dabashi, Hamid. 2013. "Can Non-Europeans Think?" *Al Jazeera.* January 15, 2103. http://www.aljazeera.com/indepth/opinion/20 13/01/2013114142638797542.html

Dalton, Harlon. 1987. "The Clouded Prism." *Harvard Civil Rights–Civil Liberties Law Review* 435–448.

Davis, David Brion. 2006. *Inhuman Bondage: The Rise and Fall of Slavery in the New World*. Oxford: Oxford University Press.

Deleuze, Gilles. 1994. *Difference and Repetition*. New York: Columbia University Press.

Deleuze, Gilles, and Félix Guattari. 1994. *What Is Philosophy?* Translated by Hugh Tomlinson and Graham Burchell. New York: Columbia University Press.

Deligiorgi, Katerina. 2005. *Kant and the Culture of Enlightenment*. Albany: State University of New York Press.

Derrida, Jacques. 2004. "Countersignature." Translated by Mairéad Hanrahan. *Paragraph* 27, no. 2: 7–42.

Des Chene, Dennis. 1996. *Physiologia: Natural Philosophy in Late Aristotelean and Cartesian Thought*. Ithaca: Cornell University Press.

———. 2001. *Spirits and Clocks: Machine and Organism in Descartes*. Ithaca: Cornell University Press.

Descartes, René. 1996. *Oeuvres de Descartes*. Vols. 1–12. Edited by Charles Adam and Paul Tannery. Paris: J. Vrin.

Doron, Claude-Olivier. 2012. "Race and Genealogy: Buffon and the Formation of the Concept of 'Race.'" *Humana Mente Journal of Philosophical Studies* 22: 75–109.

Dotson, Kristie. 2013. "Querying Harris' Insurrectionist Standards." *Transactions of the Charles S. Peirce Society* 49, no. 1: 74–92.

Dubos, Jean-Baptiste. 1719. *Réflexions critiques sur la poésie et sur la peinture* Part 2. Paris.

Duchesneau, François. 2006. "Charles Bonnet's Neo-Leibnizian Theory of Organic Bodies." In *The Problem of Animal Generation in Early Modern Philosophy*, edited by Justin E. H. Smith, 285–316. New York: Cambridge University Press.

Eccles, John C. 1973. *The Understanding of the Brain*. New York: McGraw-Hill.

Ellison, Ralph. 1980. *The Invisible Man*. New York: Vintage.

Eze, Emmanuel. 1995. "The Color of Reason: The Idea of 'Race' in Kant's Anthropology." In *Anthropology and the German Enlightenment*, edited by Katherine M. Faull, 200–235. Lewisburg: Bucknell University Press.

Fabian, Johannes. 1983. *Time and the Other: How Anthropology Makes Its Object*. New York: Columbia University Press.

Fanon, Frantz. 1967. "Racism and Culture." In *Toward the African Revolution*, 29–44. Translated by Haakon Chevalier. New York: Grove Press.

———. 2004. *The Wretched of the Earth*. Translated by Richard Philcox. New York: Grove Press.

———. 2008. *Black Skin, White Masks*. Translated by Richard Philcox. New York: Grove Press.

———. 2011. *Oeuvres*. Paris: La Découverte.

Farber, Paul L. 1972. "Buffon and the Concept of Species." *Journal of the History of Biology* 5: 259–284.

Fernel, Jean. 2005. *Jean Fernel's "On the Hidden Causes of Things: Forms, Souls and Occult Diseases in Renaissance Medicine."* Translated by John M. Forrester. Boston: Brill Academic.

Ficino, Marsilio. 1985. *Commentary on Plato's Symposium on Love*. Translated by Jayne Sears. Dallas: Spring.

Figard, Leon. 1903. *Un Médecin philosophe au XVIe siècle: Etude sur la psychologie de Jean Fernel*. Paris.

Firmin, Anténor. 2002. *The Equality of the Human Races*. Translated by Asselin Charles. Champagne: University of Illinois Press.

Fluehr-Lobban, Carolyn. 2005. "Anténor Firmin and Haiti's Contribution to Anthropology." *Gradhiva* 1: 95–108.

Fontenelle, Bernard le Bovier de. 1989–2001. *Oeuvres Completes*. Edited by A. Niderst. Paris: Fayard.

Forrester, John. 2003. Introduction. *The "Physiologia" of Jean Fernel*. Translated by John M. Forrester. Philadelphia: American Philosophical Society.

Forster, Georg. 2000. *A Voyage Round the World*. Edited by Nicholas Thomas and Oliver Berghof. Honolulu: University of Hawaii Press.

Foucault, Michel. 1984. *The Foucault Reader*. Edited by Paul Rabinow. New York: Pantheon Books.

Fouke, Daniel Clifford. 1991. "Spontaneity and the Generation of Rational Beings in Leibniz's Theory of Biological Reproduction." *Journal of the History of Philosophy* 29, no. 1: 33–45.

French, Roger. 1994. *William Harvey's Natural Philosophy*. Cambridge: Cambridge University Press.

Frye, Marilyn. 1983. *The Politics of Reality: Essays in Feminist Theory*. Berkeley: The Crossing Press.

Fuchs, Thomas. 2001. *The Mechanization of the Heart: Harvey to Descartes*. Translated by Marjorie Greene. Rochester: University of Rochester Press.

Furet, François. 1984. "From Narrative History to Problem-Oriented History." In *In the Workshop of History*, 54–68. Chicago: University of Chicago Press.

Galton, Francis. 1865. "Hereditary Talent and Character." *Macmillan's Magazine*. November 1864–April 1865: 318–327.

Garber, Daniel. 2001. "Descartes, Or the Cultivation of the Intellect." In *Descartes Embodied: Reading Cartesian Philosophy Through Cartesian Science*, 277–295. Cambridge: Cambridge University Press.

Garvey, Marcus. 1926. "Who and What Is a Negro?" In *Philosophy and Opinions of Marcus Garvey or Africa for the Africans*, volume 2, edited by Amy Jacques-Garvey, 18–21. New York: The Universal Publishing House.

Gascagione, John. 2007. "The German Enlightenment and the Pacific." In *The Anthropology of the Enlightenment*, edited by Larry Wolff and Marco Cipolloni. Stanford: Stanford University Press.

Gaukroger, Stephen. 2000. "The Resources of a Mechanist Physiology and the Problem of Goal Directed Processes." In *Descartes' Natural Philosophy*, edited by Stephen Gaukroger, John Schuster, and John Sutton, 383–403. New York: Routledge.

Gaulmier, Jean. 1981. "Poison dans les veines: Note sur le thème de Sang chez Gobineau." *Romantisme* 11, no. 31: 197–208.

Gilson, Étienne. 1951. *Études sur la role de la pensée médiévale dans la formation du système cartésien*. Paris: J. Vrin.

Girtanner, Christoph. 2013. "Concerning the Kantian Principle in Natural History: An Attempt to Attempt to Treat This Science Philosophically." In *Kant on Race: Late Eighteenth-Century Writings*, edited and translated by Jon M. Mikkelsen, 209–332. Albany: State University of New York Press.

Gobineau, Arthur de. 1983. "Essai sur l'inégalité des races humaines." In *Œuvres*, edited by Jean Gaulmier. Paris: Gallimard.

———. 1999. *The Inequality of the Human Races*. Translated by Adrian Collins. New York: Howard Fertig.

Godart, Guillaume-Lambert. 1755. *La physique de l'âme humaine*. Berlin.

Gordon, Lewis. 1999. "A Short History of the 'Critical' in Critical Race Theory." *APA Newsletters* 98, no. 2: 23–26.

———. 2007. "Through the Hellish Zone of Nonbeing: Thinking through Fanon, Disaster, and the Damned of the Earth." *Human Architecture: Journal of the Sociology of Self-Knowledge* 5, no. 3: 5–11.

Grober, Max. 1993. "The Natural History of Heaven and the Historical Proofs of Christianity: *La palingénésie philosophique* of Charles Bonnet." *Studies on Voltaire in the Eighteenth Century*: 233–255.

———. 1995. "Harmony Structure and Force in the *Essai analytique sur les facultés de l'âme* of Charles Bonnet." *Journal of the History of the Behavioral Sciences* 31, no. 1: 34–50.

Gueroult, Martial. 1984. *Descartes' Philosophy Interpreted According to the Order of Reasons: The Soul and God*. Translated by Roger Ariew. Minneapolis: University of Minnesota Press.

Gutiérrez, Gustavo. 1988. *A Theology of Liberation*. Translated by Sister Caridad Inda and John Eagleson. New York: Orbis.

Gyeke, Kwame. 1998. "The Relation of Okra (Soul) and Honam (Body): An Akan Conception." In *African Philosophy: An Anthology*, edited by Emmanuel Chukwudi Eze, 59–66. Malden: Blackwell.

Haller, Albrecht von, and Charles Bonnet. 2013. *The Correspondence Between Albrecht von Haller and Charles Bonnet*, edited by Otto Sontag. Bern: Hans Huber Publishers.

Han, Béatrice. 2002. *Foucault's Critical Project: Between the Transcendental and the Historical*. Translated by Edward Pile. Stanford: Stanford University Press.

Hannaford, Ivan. 1996. *Race: The History of an Idea in the West*. Washington, DC: The Woodrow Wilson Center Press.

Harfouch, John. Forthcoming. "Does Leibniz Have Any Role in the History of Racism?" *Philosophy Today* 61, no. 3.

———. 2017. "The Arab That Cannot Be Killed: An Orientalist Logic of Genocide." *Radical Philosophy Review* 20, no. 2: 219–241.

Harrington, Katie. 2013. "Kant and Collingwood on the Mind-Body Problem." *Collingwood and British Idealism Studies* 19, no. 1: 95–111.

Harris, Cheryl I. 1993. "Whiteness as Property." *Harvard Law Review* 106, no. 8: 1707–1791.

Harris, Leonard. 2002. "Insurrectionist Ethics: Advocacy, Moral Psychology, and Pragmatism. In *Ethical Issues for a New Millennium*, edited by J. Howie, 192–210. Carbondale: Southern Illinois University Press.

Harrison, Peter. 2001. "Scaling the Ladder of Being: Theology and Early Theories of Evolution." In *Religion, Reason, and Nature in Early Modern Europe*, edited by Robert Crocker, 199–224. Dordrecht: Kluwer.

Harveo, Guilielmo. 1666. *Excertationes de Generatione Animalium*. Ex Officiana Heredum Pauli Frambotti.

Harvey, William. 1847. *The Works of William Harvey*. Translated by Robert Willis. London: Sydenham.

———. 1949. *Exercitatio anatomica de motu cordis et sanguinis in animalibus*. Translated by Chauncey Leake. Baltimore: C. C. Thomas.

———. 1995. *The Anatomical Exercises*. Edited by Geoffrey Keynes. New York: Dover.

Hatfield, Gary. 1995. "Remaking the Science of Mind: Psychology as Natural Science." In *Inventing Human Science: Eighteenth-Century*

Domains, edited by Christopher Fox, Roy Porter, and Robert Wolker, 184–231. Berkeley: University of California Press.

Hattab, Helen. 2009. *Descartes on Forms and Mechanisms*. Cambridge: Cambridge University Press.

Headley, Clevis. 2006. "Black Studies, Race, and Critical Race Theory: A Narrative Deconstruction of Law." In *A Companion to African-American Studies*, edited by Lewis Gordon and Jane Gordon, 330–359. Oxford: Blackwell.

Hedrick, Todd. 2008. "Race, Difference, and Anthropology in Kant's Cosmopolitanism." *Journal of the History of Philosophy* 46, no. 2: 245–268.

Heidegger, Martin. 1996. *The Principle of Reason*. Translated by Reginald Lilly. Bloomington: Indiana University Press.

Heidelberger, Michael. 2003. "The Mind-Body Problem in the Origin of Logical Empiricism: Herbert Feigl and Psychophysical Parallelism." In *Logical Empiricism: Historical and Contemporary Perspectives*, edited by Paolo Parrini, Wesley C. Salmon, and Merilee H. Salmon, 233–262. Pittsburgh: University of Pittsburgh Press.

Hirai, Hiro. 2005. "Alter Galenus: Jean Fernel et son interpretation platon-ico-chrétienne e Galien." *Early Science and Medicine* 10, no. 1: 1–35.

Hoffman, Paul. 1986. "The Unity of Descartes' Man." *The Philosophical Review* 95, no. 3: 339–370.

hooks, bell. 2015. *Ain't I a Woman: black women and feminism*. New York: Routledge.

Hopper, David. 1991. *Technology, Theology and the Idea of Progress*. Louisville: Westminster/John Knox Press.

Hoquet, Thierry. 2005. *Buffon: histoire naturelle et philosophie*. Paris: Honoré Champion.

———. 2007. *Buffon illustré: les gravures de l'histoire naturelle (1749–1767)*. Paris: Publication Scientifiques du Muséum National d'Histoire Naturelle.

———. 2014. "Bioligasition de la race et racialisation de l'humain: Bernier, Buffon, Linné." In *L'invention de la race: Des représentations scientifiques aux exhibitions populaires*, edited by Nicolas Bancel, Thomas David, and Dominic Thomas. Paris: La Découverte.

Horkheimer, Max. 2002. "Traditional and Critical Theory." In *Critical Theory: Selected Essays*, translated by Matthew J. O'Connell, 188–243. New York: Continuum.

Huet, Marie-Hélène. 1993. *Monstrous Imagination*. Cambridge: Harvard University Press.

Huneman, Philippe. 2007. "Reflexive judgement and Wolffian Embryology: Kant's Shift between the First and the Third Critique." In *Understanding Purpose: Kant and the Philosophy of Biology*, edited by Philippe Huneman, 75–100. Rochester: University of Rochester Press.

Ibrahim, Annie. 1987. "La notion de moule intérieur dans les théories de la génération au XVIIIe siècle." *Archives de Philosophie* 50: 555–580.

Iggers, George G. 1982. "The Idea of Progress in Historiography and Social Thought since the Enlightenment." In *Progress and Its Discontents*, edited by Gabriel A. Almond, Marvin Chodorow, and Roy Harvey Pearce, 41–66. Berkeley: University of California Press.

Jacques, T. Carlos. 1997. "From Savages and Barbarians to Primitives: Africa, Social Typologies, and History in Eighteenth-Century French Philosophy." *History and Theory* 36, no. 2: 190–215.

Johnson, Kelly. 2010. "Developmentalism Then and Now: The Origins and Resurgence of an Enduring Grand Theory." In *Grand Theories and Ideologies in the Social Sciences*, edited by Howard J. Wiarda, 19–40. New York: Palgrave.

Jordan, Winthrop. 1968. *White Over Black: American Attitude Toward the Negro, 1550–1812*. Williamsburg: University of North Carolina Press.

Kaitaro, Timo. 1996. "La Peyronie and the Experimental Search for the Seat of Soul: Neuropsychological Methodology in the Eighteenth Century." *Cortex* 32: 557–564.

Kale, Steven. 2010. "Gobineau, Racism and Legitimism: A Royalist Heretic in Nineteenth-Century France." *Modern Intellectual History* 7, no. 1: 33–61.

Kames, Henry Home. 1776. *Six Sketches on the History of Man.* Philadelphia: R. Bell.

Kant, Immanuel. 1900–. *Kants gesammelte Schriften.* Edited by the Könglichen-preussischen Akademie der Wissenschaften, 29 vols. to date. Berlin: Walter de Gruyter.

———. 1960. *Religion within the Limits of Reason Alone.* Translated by Theodore M. Greene and Hoyt H. Hudson. New York: Harper and Row.

———. 1967. *Philosophical Correspondence: 1759–1799.* Edited and translated by Arnulf Zweig. Chicago: University of Chicago Press.

———. 1991a. "Perpetual Peace: A Philosophical Sketch." In *Political Writings*, edited by H. S. Reiss, 93–130. Cambridge: Cambridge University Press.

———. 1991b. "Reviews of Herder's Ideas on the Philosophy of the History of Mankind." In *Political Writings*, edited by H. S. Reiss, 201–220. Cambridge: Cambridge University Press.

———. 2006. *Anthropology from a Pragmatic Point of View.* Translated by Robert Louden. Cambridge: Cambridge University Press.

———. 2007a. *Anthropology, History, and Education.* Cambridge: Cambridge University Press.

———. 2007b. *Critique of Pure Reason.* Translated by Norman Kemp Smith. Boston: Palgrave.

———. 2008. *Universal Natural History and Theory of the Heavens.* Translated by Ian Johnston. Arlington: Richer Resources Publications.

———. 2009. *Kant's Idea for a Universal History with a Cosmopolitan Aim.* Edited by Amélie Oksenberg Rorty and James Schmidt. Cambridge: Cambridge University Press.

———. 2012a. *Natural Science.* Edited by Eric Watkins. Cambridge: Cambridge University Press.

———. 2012b. *Lectures on Anthropology.* Cambridge: Cambridge University Press.

———. 2013. *Kant and the Concept of Race*. Translated by Jon M. Mikkelsen. Albany: State University of New York Press.

Kassir, Samir. 2013. *Being Arab*. London: Verso.

Kawash, Samira. 1999. "Terrorists and Vampires: Fanon's Spectral Violence of Decolonization." In *Frantz Fanon: Critical Perspectives*, edited by Anthony C. Alessandrini, 235–257. New York: Routledge.

Kidd, Colin. 2006. *The Forging of Races: Race and Scripture in the Protestant Atlantic World, 1600–2000*. Cambridge: Cambridge University Press.

Kim, Jaegwon. 1998. *Mind in a Physical World: An Essay on the Mind-Body Problem and Mental Causation*. Cambridge: MIT Press.

Kirk, Robert. 2003. *Mind and Body*. New York: Acumen.

Kleingeld, Pauline. 2007. "Kant's Second Thoughts on Race." *The Philosophical Quarterly* 57, no. 229: 573–592.

———. 2012. *Kant and Cosmopolitanism*. Cambridge: Cambridge University Press.

———. 2014. "Kant's Second Thoughts on Colonialism." In *Kant and Colonialism: Historical and Critical Perspectives*, edited by Katrin Flickshuh and Lea Ypi, 43–67. Oxford: Oxford University Press.

Kleywegt, A. J. 1984. "Cleanthes and the 'Vital Heat.'" *Mnemosyne* 37: 94–102.

La Peyronie, François Gigot de. 1741. "Observations par lesquelles on tâche de découvrir la partie du cerveau où l'âme exerce ses fonctions." In *Mémoires de l'Académie royale des sciences*. Paris.

La Vopa, Anthony J. 2010. "Sexless Minds at Work and at Play: Poullain de la Barre and the Origins of Early Modern Feminism." *Representations* 109, no. 1: 57–94.

Lagier, Raphael. 2004. *Les Races Humaines Selon Kant*. Paris: PUF.

Larrimore, Mark. 2008. "Antinomies of Race: Diversity and Destiny in Kant." *Patterns of Prejudice* 42, no. 4–5: 341–363.

———. 1999. "Sublime Waste: Kant on the Destiny of the Races." *Canadian Journal of Philosophy* 29: 199–225.

Leibniz, G. W. 1976. *Philosophical Papers and Letters*. Edited by Leroy Loemker. Chicago: Chicago University Press.

———. 1989. *Philosophical Essays*. Edited and translated by Roger Ariew and Daniel Garber. Indianapolis: Hackett.

———. 1996. *New Essays on Human Understanding.* Edited and translated by Peter Remnant and Jonathan Bennett. Cambridge: Cambridge University Press.

———. 1998. *Philosophical Texts.* Edited and translated by R. S. Woodhouse and Richard Franks. Oxford: Oxford University Press.

———. 2007a. *The Leibniz-Des Bosses Correspondence.* Translated by Brandon Look and Donald Rutherford. New Haven: Yale University Press.

———. 2007b. *Theodicy.* Edited by Austin Farrer, translated by E. M. Huggard. BiblioBazaar.

Levine, Joseph. 1983. "Materialism and Qualia: The Explanatory Gap." *Pacific Philosophical Quarterly* 64: 354–361.

Locke, John. 1979. *An Essay Concerning Human Understanding.* Edited by Peter H. Nidditch. New York: Oxford University Press.

Long, Edward. 1774. *The History of Jamaica.* Vol. 2. London: T. Lowndes.

Longuenesse, Beatrice. 1994. "Logique et Métaphysique dans le Système Critique: l'Exemple de la Causalité." *Bulletin de la Société Française de la Philosophie* 88, no. 2: 65–105.

———. 2001. "Kant's Deconstruction of the Principle of Sufficient Reason." *The Harvard Review of Philosophy* 9, no. 1: 67–87.

Look, Brandon. 2011 "Grounding the Principle of Sufficient Reason: Leibnizean Rationalism versus the Humean Challenge." In *The Rationalists: Between Tradition and Revolution,* edited by Carlos Fraenkel, Dario Perinetti, and Justin Smith, 201–219. Dordrecht: Springer.

Louden, Robert B. 2014. "Cosmopolitical Unity: The Final Destiny of the Human Species." In *Kant's Lectures on Anthropology: A Critical Guide,* edited by Alix Cohen, 211–229. Cambridge: Cambridge University Press.

Lovejoy, Arthur O. 2011. *The Great Chain of Being: A Study in the History of an Idea.* New Brunswick: Transaction.

Lowith, Karl. 1949. *Meaning in History.* Chicago: University of Chicago Press.

MacDonald, Paul S. 2003. *History of the Concept of Mind*. Burlington: Ashgate.

Manley, Michael. 1983. *Up the Down Escalator: Development and the International Economy, A Jamaican Case Study*. Washington, DC: Howard University Press.

Marat, Jean-Paul. 1773. *A Philosophical Essay on Man: Being an Attempt to Investigate the Principles and Laws of the Reciprocal Influence of the Soul on the Body*. London.

Marino, Luigi. 1994. "Söemmering, Kant, and the Organ of the Soul." In *Romanticism in Science*, edited by S. Poggi and M. Bossi, 127–142. Dordrecht: Kluwer.

Marion, Jean-Luc. 1999. *On Descartes' Metaphysical Prism: The Constitution and Limits of Onto-theo-ology in Cartesian Thought*. Translated by Jeffrey L. Kosky. Chicago: University of Chicago Press.

———. 2007. *On the Ego and God: Further Cartesian Questions*. Translated by Christina M. Gschwandtner. New York: Fordham University Press.

Marx, Jacques. 1976. *Bonnet contre les lumières*. Paris: Voltaire Fondation.

Matsuda, Mari. 1995. "Looking to the Bottom: Critical Legal Studies and Reparations." In *Critical Race Theory: The Key Writings That Formed the Movement*, edited by Kimberlé Crenshaw, Neil T. Gotanda, Gary Peller, and Kendall Thomas, 63–79. New York: New Press.

Matthen, Mohan. 1989. "The Four Causes in Aristotle's Embryology." *Apreiron: A Journal for Ancient Philosophy and Science* 22, no. 4: 159–179.

Mazzolini, Renato G., and Shirley A. Roe. 1986. Introduction. *Science Against the Unbelievers: The Correspondence of Bonnet and Needham, 1760–1780*. Oxford: Alden Press.

Mbembe, Achille. 2001. *On the Postcolony*. Berkeley: University of California Press, 2001.

McCarthy, George. 1985. "Development of the Concept and Method of Critique in Kant, Hegel, and Marx." *Studies in Soviet Thought* 30, no.1: 15–38.

McDonough, Jeffrey K. 2008. "Leibniz's Two Realms Revisited." *Nous* 42, no. 4: 673–696.

McGinn, Colin. 1989. "Can We Solve the Mind-Body Problem?" *Mind* 98, no. 391: 349–366.

———. 2003. "What Constitutes the Mind-Body Problem?" *Philosophical Issues: Philosophy of Mind* 13: 148–162.

McLaughlin, Peter. 2007. "Kant on Heredity and Adaptation." In *Heredity Produced: At the Crossroads of Biology, Politics, and Culture, 1500–1870*, edited by Staffan Müller-Wille and Hans-Jörg Rheinberger, 277–292. Cambridge: MIT Press.

Meiners, Christoph. 2013. "Of the Deviate Forms of Negroes." In *Kant and the Concept of Race: Late-Eighteenth Century Writings*, edited and translated by Jon M. Mikkelsen, 195–208. Albany: State University of New York Press.

Memmi, Albert. 1969. *The Colonizer and the Colonized*. Translated by Howard Greenfield. Boston: Beacon Press.

Meyer, A., and R. Hierons. 1965. "On Thomas Willis' Concept of Neurophysiology." *Medical History* 9: 1–15.

Michael, Emily. 1997. "Daniel Sennert on Matter and Form: At the Juncture of the Old and the New." *Early Science and Medicine* 2, no. 3: 272–299.

Mikkelsen, Jon M. 2013. *Kant and the Concept of Race*. Albany: State University of New York Press.

Mill, J. S. 1998. "Considerations on Representative Government." In *On Liberty and Other Essays*, edited by John Gray, 203–467. Oxford: Oxford University Press.

Mills, Charles. 1994. "Revisionist Ontologies: Theorizing White Supremacy." *Social and Economic Studies* 43, no. 3: 105–134.

———. 1999. *The Racial Contract*. Ithaca: Cornell University Press.

———. 1998. *Blackness Visible: Essays on Philosophy and Race.* Ithaca: Cornell University Press.

———. 2005. "Kant's *Untermenschen.*" In *Race and Racism in Modern Philosophy*, edited by Andrew Valls, 169–193. Ithaca: Cornell University Press.

Moody, Todd. 2014. "Consciousness and the Mind-Body Problem: The State of the Argument." *Journal of Consciousness* 21, no. 3–4: 177–190.

Moran, Francis. 2002. "Between Primates and Primitives: Natural Man as the Missing Link in Rousseau's *Second Discourse.*" In *Philosophers on Race*, edited by Julie K. Ward and Tommy L. Lott, 125–144. Oxford: Blackwell.

Muthu, Sankar. 2003. *Empire and Modern Political Thought.* Cambridge: Cambridge University Press.

Nagel, Thomas. 1994. "Consciousness and Objective Reality." In *The Mind Body Problem: A Guide to the Current Debate*, edited by Richard Warner and Tadeusz Szubka. New York: Wiley Blackwell.

Nale, John. 2014. "Arthur de Gobineau on Blood and Race." *Critical Philosophy of Race* 2, no. 1: 106–124.

Nandy, Ashis. 1995. "History's Forgotten Doubles." *History and Theory* 34: 44–66.

Nasrallah, Sayyed Hassan. 2011. "The New Manifesto." In *Hizbullah's Documents: From the 1985 Open Letter to the 2009 Manifesto*, edited by Joseph Alagha, 115–149. Amsterdam: Pallas.

Newton, Huey P. 2002. "Fear and Doubt: May 15, 1967." In *The Huey P. Newton Reader*, edited by David Hilliard and Donald Weise, 131–133. New York: Seven Stories Press.

Nietzsche, Friedrich. 1968. *The Will to Power.* Edited by Walter Kaufmann, translated by R. J. Hollingdale. New York: Random House.

Nisbet, Robert. 1975. "Turgot and the Contexts of Progress." *Proceedings of the American Philosophical Society* 119, no. 3: 214–222.

———. 1980. *History of the Idea of Progress.* New York: Basic Books.

Nott, Josiah, and George Gliddon. 1854. *Types of Mankind.* Philadelphia: Lippincott, Grambo, and Co.

Nuzzo, Angelica. 2008. *Ideal Embodiment: Kant's Theory of Sensibility.* Bloomington: Indiana University Press.

Osler, Margaret J. 1996. "From Immanent Natures to Nature as Artifice: The Reinterpretation of Final Causes in Seventeenth-Century Natural Philosophy." *The Monist* 79, no. 3: 388–407.

Outlaw, Lucius. 1990. "Toward a Critical Theory of 'Race.' " In *Anatomy of Racism*, edited by David Theo Goldberg, 58–82. Minneapolis: University of Minnesota Press.

Pagel, Walter. 1967. *William Harvey's Biological Ideas.* New York: Karger.

———. 1976. *New Light on William Harvey.* New York: Karger.

Park, Peter K. J. 2013. *Africa, Asia, and the History of Philosophy: Racism in the Formation of the Philosophical Canon, 1780–1830.* Albany: State University of New York Press.

Plochmann, George Kimball. 1953. "Nature and the Living Thing in Aristotle's Biology." *Journal of the History of Ideas* 14, no. 2: 167–190.

Poullain de la Barre, François. 1984. *De l'égalité des deux sexes: Discours physique et moral, où l'on voit l'importance de se défaire des préjugez* (1673, facsimile edition). Paris: Fayard.

———. 2002. "On the Equality of the Two Sexes." In *Three Cartesian Feminist Treatises*, translated by Vivian Bosley, 49–124. Chicago: University of Chicago Press.

Preus, Anthony. 1977. "Galen's Criticisms to Aristotle's Conception Theory." *Journal of the History of Biology* 10: 65–85.

Quijano, Aníbal. 2007. "Coloniality and Modernity/Rationality." *Cultural Studies* 21, no. 2: 168–172.

Reiss, Timothy. 2005. "Descartes's Silences on Slavery and Race." In *Race and Racism in Modern Philosophy*, edited by Andrew Valls, 16–42. Ithaca: Cornell University Press.

Rhode, Deborah L. 1990. "Feminist Critical Theories." *Stanford Law Review* 42, no. 3: 617–638.

Richardson, Robert. 1982. "The 'Scandal' of Cartesian Interactionism." *Mind* 91: 20–37.

Rieppel, Oliver. 1988. "The Reception of Leibniz's Philosophy in the Writings of Charles Bonnet." *Journal of the History of Biology* 21, no. 1: 119–145.

Robert Kirk. 2003. *Mind and Body*. Montreal: McGill-Queens University Press.

Rodis-Lewis, Geneviève. 1950. *L'individualité selon Descartes*. Paris: Vrin.

Roger, Jacques. 1960. *Jean Fernel et les problèmes de la médicine de la Renaissance*. Paris: Les Conférence du Palais de la Découverte.

———. 1997a. *Buffon: A Life in Natural History*. Ithaca: Cornell University Press.

———. 1997b. *The Life Sciences in Eighteenth-Century French Thought*, edited by Keith R. Benson, translated by Robert Ellrich. Stanford: Stanford University Press.

Rostow, W. W. 1990. *The Stages of Economic Growth: A Non-Communist Manifesto*. Cambridge: Cambridge University Press.

Rotenstreich, Nathan. 1989. "Morality and Culture: A Note on Kant." *History of Philosophy Quarterly* 6, no. 3: 303–316.

Russell, Camisha. 2014. "Positivism and Progress in Firmin's *Equality of the Human Races*." *Journal of Pan-African Studies* 7, no. 2: 45–67.

Said, Edward. 1979. *Orientalism*. New York: Random House.

———. 1990. "Zionism from the Standpoint of Its Victims." In *Anatomy of Racism*, edited by David Theo Goldberg, 210–246. Minneapolis: Minnesota University Press.

———. 1992. *The Question of Palestine*. New York: Vintage.

Savioz, Raymond. 1948. *La philosophie de Charles Bonnet de Genève*. Paris: Vrin.

Schmaltz, Tad. 2008. *Descartes on Causation*. New York: Oxford University Press.

Searle, John. 1984. *Minds, Brains and Science*. Cambridge: Harvard University Press.

Sennert, Daniel. 1637. *Hypomnemata Physica*.

———. 1650. "Practica Medicinae VI." In *Opera omnia Vol. III*.

Serequeberhan, Tsney. 1996. "Eurocentrism in Philosophy: The Case of Immanuel Kant." *Philosophical Forum* 27, no. 4: 333–356.

Sharpe, Christina. 2006. *In the Wake: On Blackness and Being*. Durham: Duke University Press.

Shell, Susan M. 1996. *The Embodiment of Reason: Kant on Spirit, Generation, and Community*. Chicago: University of Chicago Press.

———. 2006. "Kant's Concept of a Human Race." In *The German Invention of Race*, edited by Sara Eigen and Mark Larrimore, 55–72. Albany: State University of New York Press.

Sherrington, Charles. 1946. *The Endeavor of Jean Fernel*. Cambridge: Cambridge University Press.

Sheth, Falguni. 2009. *Toward a Political Philosophy of Race*. Albany: State University of New York Press.

Sikka, Sonia. 2007. "On the Value of Happiness: Herder contra Kant." *Canadian Journal of Philosophy* 37, no. 4: 515–546.

Skirry, Justin. 2001. "A Hylopmorphic Interpretation of Descartes' Mind-Body Union." *Proceedings of the American Catholic Philosophical Association* 75: 267–283.

Sleigh, Robert. 1982. "Truth and Sufficient Reason in the Philosophy of Leibniz." In *Leibniz Critical and Interpretive Essays*, edited by Michael Hooker, 209–242. Manchester: Manchester University Press.

Sloan, Phillip R. 1973. "The Idea of Racial Degeneracy in Buffon's *Histoire Naturelle*." In *Studies in Eighteenth Century Culture, vol. 3*, edited by Harold E. Pagliaro, 293–321. Cleveland: The Press of Case Western Reserve University.

———. 1979. "Buffon, German Biology, and the Historical Interpretation of Biological Species." *The British Journal for the History of Science* 12, no. 2: 109–153.

———. "From Logical Universals to Historical Individuals: Buffon's Idea of Biological Species." In *Histoire du concept d'espèce dans les sciences de la vie*, 101–140. Paris: Fondation Singer-Polignac, 1987.

Smith, Justin E. H. 2002. "Leibniz's Preformationism: Between Metaphysics and Biology." *Analecta Husserliana: The Yearbook of Phenomenological Research* 77: 161–192.

———. 2011. *Divine Machines: Leibniz and the Sciences of Life*. Princeton: Princeton University Press.

———. 2015. *Nature, Human Nature, and Human Difference: Race in Early Modern Philosophy.* Princeton: Princeton University Press.

Solmsen, Friedrich. 1957. "The Vital Heat, the Inborn Pneuma and the Aether." *The Journal of Hellenic Studies* 77, no. 1: 119–123.

Spinoza, Baruch. *The Ethics.* Edited and translated by R. H. M. Elwes. New York: Dover.

Stone Haring, Ellen. 1956. "Substantial Form in Aristotle's 'Metaphysics' Z, I." *The Review of Metaphysics* 10, no. 2: 308–332.

Stuurman, Siep. 2004. *François Poullain de la Barre and the Invention of Modern Equality.* Cambridge: Harvard University Press.

Suarez, Francisco. 2000. *On the Formal Cause of Substance: Metaphysical Disputation XV.* Translated by John Kronen and Jeremiah Reed. Milwaukee: Marquette University Press.

Sytnik-Czetwertyński, Janusz. 2013. "Some Eighteenth-Century Contributions to the Mind–Body Problem (Wolff, Taurellus, Knutzen, Bülfiger and the Pre-Critical Kant)." *Axiomathes* 23: 567–577.

Taguieff, Pierre-André. 1998. *La couleur et le sang: Doctrines raciste à la française.* Paris: Mille et une nuits.

———. 2001. *The Force of Prejudice: On Racism and Its Doubles,* edited and translated by Hasan Melehy. Minneapolis: Minnesota University Press.

———. 2004. *Le sens du progrès: une approche historique et philosophique.* Paris: Flammarion.

Thompson, Ann. 2001. "Materialistic Theories of Mind and Brain." In *Between Leibniz, Newton, and Kant: Philosophy and Science in the Eighteenth Century,* edited by Wolfgang Lefèvre, 149–174. Dordrecht: Kluwer.

Truth, Sojourner. 1998. *Narrative of Sojourner Truth.* New York: Penguin Books.

Tully, James. 1983. *A Discourse on Property: John Locke and His Adversaries.* Cambridge: Cambridge University Press.

Ture, Kwame, and Charles V. Hamilton. 1992. *Black Power: The Politics of Liberation.* New York: Vintage.

Turgot, Anne-Robert Jacques. 1973. "A Philosophical Review of the Successive Advances of the Human Mind." In *Turgot on Progress, Sociology, and Economics*, edited and translated by Ronald L. Meek, 41–60. Cambridge: Cambridge University Press.

Unger, Roberto Mangabeira. 1983. "The Critical Legal Studies Movement." *Harvard Law Review* 96, no. 3: 561–647.

Valdez, Inés. (forthcoming). "It's Not About Race: Good Wars, Bad Wars, and the Origins of Kant's Anti-Colonialism." *American Political Science Review*, 1–16.

Voegelin, Eric. 1940. "The Growth of the Race Idea." *The Review of Politics* 2, no. 3: 283–317.

———. 1997. *Race and State*. Edited by Klaus Vondung, translated by Ruth Hein. Baton Rouge: Louisiana University Press.

———. 1998. *The History of the Race Idea: From Ray to Carus*. Edited by Klaus Vondung, translated by Ruth Hein. Baton Rouge: Louisiana University Press.

Watkins, Eric. 1995. "The Development of Physical Influx in Early Eighteenth-Century Germany: Gottsched, Knutzen, and Crusius." *The Review of Metaphysics* 49: 295–339.

———. 1998. "From Pre-established Harmony to Physical Influx: Leibniz's Reception in Eighteenth-Century Germany." *Perspectives on Science* 6, no. 1–2: 136–203.

———. 2005. *Kant and the Metaphysics of Causality*. Cambridge: Cambridge University Press.

Wattles, Gurdon. 1989. "Buffon, D'Alembert and Materialist Atheism." *Studies on Voltaire and the Eighteenth Century* 266: 285–341.

Webster, Charles. 1967. "Harvey's *De generatione*: Its Origin and Relevance to the Theory of Circulation." *British Journal of the History of Science* 3: 262–274.

Westphal, Jonathon. 2016. *The Mind-Body Problem*. Cambridge: MIT Press.

White, Charles. 1795. *An Account of the Regular Gradation of Man*. Read to the Literary and Philosophical Society of Manchester.

White, John S. 1986. "William Harvey and the Primacy of the Blood." *Annales of Science* 43: 239–255.

Whitman, C. O. 1895. "Bonnet's Theory of Evolution." *The Monist* 5, no. 3: 412–426.

Williams, Bernard. 1978. *Descartes: The Project of Pure Inquiry.* Sussex: Penguin Press.

Williams, James. 2014. *A Narrative of Events: Since the 1st of August 1834.* Mineola: Dover.

Wilson, Catherine. 2009. "Kant on Civilization, Culture and Moralization." In *Kant's Idea for a Universal History with a Cosmopolitan Aim: A Critical Guide,* edited by Alix Cohen, 191–210. Cambridge: Cambridge University Press.

Wilson, Margaret. 1978. *Descartes.* London: Routledge.

Winston, Michael. 2005. "Medicine, Marriage, and Human Degeneration in the French Enlightenment." *Eighteenth-Century Studies* 38, no. 2: 263–281.

Wynter, Sylvia. 1994. " 'No Humans Involved': An Open Letter to my Colleagues." *Forum N.H.I.: Knowledge for the Twenty-First Century* 1, no. 1: 42–73.

X, Malcolm. 1964. "Interview with Malcolm X by A.B. Spellman." *Monthly Review* 16: 14–24.

———. 1990. "On Afro-American History (January 24, 1965)." In *Malcolm X on Afro-American History.* Pathfinder: New York.

———. 1992. *By Any Means Necessary.* New York: Pathfinder.

———. 2001. *The Autobiography of Malcolm X.* London: Penguin.

Yolton, John. 1991. *Locke and French Materialism.* Oxford: Clarendon.

Yovel, Yirmiyahu. 1980. *Kant and the Philosophy of History.* Princeton: Princeton University Press.

Ypi, Lea. 2010. "*Natura daedala rerum*? On the Justification of Historical Progress in Kant's Guarantee of Perpetual Peace." *Kantian Review* 14, no. 2: 118–148.

———. 2014. "Commerce and Colonialism in Kant's Philosophy of History." In *Kant and Colonialism: Historical and Critical*

Perspectives, edited by Katrin Flickshuh and Lea Ypi, 99–127. Oxford: Oxford University Press.

Zammito, John H. 1992. *The Genesis of Kant's Critique of Judgment*. Chicago: University of Chicago Press.

———. 2002. *Kant, Herder, and the Birth of Anthropology*. Chicago: University of Chicago Press.

Zanier, Giancarlo. 1987. "Platonic Trends in Renaissance Medicine." *Journal of the History of Ideas* 48, no. 3: 509–519.

Zhang, Chunjie. 2013. "Georg Forster in Tahiti: Enlightenment, Sentiment and the Intrusion of the South Seas." *Journal for Eighteenth-Century Studies* 36, no. 2: 263–277.

INDEX